D0780300

Exquisite Masochism .

Exquisite Masochism

Marriage, Sex, and the Novel Form

Claire Jarvis

JOHNS HOPKINS UNIVERSITY PRESS   BALTIMORE

© 2016 Johns Hopkins University Press
All rights reserved. Published 2016
Printed in the United States of America on acid-free paper
9 8 7 6 5 4 3 2 1

Johns Hopkins University Press
2715 North Charles Street
Baltimore, Maryland 21218-4363
www.press.jhu.edu

Library of Congress Cataloging-in-Publication Data

Jarvis, Claire, 1977–
    Exquisite masochism : marriage, sex, and the novel form / Claire Jarvis.
      pages cm
    Includes bibliographical references and index.
    ISBN 978-1-4214-1993-0 (hardcover : alk. paper) — ISBN 978-1-4214-1994-7
(electronic) — ISBN 1-4214-1993-9 (hardcover : alk. paper) — ISBN 1-4214-1994-7
(electronic) 1. English fiction—19th century—History and criticism. 2. Marriage in
literature. 3. Sex role in literature. 4. Fiction—Technique. I. Title.
    PR878.M36J37 2016
    823'.8093543—dc23   2015031661

A catalog record for this book is available from the British Library.

*Special discounts are available for bulk purchases of this book. For more information, please
contact Special Sales at 410-516-6936 or specialsales@press.jhu.edu.*

Johns Hopkins University Press uses environmentally friendly book materials,
including recycled text paper that is composed of at least 30 percent post-consumer
waste, whenever possible.

Contents

Preface

This book began with a simple question: How do respectable novelists describe sex and still maintain a decent distance from pornography? As a formal plotting technique, marriage offers respectable cover for the secretive impulses of sex. As readers, we no longer have to worry about what will happen to a character once she marries; we know what she's in for on her wedding night. Likewise, waves, oceans, blooms, and illuminations mark the sexual act within the respectable novel and allow a writer to refer to sexual action without realistically describing the act itself. Descriptive haze lets a reader experience sex's capacity to dislocate personal experience. It alerts us to the fact of sex's occurrence, and it absolves the writer of a particular kind of obscenity, one that comes of naming things as they are. More than this, though, fuzzy metaphor locates the description of sex as internal to a character. By describing a sexual act as a bloom or a wave, an author is not describing something in the external world. Instead, she is focusing on the internal register of sexual act—on orgasm and its felt experience, on seduction and its bodily effects.[1] Metaphor, in other words, provides protection for writing about the internal experience of sex.

In the period this book covers, writers began to challenge metaphor's reign in the novelistic depiction of sex. Novelists took to new strategies—drawn in part from the threats posed to embedded, domestic Englishness by cosmopolitan, financial power—to hint at sexual impropriety, perversion, and danger.[2] This book thinks through the novel's reimagined marriage plot as sex found clearer and clearer representation in its pages. I draw my examples from the canonical core of Victorian literature and focus on the states that novelistic characters occupy on the periphery of marriage—engagement, adultery, and widowhood. Through readings of work by Emily Brontë, Anthony Trollope, Thomas Hardy, and an apparent modernist outlier, D. H. Lawrence, I concentrate on writers' varied uses of both a character type (the dominant woman) and what I term the exquisitely masochistic scene (a decadent, descriptive scene of sexual refusal); in combination, these formal elements reveal the shortcomings of both patriarchal and more equitable, companionate marriage structures. Along the way, this book tracks a representational shift in the ways novelists describe sex, from descriptive hermeneutics to descriptive clarity—from the description of Tess Durbeyfield's "mobile, peony mouth" to Connie Chatterley's blossom-covered pudendum.

In this book, I focus on a specific kind of erotic scene that's repeated, in different ways, across some of the central works of Victorian fiction. These are scenes of "exquisite masochism." The term signals these scenes' status as refined aesthetic vignettes within their respective novels, but it also reflects their capacity to represent desire as painful and worrying. Such scenes feature powerful women and submissive men, often take place in highly aestheticized environments, and, as I suggested above, work as vehicles for the respectable novel's sexual content. They stop or dislocate progress in romantic developments by taking genital sex off the representational table in favor of masochistic embraces: they are squeaky wheels in the marriage plot. These are highly charged scenes—scenes of sustained stasis, where plot and character drop out, description thickens, and a glance, gesture, or object takes on heightened relational significance. And recognizing these moments as scenes—in novels across the long nineteenth century—helps us see how the novel understands sex.

A long history of Foucauldian criticism has found sex where it didn't appear to be represented; I am interested in extending this analysis further, in reading nongenital sex as central to Victorian erotic life. Withholding sex, in the Victorian novel, is a perverse way of having it. In a novelistic milieu where illegitimacy or adultery can be the motives for serious tragedy, a fully developed sexual life presents a frightening threat. By describing erotic life in ways that avoid depicting sexual intercourse in favor of nongenital tension or intensity, novelists can render the frisson of sexual desire without the attendant plot risks. Reflection on how sex is presented in Victorian novels reveals how some novelists harness potentially disruptive elements—like sexual desire, sexual power reversals, and illegitimate pleasure—and put them to work in the service of, not just as a challenge to, marriage ideology. These novels often demonstrate an investment in the sexual power of characters (like the dominant women I describe in the following pages), but they also keep these characters from any explicitly sexual connections that would muck up their novels' respectably plotted, core marriages. Instead of presenting characters with a single frightening consequence to illicit sex—a baby or a disease—exquisite masochism disperses physicality throughout the scene, minimizing sex's risk while accentuating its thrill.

There are a number of ways to recognize the scenes that are at the center of this book. They lie at the intersection of novel form and aesthetics. Often, they are filled with "exquisite" things, objects carefully chosen, painstakingly refined and delicate. These objects, and their relationships to the bodies and other objects around them, are precisely drawn—there's a sensory scaffold that holds the whole thing together. Such scenes feel like vignettes, staged and managed for the consumption of a viewer (for the reader? the characters? a little of both?). The "staged" feeling comes, in part, from the sense that plot and action cease in these moments, freezing characters in statuesque attitudes, giving the reader an impression of a *tableau vivant* rendered in prose. Additionally, characters may be described as seeming like living statues, frozen in an attitude—static but humming with pulsing life beneath their inviolate exteriors. In a single novel, a scene like this might stand out and might trouble or resist interpretation: What is this passage doing here? But, by noticing the ways such moments appear in multiple novels across a wide historical period, one begins to see how they work as a type of scene, as a group of like scenes. And these scenes, taken together, demonstrate how, even before its clear representation on the page, the description of masochistic sex—that is, a description of an action that might not seem like sex at all—is essential to nineteenth-century plots about love and marriage.

A character's feelings, too, can be "exquisite," with a narrator, or the character herself, describing pleasure and pain mingling into a new, unsettling sensation. This experience often tips the character into an experience of fulsomeness—exquisite feelings are also intense, keen, potent, overpowering. These descriptions suggest that a character's available sensorium is shut down, obliterated by the force of the experience she is having. In other words, "exquisite" scenes are a way of presenting passion's power in novel form. But "exquisite" things and feelings aren't necessarily salutary or good. Instead, they are finely wrought, and the intensity smuggled into the minute attention to detail in such scenes reflects the asymptotic relationship to pain that they depict.

To understand the elements of the masochistic scene, consider one of the strangest moments in a very strange novel, when *Wuthering Heights'* observant servant, Nelly Dean, comes upon Heathcliff, staring, it seems, at Catherine the Elder's ghost:

> Now, I perceived he was not looking at the wall; for when I regarded him alone, it seemed exactly that he gazed at something within two yards' distance. And whatever it was, it communicated, apparently, both pleasure and pain in exquisite extremes: at least the anguished, yet raptured, expression of his countenance suggested that idea. The fancied object was not fixed, either: his eyes pursued it with unwearied diligence, and, even in speaking to me, were never weaned away. I vainly reminded him of his protracted abstinence from food: if he stirred to touch anything in compliance with my entreaties, if he stretched his hand out to get a piece of bread, his fingers clenched before they reached it, and remained on the table, forgetful of their aim. (253)[3]

Jettison for a moment the question at the heart of this brief passage (does Heathcliff see the dead woman's ghost?) and focus instead on the physical scene it describes. Nelly perceives (or thinks she perceives) Heathcliff's horror written on his face. But Nelly sees something other than horror there: rapture. Rapture and anguish, in equal portions, freeze Heathcliff in his attitude, staring at someone who may or may not be there, chilling his body so intensely that even a grasp for food fails. "Pleasure and pain in exquisite extremes"—here, the author describes a man moving—his hands "clench," rigid, before they reach food—toward a starving death. Brontë's inclusion of "exquisite" imagines there might be some kind of aesthetic satisfaction—or consummation—in Heathcliff's experience. In all of its meanings, "exquisite" develops precision and cultivation so extremely that they can tip from pleasure into pain, from beauty into fastidiousness into horror.

Pain and pleasure: they are two feelings that, in mundane experience, seem thoroughly opposed. But when Brontë modifies them with this crucial word—"exquisite"—they mean something a bit different, something that confuses the senses because pleasure and pain blend into something new, something a little closer to erotic sensation.[4] "Exquisiteness" forges a connection between the realms of aesthetics and the realms of sensation, connecting the keenness of precise description to a different kind of keenness, the needling, sharp remnant of a discomfiting sensory experience. It implicitly connects taste and display to erotic desire. The confluence of these intense feelings—in precisely these words and in words quite similar to these—is, I argue, one of ways the Victorian novel manifests sex and desire in its pages. In a number of key British novels, in a number of central scenes, these two opposed feelings occur at once, and, when they do, they create tension, excitement, and confusion in the characters that experience them.

These twinned feelings appear in scenes across a wide variety of novels. This book examines not only how the novel uses these scenes to work through ideas about the relationship between aesthetics and romance, and the relationship between romance and social life, and, further, how the novel formally navigates the sex scene before modernism made it explicit. By alloying "exquisite pleasure" with "exquisite pain," novelists found a new way to symbolize sex on the page. Joined together into an "exquisite masochism"— a pleasure that comes from pain, a pain that comes from pleasure—such scenes show how the novel demonstrated sex's dislocating and thrilling effects, even without clearly representing sex itself.

The masochistic scenes at the center of this discussion rely on tightly ordered, almost scripted, interactions. Thus, they stand out from their surrounding texts with remarkable clarity. We can read them and not mistake them for descriptions of an ocean or a flower. These are scenes about people, and about their bodily interactions. Further, the zone of sexual experience these scenes describe is quite different from that described merely metaphorically. Once we notice the way masochism makes the sex scene obvious and once we see these scenes as reproduced over many novels, the contours of sex's relation to the novel's wider project becomes sharper. Exquisite masochism gives us access to the social effects of sex on novel form. I'm not suggesting that all intense scenes are masochistic, nor am I claiming that masochistic scenes alone can be described in scenic terms. Instead, exquisite masochism gives us a clear way to see spatial or aesthetic descriptions as signs of erotic connection. What I have come to realize is that this approach develops one way of thinking about a much broader question in novel criticism: How do novelists represent vital worlds, and what things—what places, bodies, and plots—give those worlds their life?

In addition to uncovering the way episodes of exquisite masochism convey sex in the Victorian novel, I also aim to hunt for and describe something inchoate in these scenes—an atmosphere, a feeling—scenes that don't seem to contribute directly to plot or character development, scenes that appear to block or evade interpretation. Both the procedure for finding those scenes and the argumentative spoils they yield once they're located can feel insubstantial or even contradictory. In the following chapters, I make a case for thinking of these scenes together and offer some ways of reading them that highlight their formal importance in the nineteenth-century novel. What happens, for instance, when we read Heathcliff's embraces with Catherine the Elder as sex scenes rather than just as signs of sex that happens off stage? My aim here has been to give exquisitely masochistic scenes some light, and to think—sometimes loosely and in roundabout ways—about what these scenes can tell us about novel form.

Acknowledgments

My first thanks go to Amanda Anderson and Frances Ferguson, scholars whose brilliant work and equally brilliant capacities as a teachers and guides shaped this book in its earliest stages. Alex Woloch deserves special thanks for his precision, intensity, and wit and for being such a generous interlocutor and friend. Jonathan Kramnick, too, has my gratitude. His engagement and sound advice were invaluable as I finished this book.

At Johns Hopkins University Press, I'd like to thank my acquisitions editor, Matt McAdam, for his attention to and investment in my work. This book would not be the same without his eye. Catherine Goldstead, Julie McCarthy, Kim Johnson, and Carrie Watterson made the process of turning manuscript into book seamless, and Isaac Tobin designed the beautiful cover. Michael Taber prepared the index. I'm also grateful to the reader for the Press, whose insight made this book stronger in countless ways.

I have had comradeship and support at both Johns Hopkins and Stanford, and I would like especially to thank Neil Hertz, Isobel Armstrong, Gavin Jones, Rob Polhemus, Jennifer Summit, and Blakey Vermeule, who read a lot of this in a lot of forms. I am also thankful for the scholars whose work has made this book possible and for the conversations that have helped it to change and grow. Rachel Ablow, Ayelet Ben-yishai, John Bowen, Rachel Buurma, Terry Castle, Michael Clune, Michael Cohen, Elisha Cohn, Peter Coviello, Nick Dames, Ian Duncan, Elaine Freedgood, Renee Fox, Alex Galloway, Aman Garcha, Jason Gladstone, Rae Greiner, Mark Greif, Richard Halpern, Nancy Henry, Mark Algee-Hewitt, Jane Hu, Michelle Karnes, Evan Kindley, Ivan Kreilkamp, Jos Lavery, Allen MacDuffie, Sandra MacPherson, Doug Mao, Ian Martin, Monique Morgan, Paula Moya, Sharon Marcus, John Marx, Elsie Michie, Franco Moretti, Sianne Ngai, Vaughn Rasberry, Catherine Robson, Ramón Saldívar, Jordan Stein, Hannah Sullivan, Sam Tobin, and Karen Zumhagen-Yekplé all deserve my gratitude. Kathleen Frederickson, Stephanie Insley Hershinow, and Adena Spingarn merit keener thanks for reading much of this in draft form.

My students at both Johns Hopkins and Stanford have impressed me with their thoughtfulness and excitement about English literature. I'm grateful for the work and insights of the wonderful sets of students in my Hardy and Lawrence seminars, as well as the students in my seminar on the Palliser novels, whose enthusiasms were educational and inspiring.

The faculty and students of the Dickens Universe at UC Santa Cruz were an institutional home away from home, and I'm particularly indebted to Catherine Robson and Jim Adams for the opportunity to sketch out some of these ideas in a lecture there in 2011. At Stanford, the Center for the Study of the Novel was a welcome proving ground for my Lawrence chapter in its early stages, and I thank the Stanford graduate students and John Marx for the stimulating conversation about that work. In addition, Berkeley's Nineteenth-Century Colloquium and Cornell University both hosted me as I presented portions of this book. Those conversations, too, came at crucial times in the revision process. My research at the Ransom Center at the University of Texas at Austin and the Berg Collection at the New York Public Library were instrumental in finishing this project, and I am thankful for the support of my department and deans in providing me with the funding to complete this portion of the work.

Alyce Boster, Dagmar Logie, Laura Ma, Katie Dooling, Judy Candell, Nelia Peralta, Nicole Bridges, and Katie Oey were and are the administrative staff in the Stanford English department, and their work and care have supported me in ways big and small as I transitioned from being a graduate student to a faculty member.

A wonderful group of women, Kyla Wazana Tomkins, Sarah Mesle, Sarah Blackwood, and Hester Blum, became boon companions in the last few years, and this book bears their collective mark. Teleunits kept me going when it didn't seem possible to go any further (forty-five minutes at a time). The Van drove me there and back again. For sustaining me in big and small ways, often with cake, I thank Michelle Polzine, Franz Kunst, Nancy Ruttenburg, Greg Lowry, Naomi Fry, Ohad Meromi, Dana Kletter, Neal Fisher, Mary McDonough, and Charlie Speight. I am grateful for your friendships and for your patience. The 20th Century Café and Grand Coffee gave me knishes and coffee when I needed them, which was often. My family—all the Jarvises, Harts, Cannons, and Murphys—also have my thanks.

One of the central arguments of this book is that relationships are fragile and that a thoughtful life must accept this fact. This might seem like a frightening prospect, especially in a world full of such dismal daily reminders that a lack of security can jeopardize even the most stalwart institutions. But this does not have to cause fear. In the writing of this book, I have had the great pleasure of living in a family that reminds me daily of the pleasures that a willingness to accept vulnerability can bring. Vince and Cecil Cannon have my greatest, deepest appreciation. I could not have written this book without them, and I wouldn't recognize myself without their presence. I am grateful in ways that can't be properly acknowledged, but I hope this thanks will do.

My parents have always supported me, even when I chose to do perverse things. I owe them everything.

Exquisite Masochism

1

Making Scenes

This chapter lays out the theoretical and critical foundations of this project. Over the course of this book, I argue that by analyzing a specific kind of descriptive scene, the exquisitely masochistic scene, we can learn some of the ways the novel uses description. In the first half of the chapter, I'll give a brief synopsis of how description relates to the marriage plot, a key plotting form in the nineteenth-century novels I treat. Then, I'll move to a short close reading of Anthony Trollope's Phineas Finn novels as a way to demonstrate the importance of formal (as opposed to historical or contextual) analysis in this kind of literary criticism. In the chapter's second half, I'll discuss the specific genealogy of masochism I'll be using in this book as well as the literary critical conversations in which this book takes part. Because the concept of masochism in this book shares little with either Freudian masochism or the pragmatic sadomasochism conceptualized in the work of Michel Foucault and Leo Bersani, it bears some clarification. And because this kind of masochism helps structure the scenes I am going to be discussing, it's worthwhile to begin with an explanation of how these scenes relate to the novels in which they are found.

Describing Desire

This book is about a period in the history of the novel—the nineteenth and early twentieth centuries—in which the dominant form of the marriage plot did as much as possible to erase the material—money, looks, and property—from its pages in favor of an intangible notion of the loveable character.[1] The realist novel is full of warnings about the dangers of focusing too much on the material world—either financial or fleshly matter—

in love.[2] But if this is the novel's new ideal image of marriage, how do we read evocative, materially descriptive passages that draw our attention to the novel's material conditions?

I argue that the domestic novel's materialism—by which I mean its emphasis on the financial and physical realities that most often motivate the romantic plot—is directly related to its form. Passages of deep erotic description, when plot stops and the narrative eye tracks the minute gradations of embodied life, offer insight into the novel's dependence on substance and not just spirit, on body and not just mind. If much of the theory of the novel focuses on the many ways novelists depict minds, this project turns to read the frames, the bodies, that house those imagined minds. When Catherine the Elder forces Heathcliff to his knees in *Wuthering Heights*, when Glencora Palliser compels Burgo Fitzgerald to return to her side in *Can You Forgive Her?*, when Sue Bridehead tries, but fails, to call Jude Fawley back to her after their children's deaths in *Jude the Obscure*, when Hermione Roddice strikes Rupert Birkin with a lapis lazuli paperweight: these encounters hold or explode erotic charges that make explicit the sexual connections—and those connections' limits—between the characters.

This argument takes historical shape without resting on a historical foundation. Between the 1840s and the 1930s, the novel's status as a central cultural form was consolidated and normalized; also in this period, marriage's legal margins changed radically.[3] While what follows describes how the novel form develops in concert with these social and legal transitions, my argument stresses the formally conspicuous scenes that, I argue, link these disparate texts. Between 1847, when Emily Brontë imagines Catherine the Elder and Heathcliff enmeshed in a clinch that produces a "strange and fearful picture," and 1920, when D. H. Lawrence writes of the "infinite relief" that the "living effluence" of sexual life could bring, novelists change not only what aspects of sex can be represented in the novel's pages, but also how sex's representation connects to the novel genre's moral and social project (Brontë 124; *Women* 344–45).[4]

Between these two publication dates, the clinch, the grip, and the embrace—all ways of representing the discombobulating effect of sex on the self's equilibrium—give way to a dramatically more explicit representation of sex's dynamics. In Brontë's novel, the extramarital grasps of Catherine the Elder and Heathcliff buoy their romance up against the worryingly deadening effects their marriages have on them. But by the time we read Lawrence, nongenital sexual expressions, like those of Hermione Roddice in *Women in Love*, appear warped and psychologically damaging. Exquisitely masochistic scenes find their fullest flower in novels focusing on marriage and marriage's capacity to order a life (for good or ill).[5] The intersection between novelistic and sociohistorical development is not the primary focus of this book, but legal and social adjustments in the status of women do contribute to the marriage plot's centrality, and to that plot's alteration, over the long century between Romanticism and modernism.

In many Victorian novels, erotic connection is best inspired through rejection. This counterintuitive point develops in a world in which sexual desire is a key to a successful marriage plot but in which respectability demands that "good" characters resist their desires if they lack marriage's sanction. In the period from Victoria's reign into the early twentieth century, an important strategy for oblique sexual description involves using sexually powerful women characters to challenge prevailing sexual norms. Scenes of sexual pain and delay allow novelists to manage the erotic paradox at the core of a realist form that values accurate erotic representation while it also avoids explicit sexual depiction. At the height of the novel's cultural dominance, the most potent material sign of a couple's sexual connection was the appearance of a baby, not anything like a current novel's sex scene. During this period, too, sexual plotting—illegitimacy, bigamy, and adultery—became more and more central to the novel's form. Exquisitely masochistic scenes represent one way that novelists staged the forceful pull of sex on their respectable characters.

Because sexual life is so often posed against marriage in realist novels, particularly in the well-discussed forms of fallen women or demimondaines, readers sometimes perceive marriage as a respite from eroticism's destabilizing energies. But sexually powerful women characters don't simply provide a model of sexual life against which angelic Victorian heroines define themselves. These women and the erotic scenes they conduct drastically alter the marital model available to the normative couples located at the centers of Victorian marriage plots. Explicitly sexualized characters highlight the volatility inherent in marriage while also demonstrating the importance of sexual compatibility in ideal marriage. Consider characters as varied in their powers as the frightening, jilted Miss Wade in *Little Dorrit*, the attractive but mercenary, Rosamond Vincy in *Middlemarch*, and the voracious Lucy Westerna in *Dracula*. Despite their differences, these characters have one thing in common: they persistently disturb the desexualizing, companionable impulses traditionally thought to be central to the conventional marriage plot. To explain further what noticing exquisitely masochistic scenes can do for criticism and to describe their contours in some detail, I'll turn now to a brief account of some scenes in Anthony Trollope's Palliser series.

Warming the Blood

Late in *Phineas Redux* (1873–74), Trollope's second novel about Phineas Finn, the author describes the frustrated mind of a woman rejected—gently rejected, but rejected all the same—by the man she loves. Lady Laura Kennedy, née Standish, has been in love with Finn since before her marriage. Her love for him has survived her marriage as well as Finn's, and it continues through his wife's death and into Lady Laura's scandalous widowhood. That Lady Laura loves Finn is a truth her late husband flushed out, and the fact of that love casts a disgraceful pall over most of *Redux*. Lady Laura fantasizes about what she would do should Finn declare himself, and imagines an ideal scenario: "Had he then professed a passion for her she would have rebuked him, and told him that he must go from her,—but it would have warmed the blood in all her veins, and brought back to her a sense of youthful life" (*Phineas Redux* 500).[6]

In that "but" lies the premise of this book. Lady Laura wants to be able to push Finn away, and it is that desire for repulsion, she senses here, that spurs on her erotic attachment. The Victorian novel is full of impossible love scenes, but they're often impossible in just this way. Characters refuse erotic advances not in the interest of shutting them down but in the interest of prolonging and never escalating the experience of their approach—in *Phineas Redux*, Lady Laura imagines herself spurning Finn in the hopes that her refusal returns him to her with even more passion. Victorian novels also invest in the sense that emotional seesawing actually produces erotic heat—here, Lady Laura predicts such an experience would "[warm] the blood in all her veins."

As I have suggested, efforts to describe sexual life have had remarkable effects on novel form, a point that becomes more clearly recognizable if we turn, briefly, to a passage about a different kind of bodily description. About a third of the way through *Phineas Finn* (1867–68), Anthony Trollope gives an extended account of Finn's anxious feelings leading up to a much-hoped-for first speech:

> He was going to do something which he longed to achieve, but the very idea of which, now that it was so near to him, was a terror to him. To be in the House and not to speak would, to his thinking, be a disgraceful failure. Indeed, he could not continue to keep his seat unless he spoke. He had been put there that he might speak. He would speak. Of course he would speak. Had he not already been conspicuous almost as a boy orator? And yet, at this moment he did not know whether he was eating mutton or beef, or who was standing opposite to him and talking to him, so much was he in dread of the ordeal which he had prepared for himself. As he went down to the House after dinner, he almost made up his mind that it would be a good thing to leave London by one of the night mail trains. He felt himself to be stiff and stilted as he walked, and that his clothes were uneasy to him. When he turned into Westminster Hall he regretted more keenly than ever he had done that he had seceded from the keeping of Mr. Low. He could, he thought, have spoken very well in court, and would there have learned that self-confidence which now failed him so terribly. It was, however, too late to think of that. He could only go in and take his seat. (1:179)[7]

Trollope tracks the young parliamentarian's anxiety, which floats from his assessment of himself (he has already been "conspicuous almost as a boy orator") to his failure to perceive what's around him (he can't tell if he is eating mutton or beef) to his actual movement through space (he is "stiff and stilted" as he walks to Parliament).[8] But the central point of this passage is Finn's symptomatic anxiety about speaking: "He had been put there that he might speak. He would speak. Of course he would speak." Trollope's first Phineas novel tracks the uninitiated young Finn from his circumstantial election to his eventual return as the MP for a pocket borough. The novel's readers will recall with some pleasure that this passage does not, in fact, represent the occasion of Finn's first, muddled speech nor even his second, pat speech. Instead, it marks a puzzling stopping point on the way to his embodiment as a robust, speaking member of Parliament. This is a description of an uncomfortable feeling—anticipation—that is directly related to Finn's worries for his progress in the avenues of power. The novel is full of depictions of this concern, which alternately is represented as dislocating, confusing, and physically miserable. If all anticipatory moments were thus, this book, the book you're reading now, needn't have been written. There is a difference between this first anticipatory mode and a second, described later in the novel as Phineas waits for Madame Max Goesler—a difference between anticipation about a job or a career or a public face, and anticipation about love and sex.

Sex and desire make the experience of anticipation pleasurable, even if it's uncomfortable. This observation lies at the core of *Exquisite Masochism*: by blending pleasure with pain, sex makes waiting fun. Flick through another fifty-odd chapters of Trollope's novel, and we see this point laid bare when once again Finn is waiting for something. This time, though, the narration emphasizes a different aspect of Finn's experience as he goes to disentangle himself from Madame Max at the end of *Phineas Finn*:

> "She shall be down directly," said the girl. "I shall tell her who is here, and she will come."
>
> It was a very pretty room. It may almost be said that there could be no prettier room in all London. It looked out across certain small private gardens,—which were as bright and gay as money could make them when brought into competition with London smoke,—right on to the park. Outside and inside the window, flowers and green things were so arranged that the room itself almost looked as though it were a bower in a garden. And everything in that bower was rich and rare; and there was nothing there which annoyed by its rarity or was distasteful by its richness. The seats, though they were costly as money could buy, were meant for sitting, and were comfortable as seats. There were books for reading, and the means of reading them. Two or three gems of English art were hung upon the walls, and could be seen backwards and forwards in the mirrors. And there were precious toys lying here and there about the room,—toys very precious, but placed there not because of their price, but because of their beauty. Phineas already knew enough of the art of living to be aware that the woman who had made that room what it was, had charms to add a beauty to everything she touched. What would such a life as his want, if graced by such a companion,—such a life as his might be, if the means which were hers were at his command? It would want one thing, he thought,—the self-respect which he would lose if he were false to the girl who was trusting him with such sweet trust at home in Ireland.
>
> In a very few minutes Madame Goesler was with him, and, though he did not

think about it, he perceived that she was bright in her apparel, that her hair was as soft as care could make it, and that every charm belonging to her had been brought into use for his gratification. (2:313–14)

Phineas's waiting differs here. It's pleasant. All good things in his vision seem to come from Madame Max's organizing power, including the neighbor's gardens (even if they are drawn in distinction to industrial pollution): "as bright and gay as money could make them when brought into competition with London smoke."

Despite her apparent uniqueness in this passage, Madame Max is a type, a type that appears frequently in the Victorian novel. In almost every case, novelists grant great authority to these characters' aesthetic choices, choices that are described as unusual, distinct, or out of step with the current fashion. If we think of the many ways that sexualized power gives characters additional mobility or authority in their novel worlds, we begin to see how passages that might, at first glance, be dismissed as mere (actually) material description instead develop an unconventional aesthetics that signals a character's capacity to understand and use sexual power.[9]

If in the first passage Phineas Finn considers his status and the expectations surrounding his political career, in the second, he pays close attention to his surroundings, noticing in (and reading into) the seats and art and precious toys Madame Max's vision for his enjoyment of the space and, more than this, a vision of Madame Max's view of him. Of Phineas Finn. Anticipation is, in all its forms, tied up in expectation—in what one expects for oneself and what is expected of one by other people. The trick of *Phineas Finn*'s final, but still anticipatory, meeting and parting between Madame Max and Phineas, of course (a trick that Trollope himself can't yet know when writing this passage), is that in *Phineas Redux*, the fourth Palliser novel, Phineas and Madame Max do indeed marry, and that the widow's appeal retains its sweet entreaty even through the death of Finn's first wife, charges of murder leveled against him, and Madame Max turning detective.

Clearly, while both anticipatory modes, waiting for one's professional future and waiting for love, structure the realist novel, there are some significant differences to how they build that structure. When an author translates sexual tension into a scene, there is little emphasis on future action or the possibility of change. Instead, the narrative halts, producing a descriptive *tableau vivant* in which characters' physical and sartorial attributes take on significance. Another way to say this might be that in the first scene, when Finn contemplates his parliamentary career, his anxiety focuses on what will happen in the plot, on what comes next for him. Whereas in the scene in which Finn sits, waiting for Madame Max to appear, his anticipation is pleasurable, connected neither to the future nor to plot. Remember, after all, that these two don't end up together at this moment and that, once their meeting concludes, their relationship remains as it has been, one of gentle, static anticipation.

But here, when Trollope first brings Madame Max into the room and we see the intention that Finn reads into her dress ("every charm belonging to her had been brought into use for his gratification") reflexively cast back over the description we've just read of the room. Then, the softness and indeterminacy of the space (that "two or three gems of English art" adorn the walls is a perfect example of the elasticity of the décor) appears to have been intended to produce an effect in Finn. By virtue of that last, reflexive paragraph, the topic of the passage becomes Finn's pleasure and Madame Max's pleased investment in orchestrating an experience that generates such pleasure. While Finn's pleasure here is borne of stasis—on the absence of future plans from the various considerations Madame Max's room encourages—the fullness of these examples is only really evident if we have recourse to plot. The appeal of Madame Max's room can only be perceived when we remember that this scene, as managed as it seems to be, changes nothing about these two characters' relationship. Somewhat similarly, in moments of anticipation not connected with sexual life, as the first example above, the narrator's perspective maintains its distance from its narrated object. While the narrator has clear insight into the confusion Finn feels, the voice does not blend with Finn's; Trollope's narrator sees more than Finn sees and comments on his discombobulation with authority.

As I noted earlier, as odd as Madame Max might appear to be in the milieu of the Palliser novels' Liberal country houses, her powers of personal display mark her as a clear example of a character type given great structural weight in the realist novel, a figure I'll describe alternately as the dominant, sexually powerful, or masochistic woman. As I'll explain in greater detail later in this chapter, here "masochistic" describes characters engaged in masochistic scenes that demand their dominance and their lover's submission. Madame Max's dominance takes a number of forms. She has a perfect command of the problems other characters face and can see solutions for those problems well before the troubled characters themselves. Her status, as a wealthy widow of European (possibly Jewish) extraction, marks her as the kind of liberal cosmopolitan that Amanda Anderson argues marks the "critically detached" character in the nineteenth-century text.[10] Trollope's narrator further marks out Madame Max's self-presentation as peculiar and enticing in its peculiarity:

> Though she was the only woman so clad now present in the room, this singularity did not specially strike one, because in other respects her apparel was so rich and quaint as to make inattention to it impossible. The observer who did not observe very closely would perceive that Madame Max Goesler's dress was unlike the dress of other women, but seeing that it was unlike in make, unlike in colour, and unlike in material, the ordinary observer would not see also that it was unlike in form for any other purpose than that of maintaining its general peculiarity of character. In colour she was abundant, and yet the fabric of her garment was always black. My pen may not dare to describe the traceries of yellow and ruby silk which went in and out through the black lace, across her bosom, and round her neck, and over her shoulders, and along her arms, and down to the very ground at her feet, robbing the black stuff of all its sombre solemnity, and producing a brightness in which there was nothing gaudy. (2:25–26)

Madame Max's costume demands notice ("inattention to it [was] impossible"), but it is not overtly seductive. The strangeness of her clothing, and its richness, mark her attention to detail in such a way as to imply that though one might read this clothing, understanding its full meaning is impossible. Instead of using clothing to showcase a favored feature or to downplay a weak part, Madame Max's aesthetic choices work to highlight her character's indecipherability. So much so that the perceptive narrative voice fails in its descriptive project: "My pen may not dare to describe the traceries of yellow and ruby silk." Confoundedly, the very features that are especially compelling about Madame Max's costume defy description, even though the narrator can recognize enough about that costume to give us extraordinary detail, down to the color of the thread ("yellow and ruby") that creates these mysterious "traceries" in her black gown.

We can see very quickly how a historically attuned reader might approach these two passages from *Phineas Finn*. She might, for example, think about the status of the Irish member in an English parliament; she might think about Finn's shift from being an Irish member to becoming the member for an English pocket borough; she might think about how young men were trained in the law, and what kind of figure Mr. Low might represent; she might consider the stances of various political groups in relation to household representation or naval stores or the quest for the ballot (the actual subject of Finn's speech). Each of these approaches gives us evidence for why Finn would be anxious about making a clear, persuasive parliamentary speech; historical attention gives a number of avenues into this novel, and into this passage.

But if we turn to the second passage, which details Madame Max's room and its special appeal to Phineas Finn, we might run into some interpretive difficulty.[11] Or, if not precisely difficulty in interpretation, then difficulty in recognizing this passage as one worthy of critical analysis. Of course, history might give us an account of the room's shape and style, of the kinds of furniture and knickknacks that would produce such a warm, inviting environment. We can imagine an account that focused careful attention on the gusting industrial chimneys beyond Madame Max's window, generating all that London smoke, or we might consider the important detail that Madame Max's servant is German, not French or English. Such investigations get us quite a long way into this passage, and we can certainly assemble a close reading from such historically inflected observations. But, in so doing, we miss the attenuated pull that Madame Max's sitting room has on Phineas Finn, and if we miss that delicate draw, we miss the purpose of the passage.

Masochism's Exquisite Forms

In a book focused on how novelists represent sex on the page, masochism may seem a peculiar argumentative wedge given its pride of place in the psychoanalytic tool kit. In Freud's earliest terms, masochism is a perversion: it is sadism dangerously turned on the self, a sign of a confused identification with the submissive mother, rather than the aggressive father. For Foucault and other poststructuralist critics, masochism is a substantial part of S/M behavior, a method by which the body learns new pleasures and where new pleasures can be found in causing another body pain. But, from its earliest uses by sexologists, the concept of masochism has been connected to literary analysis.[12] For my purposes, masochism offers a site of conceptual clarification.

Following on work by Gilles Deleuze and Frances Ferguson, the masochism

I describe is entirely separate from sadism.[13] Exquisite masochism is organized into scenes with carefully ordered roles and accouterments. Furthermore, masochistic scenes feature sexual relationships that develop through ongoing negotiations and that involve partners' persistent reexamination of their sexual and romantic connections.[14] Ongoing negotiation centrally defines exquisite masochism, a form that also can include decadent, performative scenes of humiliation, the delay or refusal of genital gratification, the use of an array of masochistic props (epitomized by the raised whip), and investment in a frozen, or suspended, sexual charge (epitomized by luxurious furs). These elements stress the frozen, suspended qualities of this sexuality.[15] Together, these masochistic features allow writers to reference sexual desire without representing sexual acts. The respectable nineteenth-century novel may not (often) graphically depict sex acts, but the sexual charge of the masochistic scene enables a novelist to detail sexual connection without an explicit account of it.

The "masochistic" aspect of such scenes further arises from the disquieting tension that they produce in their participants, an experience that can cause torturous emotional sensations. This is an effect Bram Stoker's Jonathan Harker explains as he describes Dracula's vampire brides: "[i]t was like the intolerable, tingling sweetness of waterglasses when played on by a cunning hand" (45). Exquisite masochism is a relational masochism: it demands two participants, and it separates them in a dyad, suspended and cordoned off from the rest of the social world. Sometimes the participants in these scenes are the only people in the room, as in the climactic scene between Catherine the Elder and Heathcliff in *Wuthering Heights*. On other occasions, the scene works to set off the pair from the social background, as Anthony Trollope likes to do in his hunting and party scenes.

On the level of language, these scenes share a discourse. Words like "exquisite," "queenly," "imperious," "cruel," "quivering," "palpitating," "trembling," "shivering," and "flushing" mark the masochistic scene across a variety of texts. The discourse of exquisite masochism brings together language indicative of cruelty—particularly feminine, queenly cruelty—and language that describes equivocal states of being.[16] This shared discourse underscores the heightened anticipation that is vital to the masochistic scene.[17] Stasis, in these scenes, is not a lack of movement but a movement curtailed—a thrum that signals tension while also marking a body's lively vitality. In response to reading such a scene, a reader might experience "intensity," "thickness,"

"density," and "potency," although she might also be unaware of what, precisely, prompts these feelings. The atmosphere of exquisite masochism is
one of fullness and coalescence, of gravity. Time's passage stops or at least
is slowed: plot drops out, as does the novel's capacity to register internal
thought; the senses dominate, and description reigns.

Along with a shared discourse, close attention to the aesthetic choices of
feminine or female characters, and the particular character of such choices,
mark these scenes. In the novel, appearance often works as a shortcut to
developing a character—think of how meaningful costuming is to giving
insight into a character's political views or class position or how important
brief passages of physical characteristics can be to getting a picture of a character in one's head—and these scenes are no exception. However, in exquisitely masochistic scenes, the aesthetics are of a minor or demotic type:
clothes are dark and heavy, not light and filmy; expensive and exotic, not
only beautiful. If a dominant woman's clothing is luxurious, it is also peculiar. In fact, peculiarity trumps luxury in masochistic aesthetics. Often, the
masochistic heroine is set off from other women by virtue of her strange
apparel. The masochistic heroine's clothing emphasizes her body's closure,
its resistance to prurient notice. Masochistic heroines are buttoned up, and
their tightly controlled—exquisite—physical displays contrast with more
obviously voluptuous demonstrations.

Using a term like "masochism" implies a strong theoretical connection
to psychoanalytic frameworks, especially when examining novels produced
in the period that also occasions the rise of sexology. While the term has a
potent psychoanalytic charge, my interest is primarily formal, not psychological. As a formal device, exquisite masochism rests on the adoption of
complicated (and sometimes individual or idiosyncratic) symbolic logics, in
suspension or sexual delay, in deferred or denied sexual gratification, and
in an investment in contract and its failures. More, as I suggested in the
preface, "exquisite" masochism can be recognized through its dependence
on aesthetically minded, dominant women, its heightened erotic tension
and its scenic display. All of these can be staged in a signal feature of this
masochistic mode, the sexualized scene. What results from these scenes are,
alternately, stories focused on female rule and male supplication—a plot-
level delay of genital sex in favor of sexual pleasure through pain—and
scenes or spectacles with no normatively satisfying resolution or consequence. Exquisitely masochistic scenes rely on a refusal of event, on scene

building for its own sake. But this dependence also delineates masochism's eventual failure. Genital sex, tied as it is to reproduction and familial life, often exerts a pull on the masochistic couple. Nongenital sex can, eventually, fail to provide a sexual thrill. If, as I propose, we imagine masochistic scenes as spaces that allow for radical, generative formations of romantic attachment to develop, we must also imagine them as limited by their differences from the outside worlds they hamper. Conceptually, masochism has had an interesting history since the turn of the twenty-first century. Some critics have attacked the perversion inherent in masochistic sexuality, either because it tends to mimic patriarchal heterosexuality or because masochism typically associates sex with violence and pain. Alternately, queer scholarship on sadomasochistic culture claims an equalizing potential in masochistically charged sexualities that emphasize role reversal and flexible sexual practice. The exquisite masochism on which I focus does not fit into either of these classifications, but it is my contention that masochism's tightly structured scenarios belie its productive potential.

Adherents to a notion of S/M role reversal's liberating effects ignore the ways in which such role reversal avoids a real encounter with negotiation. Flexible positions reduce the need to agree about anything other than the position one occupies during an individual encounter. Instead of arguing about their actual positions, then, partners come to debate the momentary occupation of a position. The dyads I discuss, by contrast, fully negotiate the fixed power positions common in Victorian novels. Furthermore, because the power dynamics in the masochistic dyad contribute to the viability of the sexual relationship, one cannot disentangle sexuality from a discussion of power. Instead of imagining ideal sexuality as separable from power, then, masochism's investment in contract and negotiation forces its participants to negotiate the role of power in the relationship. If power remains a constant aspect of sexual relationship, negotiation assumes a special prominence. In this way, masochistic agreements offer useful correlatives to more conventional contractual relationships, such as marriages. Instead of securing relationship, the legalistic or social contract imagines a fixity that endures no matter how dissatisfied the constituents become. Marriage, as we will see, offers a false security that masochistic agreement exposes.

Because masochistic scenes are conceptually transparent, that is, because the negotiations between two people are central to all interaction within the masochistic scene, I use these moments to explore the ways this group of novelists depicts scenes of heightened sexual, and thus embodied, awareness. My aim is not, or is not primarily, to catalog these scenes or to group these writers under the aegis of "masochistic authorship." Again, psychoanalytic masochism itself does not illuminate these scenes. Instead, the structures that masochism needs to develop its erotic charge allow us to see the novel's somatic medium.[18] By noticing masochistic scenes, one comes to see a bit more clearly how scenic-ness—broadly construed—works in the novel. In the novels I discuss below, masochistic scenes take place in a sexual milieu that centers on the marriage plot.

This book hinges on a version of masochism related to the earliest descriptions of this pathology's investment in the "supersensual." Masochism, like sadism, is a pathology with a peculiarly literary history. The word is derived from the name of Leopold von Sacher Masoch, the German pornographic author, and his novellas and stories are useful in delineating the concept. "Supersensual," for instance, appears regularly in Masoch's 1870 novel *Venus in Furs* to describe the intense sensual experience Severin von Kuziemski, the novella's protagonist, seeks.[19] *Venus in Furs* catalogs Kuziemski's successful campaign to install the elegant Wanda von Dunajew as his "Venus in Furs," his vision of a cruel and despotic mistress who will treat him as a slave in a contract-ridden, sexualized, perverse exchange.[20] The phrase captures both the intense nerviness of the masochistic pair and any such couple's heavy investment in accouterments that fascinate or excite sensation.[21] Sometimes, Sacher-Masoch's scenes do indeed feature whips and boots and insulating furs, but more often they focus on the arrangement of the couple's bodies in space, and on the relational tensions acting on those bodies. In charting the difference between supersensual masochism and what I call exquisite masochism, I am also diverging significantly from most Freudian or post-Freudian iterations. In his early theory, Freud describes masochism as sadism turned inward. Even in a later account of what he calls "moral masochism," Freud divorces his notion of primary masochism from sexual expression; the moral masochist interests herself with humiliation rather than sexualized pain.[22] Alternately, in my account, literary representations of sadism and masochism develop differently, specifically in regard to how their writers represent bodies.

Given their shared emphasis on cruelty's connection to sexual life, masochism is often connected to sadism in the popular imaginary. It's true that these two sexual concepts share a similarly literary genealogy. But if we separate sadism from masochism, as Gilles Deleuze's intervention suggests we might, we can see these two sexual types spring from entirely oppositional desires: the sadist abuses others from an institutional distance, while the masochist abuses himself within a carefully constructed contract.[23] In their literary works, if Sade emphasizes a sexual hierarchy brought to bear on individual bodies, Masoch emphasizes a suspended scene orchestrated (and limited) by contractual agreement (Ferguson 57–95). While Deleuze's separation of masochism from sadism chimes with my concept of exquisite masochism—I agree that these concepts offer radically different approaches to an ideal version of sexual life—my account of the broader structure of masochism departs from Deleuze's in a crucial way. Counter to Deleuze, a close reading of the sexual dynamics of Sacher-Masoch's *Venus in Furs* suggests that the masochistic dyad is constructed by two active participants, not one. Further, these two participants are equally engaged in the creation of the complicated scenes that form masochism's center. Otherwise, how might one account for the question Wanda eventually puts to her lover: "Was it my idea or yours?" (201). Until this point, late in the novella, Wanda repeatedly denies that her "nature" is in any kind of sympathy with Severin's desire for abuse and tyranny, but, quickly after the exchange, the reader is given a different account of Wanda:

> "You are mistaken," I continued, "you are making yourself out to be more evil than you really are; you are far too good, far too noble by nature . . ."
>
> "What do you know about my nature?" she interrupted violently. "You will get to know me as I really am." (201)

Deleuze reads these exchanges as places where Severin's mistress beautifully enacts his masochistic fantasy; for Deleuze, Severin never relinquishes control, though the illusion of that control's relinquishment is one of the most exciting attributes of the affair. But Wanda's repeated insistence that she disdains "play acting" and "melodrama," as well as her "violent" eruption during Severin's assessment of her character, point to another possibility. In other words, where Deleuze sees one subject controlling two bodies, Masoch's text offers two strongly marked subjects operating in relation to one another. The threat of Masoch's novella, in my view, is that an effort to produce a safe master-slave relationship fails; safety is never part of a sexual equation. The erotic scenes of Masoch's novellas, and of the English novels I treat, focus on the orchestrated nature of sexually charged scenes. But they also emphasize the erotic need for an element of surprise and disorder. Though submissive men may carefully manage and orchestrate the scenes at the core of their masochistic scenarios, there must also remain a potential for surprise, scenic revision, or even the possibility of a complete disregard of the negotiated rules. This threat of disorder adds to the sexual charge, and it is this threat that indicates the necessity of both participants' agency in the dyad.

The novelists I examine use masochism's elements to emphasize the contract's failure to secure relationships, the need for compatibility between partners' sexual desires, and the conflict between the paired Victorian ideals of isolating, dyadic marriage and public, reproductive marriage—think of the salutary effect that the birth of a child brings to the last pages of novels as diverse as *Dracula*, *Middlemarch*, and *Bleak House*. Unlike marriage, the masochistic contract does not look to a greater legal or political body for endorsement. Instead, it exposes a larger issue with thinking about relationships in contractual terms. In the chapters that follow, I describe a number of novelistic encounters with this problem. A major difficulty with imagining relationship, especially sexual relationship, as contractual is that relationships of all kinds contain within themselves an anxiety about their dissolution or scarcity. One way to push against this fear is to naturalize relationship. And when masochistic contracts come into conflict with these newly naturalized contracts, such as the contract between parent and child, or even the contract between husband and wife, participants find themselves party to more contracts than they can acknowledge or reconcile.

Masochism, too, offers a useful tool for locating these scenes in novels because its forms so clearly emphasize characters' physical interactions, particularly how their imagined bodies relate to one another in their imagined worlds. Masochistic scenes freeze figures in attitudes suggestive of sexual or erotic experience, which in turn slows down action and allows a reader to develop her sense of the somatic schematics necessary to an interaction between characters. Novels give plenty of examples of such discreetly limited sexual scenes. Occasionally, these scenes are even linked explicitly to *tableaux vivants* or painted portraiture.[24] But these are not the only versions of masochistic scene building. Masochistically inflected scenes focus on characters' abilities to work the sexual hierarchies in which they find themselves: hierarchy's upheaval—even if temporary—is the aim of the masochistic scene. Sometimes, these interactions look like parodies of the marriage contract. At other times, the scene's deployment fractures any semblance of relationship—the upheaval is too powerful for the characters to accommodate. The fragility of masochistic dyads demonstrates the general difficulty of expecting the sexual contract to be enduring and stable; agreement only remains as long as each partner's desires are met. For the writers I treat, masochistic sex crucially exposes the way negotiable sexual debate is key to ongoing romantic attachment.

Masochism, particularly male-submissive, heterosexual masochism, forces us to grapple with questions of sexual power, sexual dominance, and gendered sexual subjectivity. The novels I discuss resonate with this concept because they demonstrate how authors explore the various possibilities that the marriage plot offers for imagining a contract that secures lasting sexual connection. All of these novels give readers clear examples of delineated scenes, frequently imagining carefully constructed tableaux. Additionally, the writers on whom I have focused tend to emphasize their characters' negotiated sexual interactions: all of these novelists place sexual and romantic stories at the centers of their plot systems, even if those plot systems ostensibly focus on more institutionally ordered spheres. The discreet contours of the masochistic dyad light up both its self-sufficiency and its vulnerability to outside observation or manipulation. If the dyads I describe emphasize reciprocal, dialogic exchange, they also—perhaps because of this—are fragile when placed in relation to larger social orders or institutions, especially marriage. Coverture, for example, forces a clear hierarchy on married relationship that counters the equalizing effects masochism may have. What an attention to these dyadic structures can show, then, is that while representations of conventional Victorian marriages may appear to be defined against such perverse, nongenerative masochism, they often include masochism's elements. Exquisite masochism both situates and complicates Victorian marriage ideology's more conventional focus on a productive, nation-building ideal and offers insight into Victorian debates around illicit sexuality, marriage, and feminism.

A reader may wonder why I've limited my analysis to novels from the long nineteenth century, since surely such scenes appear in a variety of texts across a much wider historical frame. This book focuses on the Victorian novel for two key reasons. First, the long nineteenth century marks the apex of the novel's cultural power. As novelists experimented with a capacious realism, the novel became an aesthetic form closely aligned with wide-ranging social observation and critique, much of it about the changing status of women and marriage. Second, while sex became a central motive for novelistic plots, the novel's newfound respectability demanded sex's cover in metaphor and euphemism. As the novel's representation of sex changed, so did the power of exquisite masochism to shape the novel form: my inclusion of D. H. Lawrence shows what happens when the dominant woman loses her structural and political power.

In other words, we see description's formal power most clearly when we see its effects on the marriage plot, one of the Victorian novel's most defined plot systems. I've chosen to focus on the coded erotic scenes that structure the representation of sexuality in these novels because they demonstrate my point most explicitly. Scenes and characters like the ones I describe in this book seem, many times, to be outside or to the side of the marriage plot, but they also shape and challenge it. Exquisitely masochistic characters may present an alternative to traditional marriage structures, but they also confirm the vibration of the real—of sexual life's significance—in the center of the marriage plot. If the marriage plot is a powerful engine for the novel, exquisite masochism stokes its fire.

Sex, Marriage and the Victorian Novel

This project trains its attention on literary form. Because of this, my methods emphasize close readings and interpretation over breadth and explanation. One aim of this book is to mount a robust defense of the case study as an analytical, not just descriptive, method. In much literary criticism, a pastiche approach to exemplary material has become increasingly common.[25] The appeal of this approach is clear: one can quickly demonstrate the power of one's claims across a wide variety of texts. But one side effect of this method is a diminution in the value of the literary in favor of an elevation of the historical. If the argumentative aim is to show a concept's broad cultural effect, the aim of the example is to secure that breadth. More, though, an argument developed through a wide-ranging use of textual examples can devolve into a kind of faulty dialectic, wherein one category of knowledge actually takes the pride of place, working as a weight against which the other category's limitations come into clearer view.[26] Often, nonliterary discourses (sciences, sociology, anthropology) are positioned as more authoritative so they're granted privileged insight into literary production.[27] While this method powerfully establishes the depth and breadth of

Victorian thought, the central aim of these related methods is to illuminate something about history. And history gives us one clear rationale for rereading novels from the past: it helps us better understand that past. But, in a historicist argument, the novel is just one kind of cultural form, if a privileged form, about which a scholar can speak.[28] Alternately, I'm interested in what happens when we turn, with sustained, prolonged attention, to specific pieces of literature. In particular, the abstract modeling of marriage plots (man and woman meet; courtship ensues; marriage may or may not happen) means that books that use this kind of plotting lose distinction when read this way. Another benefit of a case study approach is that one can train one's attention on longer passages of text. My focus on scenes requires attention to longer passages; analysis of shorter quotations can't produce the same work of showing the shape of a scene, and it is the material shape—the ways the bodies interact in a space over a period of time—that I want to emphasize in my readings.[29]

Novelists often use sexualized scenes to demonstrate the conditions for and capacities of sexual attraction. In the novels I treat, sexual attraction is either a precursor to, or a blockade against, marriage (sometimes it's both). Marriage, as I've already claimed, has a privileged status in the history of the novel, and critics from Nancy Armstrong to Elsie Michie have examined the ways novel plotting and marriage contracts coincide. Marriage occupies a special status in contract theory, too, in part because marriages emerge from scripted performances that highlight the performativity inherent in any contract.[30] This project works in conversation with a strong tradition of feminist formal criticism. Sandra Macpherson's account of the relationship between harm and contract in literary form suggests that the novel as such depends on causal plotting, not character, a concept she ties to legal theories of strict liability. In her far-reaching view, strict liability offers a conceptual framework for understanding that "to be a woman is to be engaged in an undertaking—reproduction—so dangerous that one is never delivered of its burdens: the burden of care and the corresponding burden of liability" (47). Macpherson's model of emplotment, in which characters are tragic if their novels recognize them as causes and not subjects, would seem to offer a strong account of narrative progression (for example, in *Jude the Obscure*, the children's murder could be seen as "caused" by the first fateful meeting between Arabella and Jude). But the novels on which I focus make it quite clear that this is not the best way to read such apparently causal plots. Instead, these novels' plots point to causality to dismiss it, in the same way that novels point to heredity to deny its power to order lives. The twinned problems of choice and will, represented at the novel's every turn by written and unwritten contract (marriage, sexual union, parenthood, etc.) mean that narrative development is not linked to any logical chain, causal or otherwise. In other words, while it may seem to be the case that novels oscillate between poles of plotted determinism and characterological choice, they actually group determinism and choice together as conceptual blockages to the real problem of the novel: that no security—relational or otherwise—can be found. If the marriage plot often appears to be a way to make sexual relationships secure—especially as regards childbearing, childrearing, and the consolidation of property—masochistic elements draw attention to sex's basic insecurity.

This project also addresses the place of sexual life in recent critical work that locates the ongoing cultural importance of the Victorian novel squarely in the articulation and development of a progressive worldview.[31] For example, critical accounts of the emergence of Liberalism place special emphasis on the part played by social problem novels, journalism, and essays in the nineteenth century's political fortunes.[32] And these forms do shed crucial light on problems brought about by inequality and covert political action. But I argue instead for a reinvestigation of a daemonic canon developed in the work of two somewhat oppositional figures, Raymond Williams and F. R. Leavis. Taken together, these two writers clarify the conceptual stakes of my project's object choices: *Exquisite Masochism* leavens Leavis's aggressively focused *The Great Tradition* with an emphasis on women's fortunes and extends Williams's assessment of the changing fortunes of common British life to the edges of the marriage plot. When viewed with Leavis and Williams in mind, the odd man out here is Anthony Trollope, a novelist deeply invested in embedded traditionalism, but who grapples with the scene-chewing energies that masochistic characters bring to his novel worlds. By focusing on perverse sexuality's representation within this iconoclastic canon, we begin to see how the liberal tradition, broadly construed, pushes dislocating sensual representation to the side in favor of consciousness, awareness, and social engagement. My suggestion is that we reimagine a liberal state that allows us access to those destabilizing zones of absorption, suspension, and reverie.[33] Intensity, in my account, is not a counterweight to clear-sightedness; it is its engine.

In a recent critical example, Sharon Marcus develops a concept of female marriage as ballast against the psychic destruction Victorian marriage ideology all but demanded. Marcus argues that female companionship was often the most powerful emotional support for Victorian women.[34] By exposing the ways nonmarital heterosexual encounters organize and structure the sexual plots of the Victorian novel, I am not dismissing the cultural importance of female-identified desire in the lives of Victorian women. Instead, I am suggesting that these exquisite dynamics offer another way of seeing female domination in an environment that did much to minimize female power and authority. Marcus writes of "desire—not as an antisocial force but as a deeply regulated and regulating hierarchical structure of longing" (5), whereas the versions of desire that the exquisitely masochistic dyad licenses are utterly contrary not just to social order but to any connections that threaten the dyad itself. Rachel Ablow's *The Marriage of Minds* focuses on how a "conservative ideology of marital sympathy" emphasizes the failures of "psychic interpenetration" in the novels (122). And while nineteenth-century depictions of sexual desire often tip quickly into unpleasant psychic dominance on the part of the male partner and submission on the part of the woman, as Ablow suggests, there is a space for something like sexual sympathy at work in novels that present sexual relationships that depend on power imbalances. Or, perhaps more specifically, my readings show sexual sympathy as an idealized state that finds narrative development, albeit rarely. In part, this is because sexual sympathy is most evident at the moments when bodies are in closest proximity to one another, when description thus becomes attentive to the relationships between bodies rather than souls. For example, in Anthony Trollope's *Can You Forgive Her?*, Alice Vavasor "shudders" at moments of embodied intersubjectivity—when she hears John Grey's voice after a long absence and when her cousin George asks her for a kiss.

Of course, there is a difference between hearing a voice and kissing a mouth, and while the shudder indicates an aspect of Alice's desire, it also indicates an aspect of her revulsion. Alice is, as it were, caught in the interstices of moral love and sexual love: she evinces desires for both men, but George's moral debasement over the course of the novel troubles her. The complex relationship between moral and sexual value is often the source of some worry in the nineteenth-century novel. More recently, Elsie Michie's *The Vulgar Question of Money* explains the ways "the marriage plot allows the novel to make a clear statement about where its values lie" (19). Michie's assessment focuses on the ways novelists of manners present rich women as potential marriage partners for their protagonists in order that they might draw attention to the "middle-class virtue" encoded in characters like Austen's Elizabeth Bennet (17). For my purposes, Michie's readings of Trollope's heiress heroines, whose relationship to wealth is vastly different from that of the heiresses in the novels of manners that came before his, offer a wedge into a discussion of material wealth's importance to exquisite masochism. As Michie notes, these heiresses are unusual in the history of the novel because their great wealth does not mean they are morally or ethically suspect. Unlike the Caroline Bingleys and Miss Greys of Austen, Trollope's newly minted heiresses women do not work as foils to virtuous middle class protagonists, an alteration that Michie connects to the increasingly abstract notion of money.[35] However, *Exquisite Masochism* argues that, shifting our gaze to the ways sexual desire works in these plots, a slightly different category appears. While the wealthy woman and the poor woman create one model of differentiated desires for Victorian protagonists, so do dominant women and submissive women. More, while there is often a connection between the kind of wealth Michie discusses and the aestheticized buying power of my dominant women, there is no necessary correlation, as my discussions of Hardy and Lawrence will show.

Anne-Lise François has written cogently on the aesthetic countertradition that she calls the writing of "recessive action," which emphasizes objects and manners that are "minor, nugatory, unworthy, insignificant, unreal" (25).[36] But, rather than locate reticence and recession in character systems or types that avoid or refuse the liberating ethos associated with modern protagonists, I instead locate resistance in characters that aggressively chafe against norms they encounter. The plots variously arranged for these characters are the plots of the outsider, the sexual threat, the seductress, and the pervert. Resistance to progressive ideals can take many forms, especially when such resistance is located in feminine or female characters. But while the steely submission we associate with, perhaps most evocatively, Charlotte Brontë's maddeningly reticent heroines offers one clearly recessive iteration of this countertradition, I argue that even a more explosive figure— say, Emily Brontë's Catherine the Elder—similarly resists liberal ways of being. This book focuses attention on the powerful ways that sexual desire and pleasure license unmanaged or excessive actions, feelings, and thoughts for characters in these novels. By so doing, I hope to illuminate some of the excessively recessive forces at work in these texts and to think hard about how passages that at first seem resistant to plot's organizing power may actually help bolster plot's power over novelistic description. To return to the examples I discussed above, we might think about how differently Phineas anticipates his parliamentary speech than Madame Max's entrance into her sitting room, about how his hopes for progress are different from desire.

Finally, I'm suggesting we grapple with scenes that often halt critical engagement rather than prompt it. Suspense is often imagined as coalescing around scenes that excite readerly interest. Caroline Levine suggests narrative suspense encourages readers to suspend their judgment, training readers to understand that the real world does not always confirm one's beliefs (2–3).[37] But, in my examples, suspense—what most readers mean by suspense, that tense excitement to know what happens next—is absent. There is tension in these scenes, but it is a tension marked off by and experienced by characters. If these scenes produce a tension in the text's characters, what they often produce in readers is more closely akin to boredom. These scenes do suspend convention, it's true—they are often the most erotically charged scenes in novels that can't quite represent erotic life—but they depend on assumptions of authority that deeply structure those erotic connections. The pleasure Levine's reader feels in "[waiting], suspended, to see whether or not the [novel's] future will bear out our suppositions and desires" (9) is at odds with the soporific effect scenes of exquisite masochism tend to have. These scenes bore and frustrate readers, both because they are often unconnected from plot-resolving marriages and because they tend to recur over the length of a novel. Importantly, writers separate such scenes from the processes of unfolding their novel's narrative future—such tableaux are marked off as scenes by the virtue of both their densely descriptive prose and their status as isolated vignettes in their novels.

Examining these particular novelists together shows how they all value a sexuality organized around and constructed by erotic tableaux. This is to say that Trollope's eroticized descriptions, of horse racing and midnight "crushes," correlate to the apparently more antinomian, and apparently more antisocial, intensities at play in Brontë's, Hardy's, and Lawrence's novels. In some ways, Trollope's descriptive scenes stand as a bridge between the erotics central to Brontë's project and the more measured negotiable energies of Hardy's dialogic novel. If Trollope's novels imagine the problems of sexual relationship in a social milieu, Hardy's and Brontë's novels imagine the difficulty of contracting sexual relationships entirely at odds with their communities, and Lawrence's novels present the sexual lives of their characters as ballast against creeping social rules. *Wuthering Heights* focuses on a hermetic world that not only disallows entry to outsiders but that features at its center a pairing so private it resists even this minimal community's interpretation. And Hardy's novel indicates that the private, intimate relationship that Sue and Jude construct is susceptible to even the most minimal exposure. For both of these writers, then, public exposure threatens or explicitly damages the masochistic dyad. Trollope's novels, quite differently, do not imagine the social world as totally disruptive to masochism, though the social webs his characters inhabit require masochism's sexual character be dampened in order for its productive anticipatory potential to be realized. And, finally, in Lawrence's sexualized social worlds, a sexual act makes a character neither a social pariah nor a revolutionary. Instead, we see sexuality as problematic only when connected to a character's philosophy: overthinking destroys sexual life for Lawrence. Not all of these novelists imagine a separation between masochism and ideal relationship. Emily Brontë, for example, offers a strong critique of normative marriage via her vision of painful, and painfully erotic, romance. By moving from the mid-nineteenth to the early twentieth century, I'll explain how the masochistic dyad gives a variety of canonical novelists a form against which they can ballast their ideal views of sexual companionship and, by proxy, marriage. By the time we get to Lawrence, the masochistic pair has lost its sexual charge, and the dominant woman, her narrative power and interest. But how productive is the figure that develops in her place?

2

The Grasp of *Wuthering Heights*

In moving to Emily Brontë's 1847 novel *Wuthering Heights*, I turn to one of the most written about, and most demanding, novels of the midcentury. Brontë's novel has, in many accounts, been read alongside her life. Beginning with Charlotte Brontë's 1850 introduction and Elizabeth Gaskell's *The Life of Charlotte Brontë*, critics have elided Emily Brontë's apparently iconoclastic, intense life with her similarly estranging novel. Because the novel produces such a hermetic world, critics find themselves turning biographer, trying to imagine how *this* woman wrote *this* book. *Wuthering Heights* is read as singular—for its erotic explicitness, for the difficulty in parsing the character of its antihero, Heathcliff, and for the violence that peppers the text. Because masochism, as I've described it, focuses so intensely on frozenness and suspension instead of pain or violence, *Wuthering Heights* may seem like an odd choice with which to begin. The novel's insistence on a generalized experience of extreme violence (consider not only the beatings Heathcliff gives Isabella and Catherine the Younger but the animal carcasses that litter the text) seems at odds with the kind of exquisite masochism I discussed in the introduction. But this violence actually highlights one of the key reasons it is crucial to my account. Brontë aligns much of the novel's explicit violence with a sadistic model of legal marriage, instead of the frozen, positively valued masochistic dyad of Catherine and Heathcliff at the novel's center. In fact, this central, masochistic couple turns to increasingly private, frozen scenes to buttress their relationship against the sadistic marriages that populate the plot.

Most accounts of Brontë's novel that discuss sadism or masochism attach sadistic impulses to Heathcliff and self-denying, masochistic impulses to Catherine. I suggest that while these accounts may adhere to the models explored in Heathcliff's and Catherine's *marriages*, their private relationship depends instead on the cultivation of a masochistic dyad along the Deleuzean lines I sketched briefly in my introduction. I consider one of the hermeneutics of the text—the central relationship between Catherine and Heathcliff —to be the novel's main structuring system. Masochism illuminates the closed-off quality of this pairing beyond the scope of Brontë's biography.[1] Indeed, by fixing aspects of the novel to Brontë's life, we ignore the novel's prominent models of suspense or frozenness, and we do not fully engage with the significance of Catherine's grasp on Heathcliff or of Heathcliff's decline into stone at the novel's end. The differences between Catherine and Heathcliff—instead of hampering the development of romantic attachment —help construct a masochistic dyad at odds with the novel's legitimate marriages.[2] By separating sadistic marriages from masochistic relationships in *Wuthering Heights*, Brontë anticipates Deleuze's major innovation on Freud and privileges a masochistic version of sexuality—though, by the novel's end, she also gives an account of masochism's tendency toward failure.

As I claimed in the introduction, this tendency is one of the key reasons masochistic dyads have special importance in relation to nineteenth-century marriage plots. Masochism's propensity to dissolve lights up not only the difficulty of imagining sexual relationships as contractual relationships but also the contract's failure to act as a corrective to such dissolution. If, for example, the negotiable, unwritten contracts of the masochistic dyad tend to break down when faced with internal or external challenges, how might the legal contract—less flexible by far—fare when tested? Further, *Wuthering Heights*, by virtue of its hermetic qualities, gives clear examples of some of the major problems facing romantic dyads. In Brontë's novel, problems of exposure are typified by the dyad's disclosure of its status to a community that demands married fixity in sexual relationship. And, by characterizing the novel's central pairing as one of frozen intensity, Brontë imagines this relationship in uncannily masochistic terms. Because of this, a masochistic lens can clarify a number of the most difficult aspects of Brontë's novel—the violence, the cryptic central relationship, the place of the animal, even Catherine and Heathcliff's frozen, bloodless deaths. As we shall see, masochism eventually drains both Catherine the Elder and Heathcliff of blood. But, their bodies' eventual bloodnessness is an extension of their masochistic freezing, and, as such, Brontë does not imagine this process as *fully* destructive, though it ends in death. By suturing death to frozenness, Brontë imagines a possible future for the masochistic dyad even when she also relegates the two partners to the grave. But Catherine and Heathcliff are not vampires; they do not absorb energy from the world beyond their dyadic bounds. Instead, the narrative emphasis on their bodily stiffness makes them more like interred stones: unreflecting, immovable, but permanently present. This particular kind of frozenness illuminates the endlessness of the pair's connection.

Other critics have commented extensively on the lack of significant movement in the novel's plot. The "gypsy" outsider Heathcliff enters the closed world of the moors; the Heights expels the outsider. One Hareton Earnshaw built Wuthering Heights in 1500; another Hareton Earnshaw will reclaim the Heights upon his marriage in 1803. Marriage hinders the core relationship of the novel; at its end, marriage appears to be a recuperative salve. Catherine Earnshaw imagines becoming Catherine Heathcliff but instead becomes Catherine Linton; Catherine Linton becomes Catherine Heathcliff only to be widowed, and at the novel's close is poised to become Catherine Earnshaw—reclaiming her mother's name as she moves to her mother's married home and returns to her own childhood home.[3] *Wuthering Heights* begins, in many ways, as it ends; but this doesn't, somehow, dampen the strange energy of the novel. Brontë's novel is one of anticipation.

In the pages that follow, I suggest that the energetic machine moving *Wuthering Heights* forward is not plot, as might be expected in a midcentury British novel, but an anticipatory model that mimics, in many ways, the exquisite masochism I set out in my introduction. The novel separates reproductive, legal, marital relationship from the sterile, illicit, unmarried relationship at the novel's center. The novel's marital relationships correspond to a sadistic logic, while the relationship between Catherine and Heathcliff is masochistic. The anticipatory form of the novel does not depend on the lack of clarity surrounding the novel's events—it does not much matter, in the world of the novel, what happens next (a point driven home by the circuitous, gap-filled tale-telling that Lockwood, Nelly, and their various interlocutors engage in over the course of the novel). Instead, it's clear that while Catherine the Elder and Heathcliff expect and want consummation from the first moment of their sensual embrace, they also build the intensity of their relationship through a series of masochistically inflected, erotic scenes. The anticipatory logic is so strong that, even after death, the yearning that structured the relationship during life remains.

If Brontë constructs a world structured by expectation, it is also a world that often lacks either antecedents or solutions to that expectation. Thus, the images of hanging that scatter the text (Hareton hanging cats, Heathcliff hanging Isabella's dog, the hanging lattice that catches the dead Heathcliff's skin, ghostly Cathy's hand's "tenacious gripe" on Lockwood's arm) emblematize the novel's action. All of these images belong to Brontë's strange system of signs; all are loaded with indistinct meaning. But, instead of parsing the significance of each emblem individually, I want instead to emphasize the structural relationship these images privilege. Hanging, like grasping or holding, as I'll claim, is a suspended action. Once begun, these actions might last indefinitely; and their everlasting aspect suggests, among other things, the possibility of endless continuation within the world of the novel. These gestures also signal the development of erotic tableaux, specifically scenes of domination between Catherine the Elder and Heathcliff. *Wuthering Heights* presents the reader with an interlocking nest of anticipatory signs; characters and objects are suspended in the action, waiting for the next development—the next adjustment to their scene.[4]

At the end of the novel, in her description of Heathcliff's life-ending illness, Brontë aligns his deathbed condition with that of Catherine the Elder, imagining both as progressive, bodily hardenings that eventuate in a final consummation. The pair imagines such a consummation beyond the grave (Heathcliff's plan for disintegration means that Catherine is right that Heathcliff is "more myself than I am"); the demands of masochistic anticipation prove too much for the world in which they live.[5] When the second generation's love plot develops, however, it adjusts the novel's earlier model of sadistic marriage to one of instructive, but not cruel, marriage. The sadistic model drops off when an institutional power, in the form of a slightly recuperated model of pedagogic marriage, asserts itself at the novel's end. But Brontë's decision to end the novel with a proposed marriage between Hareton Earnshaw and Catherine the Younger transforms that pairing's initially private, contractual relationship into one fixed to institutionality, and thus outside the masochistic logic so prized in the first generation. As they set about to improve the manner of life at the Heights, Catherine the Younger and Hareton develop a sense of security in marriage's contractual power in part because they *see* examples of partnership's success in transforming the world around them (windows open, gates yield to visitors). I contend that Brontë sees this as false security. In the world of *Wuthering Heights*, the contract's power to secure relationship is always tainted by sadistic violence, even if that violence can be channeled into productive, pedagogical aims. Instead of imagining an ideal social world as receptive to outsiders, Brontë conceives of the closed-off pair as an ideal at odds with a community hostile to interlopers. By the novel's end, contract is forced into institution; the idealized masochistic union of Catherine and Heathcliff is over, unsustainable outside of the grave.

Like many Victorian novels, *Wuthering Heights* does not mesh its plot resolution to its system of value. If Heathcliff dies at the novel's end, it is with the possible promise of his further satisfaction beyond the grave. And if Catherine the Younger and Hareton's marriage seems imminent, its positive potential is dampened by the intense narrative interest in Catherine the Elder's relationship with Heathcliff. It thus becomes clear that while the first generation's masochistic intensity no longer has a place in *Wuthering Heights*, it is also the ideal version of relationship within the novel. I want to focus attention on the ideation of this central relationship; the novel's major loss is, of course, this pairing. Catherine the Elder and Heathcliff are consigned to the novel's periphery where they were once its center.

Heathcliff describes his illness at the novel's end as an absorption into a yearning so intense that it obscures even involuntary processes:

> "And yet I cannot continue in this condition! I have to remind myself to breathe—almost to remind my heart to beat! And it is like bending back a stiff spring; it is by compulsion that I do the slightest act not prompted by one thought, and by compulsion, that I notice anything alive, or dead, which is not associated with one universal idea. I have a single wish, and my whole being and faculties are yearning to attain it. They have yearned towards it so long, and so unwaveringly, that I'm convinced it *will* be reached—and *soon*—because it has devoured my existence. I am swallowed in the anticipation of its fulfillment." (248)

The length and depth of his anticipation intensifies to the point where his bodily functions fail ("I have to remind myself to breathe"). The tension of expectation has stretched even Heathcliff beyond his limits, and he is fully absorbed ("swallowed") in an attitude of frozen waiting. Compulsion, importantly, does not relate to the absorbing anticipation Heathcliff describes here; he must compel his body to continue the basic operations required for survival, but he "yearns"—wants, chooses—to anticipate his reacquaintance with Catherine. And, for all their similarity of form, Heathcliff's condition features strikingly different symptoms from those of Catherine's life-ending illness. Although both stiffen bodily, Catherine's heart beats "visibly and audibly" (124), while Heathcliff must "remind [his] heart to beat." If Catherine's response to her body's increasing frozenness is to compel it to keep living, to extend her hold on the physical world, then Heathcliff's is to relinquish his hold on life and to join Catherine in the grave. But the pair's different symptoms (vivified in Brontë's language so that the internal bodily changes the pair undergo are brought to the surface and made visible) also point to the different positions they occupy within the masochistic pair. While the aim of the masochistic pair is to suspend itself in an erotic tableau, each partner maintains a different stance within that picture—Catherine fixes her grasp on Heathcliff, and Heathcliff yearns toward her.

As I've been indicating, *Wuthering Heights* features a pairing whose complicated system of catch and release relates to the account of masochism I began to lay out in the introduction. Masochism makes clear marriage's failure to secure relationship, imagining instead an extralegal model of contract that depends on ongoing negotiation. Describing the operations of this model in *Wuthering Heights* requires that I focus on Catherine the Elder and Heathcliff and the peculiarities of their relationship, but attention to the masochistic elements in this dyad also exposes the sadistic qualities in the novel's satellite marriages and relationships. As we have seen, the version of masochism most useful in reading the nineteenth-century novel emphasizes contractual and sensually frozen elements, both of which become significant in Emily Brontë's novel.[6] *Wuthering Heights'* principal relationship similarly stresses stasis and suspense, but Catherine the Elder is crucially invested in its creation and maintenance. In this way, Brontë's novel shows the importance of considering the female partner's agency in the masochistic dyad. If *Wuthering Heights'* sexual framework separates sadism from masochism, it also imagines a sensual frozenness as masochism's major attribute. Both of these aspects are important to the characterization of the novel's central romance.

Brontë's novel features at its core a version of sexual relationship that can be illuminated by Gilles Deleuze's account. The contractual dyad Heathcliff and Catherine develop leads them, ultimately, to a consummation only in death. While Catherine and Heathcliff's relationship features incredible pain, Brontë differentiates the pain these two feel from the other versions of sexualized pain explored in the novel. In my reading, Catherine and Heathcliff commit themselves to a contractual, masochistic pairing *against* an institutionalized and sadistic model of marriage; but, at the end of the novel, the world of *Wuthering Heights* has altered so materially as to make such a contract untenable. Brontë aligns the second generation's marital couple with a pedagogical model, in which Hareton is educated into his already confirmed hierarchical place. But this pairing also reduces the place eroticism has in the novel. While Catherine the Younger's slaps and kisses mimic Catherine the Elder's erotic grasps in some ways, they are always in the service of stabilizing and confirming community. The world of *Wuthering Heights*, then, no longer supports the boundless erotic energy that Catherine the Elder and Heathcliff were able to cultivate; eroticism is always, by the novel's end, in the service of something else: education, community, family order. If, at the novel's opening, Catherine and Heathcliff could imagine an extralegal contractual bond, by the novel's end Catherine and Hareton must have recourse to legal marriage. Terry Eagleton suggests that the novel "end[s] on a note of tentative convergence between labour and culture, sinew and gentility."[7] If the novel secures a version of middle-class value in this final marriage, it also retains a sense of loss in regard to Catherine the Elder's relationship to Heathcliff. But the gesture taken to be reconciliatory, that is the marriage that rejoins Catherine the Younger to the Earnshaw line, remains haunted by the novel's earlier accounts of sadistic marriage. What's left at the novel's end, then, is a marriage that imagines itself as surpassing sadism but that borrows its formal contours from the earlier, violent model. In contrast, Catherine and Heathcliff's unmarried commitments eventually end in the grave; the masochistic contract is taken too far, beyond suspension into utter lifelessness. The second generation's central couple forms a relationship that *institutionalizes* contract; both the flexibility and the negotiable quality of the earlier model are lost. Brontë's novel presents a masochistic ideal that cannot be reclaimed, though it is mourned.

Catherine the Elder and Heathcliff organize their relationship contractually, by mutual consent and agreement, but the first generation's marriages fit securely into an institutional model, wherein consent is foreclosed or limited. Catherine's marriage to Edgar corresponds to a damagingly conventional patriarchal model, while Isabella's marriage to Heathcliff extends this model to explicit sadism. It is no accident that the satellite relationships in the novel's first generation are marital; again, the legal requirements of marriage, instead of a purely interpersonal agreement or contract, order the relationship. In the second generation, and almost as an illustration of marriage's institutionality, Catherine the Younger's marriage to Linton Heathcliff appears to be not only purely formal but also contracted by Heathcliff instead of by either of the marriage's partners. This is a kind of limit case for how marriage works in the novel: it takes the form of a contract, but in Linton and Catherine the Younger's case, that contract has little to do with their intentions, desires, or choices. Linton, however, lacks either Heathcliff's or Catherine's power; his impotence reduces his marriage to Catherine the Younger to form. Linton's apparent sadism is rerouted through an infantile pettishness; he lacks either Heathcliff's energy or his desire to "experiment" on human victims.

Wuthering Heights presents two logics of interpersonal contact that underscore the difference between a sadistic sexuality and a masochistic one. The masochistic model I've been describing appears, in Brontë's novel, to be structured around frozen suspense and contract. Alternately, the sadistic model is one of institutionality and perpetual motion. These are typified in *Wuthering Heights* in the difference between the grasp and the slap. If Catherine the Elder's masochistic holds on others are signaled by her intensely fixed grasp, Catherine the Younger's slaps ring out with the institutional, pedagogical energy she assumes later in the novel. I will discuss the ways these gestures are mobilized at length below, but I first want to turn to one of the major difficulties in any critical consideration of Brontë's novel, its apparently unrelenting characterological and scenic repetitiveness.

"When I Am in the Earth"

The interwoven plots of *Wuthering Heights* tend to produce the appearance of closer connections between characters than is strictly accurate. How, for example, does one represent the two Catherines? They share two names, Catherine Earnshaw and Catherine Linton, and the younger Catherine has the added distinction of being called—for a time—the one name the elder Catherine cannot claim, Catherine Heathcliff. This repetition has the effect of enforcing a closer relationship between these two than actually exists. Further still, the moments in the novel when the two characters are aligned explicitly, specifically the moments when they slap potential partners, are misleading. Similarly misleading is a strong trend in the criticism to imagine that Catherine forms an identic bond with Heathcliff.[8] Catherine the Elder and Heathcliff are not *versions* of one another, any more than the Catherines are, or Catherine the Younger is a version of Hareton Earnshaw. Instead, there are significant departures in Catherine the Elder's vision of her relationship with Heathcliff from Heathcliff's own understanding. The scarcity of names in the novel drives home the problem of the novel's apparently limited scope. As Sandra R. Gilbert and Susan Gubar have argued, the plot of the Catherines in the novel charts the elder Catherine's movement from Earnshaw to Linton, and the younger Catherine's return to her mother's original name through marriage (392).[9] And Heathcliff is famously named after a dead Earnshaw son (Dellamora 537–38). Additionally, J. Hillis Miller has argued for the centrality of such repetitions in the novel's impenetrability: "Each emblematic passage in the novel is both a seeming avenue to the desired unity and also a barrier forbidding access to it." In Miller's account, the novel becomes a "dreadful collection" of "memoranda"; full of significance but lacking any clear meaning (67). The danger of accepting a deconstructive account of the novel, though, is that the only options available to characters would be to form identities with or oppositions to one another. And Brontë's repetitions are always partial; to imagine the generational changes as doubling or copying each element of the previous generation is to ignore the very palpable differences in characters or their functions. The differences between the two Catherines will become more significant later, but first I want to consider the importance of Brontë's alignment of Catherine Earnshaw with Heathcliff.

As is already clear, *Wuthering Heights*' central pair presents significant problems to the novel's critics. How might one characterize the relationship between Catherine Earnshaw and Heathcliff? In Joseph Allen Boone's account, Brontë's valuation of the central pair's "erotic identification" is at odds with the more normative "antagonistic" marital relationships that surround it (153–55).[10] In a similar vein, Nancy Armstrong claims both that the pair's "emotional similarity" marks them as "too endogamous to become husband and wife" but that the marital relationships in the novel seem, in contrast, too exogamous for the primitive world of the moors (173).[11] In contrast, Ivan Krielkamp has argued that Heathcliff's relationship to Catherine resembles that of a pet, which allows his body to become "an experimental object for investigation into pain and suffering" that in turn compels readers and observers to sympathize with the spectacle of pain he and Catherine create (99).[12] For Richard Dellamora, Heathcliff's representation indicates Brontë's investment in the psychology of a slavery borne of physical and economic difference, and he argues that the relationship between Catherine and Heathcliff is "troped in terms of the master-slave relation" (539). And, for Susan Meyer, Heathcliff's racialization allows Brontë to extend her critique of empire and to imagine a scenario in which Heathcliff's misogyny "hideously mimic[s] the ugly brutality of British imperialism" (116).[13] Leo Bersani claims Catherine's intense feeling for the foundling Heathcliff indicates a decision to identify beyond the bounds of the family; it is her extreme difference from him that makes her identification with him so radical.[14] In all of these accounts, Heathcliff's marked difference from Catherine (and the other inhabitants of the moor landscape) lends affective power to her identification with him. I, too, read Catherine and Heathcliff as differentiated in significant ways, in both their temperaments and in their visions of their relationship, but I see these differences as producing a masochistic configuration for the pair that links to both the contractual and frozen elements of masochism. My focus, then, is on the figure of the relationship rather that its constitutive parts. While for Catherine their relationship indeed looks more like an identity, Heathcliff's vision depends on a constant model of unrelieved anticipation that precludes identity entirely. But if we imagine the master-slave rhetoric of the novel as *only* occupying a relation to Brontë's political or social sympathies, we ignore the peculiar ways in which this rhetoric overlaps with the sexual elements in the novel. Part of the novel's impenetrability, indeed, is that its systems are so self-contained, even after critical interventions expose the myriad ways Brontë incorporates midcentury political and social concerns. And part of the deconstructive response to the novel develops from this residue of incomprehensibility. An account of *Wuthering Heights* must consider the structuring relationship at the novel's core as a relationship built on an internal accord that is, by its nature, mysterious to outsiders, even within the world of the novel.

Readings that accentuate Heathcliff's difference and separation from the Earnshaw family and represent Catherine's desire as a desire for exogamous sexuality ignore or simplify the discrete contours of the erotic relationship at the novel's center. If we imagine characterological difference as a sexualized antagonism that hampers conventional marriage or, alternately, as the key attribute that makes such marriage possible, we ignore how in *Wuthering Heights* such difference lays a foundation for the construction of the fixed masochistic relationship at odds with, but bolstered by, conventional marriage. While most accounts read either Catherine or Heathcliff as the novel's central character, I read their relationship as the figure most central to Brontë's project.[15] Thus, it's necessary to tease out the differences in their separate visions of the relationship and important to notice that the central importance of Catherine's relation to Heathcliff is in its contours—in what it contains within its sphere. As Bersani rightly argues, "[C]ertain configurations of characters begin to compete for our attention with the individual characters themselves" (199). This feature makes it almost impossible to imagine any of the characters individually; the world of *Wuthering Heights* does not allow individuals to develop in a vacuum and instead suspends them in constant exchange with the personalities surrounding them. This also explains, in part, why the frozen tableaux that order Catherine the Elder's relationship to Heathcliff are so palpably different from the satellite relationships that are, more often than not, characterized by a sexuality based on action and mobility. Again, if the masochistic tableau depends on frozenness, the Sadean tableau emphasizes action.[16] Both of these scenarios imagine staged combinations of sex and violence. But if the sadistic scene involves an actor experimentally directing a number of submissives, the masochistic tableau includes two figures involved in a private fantasy. The formal distinctions in the structures of sexual scenes relate to the different versions of subjectivity available to their participants. This explains, in part, the careful attention paid to aesthetic choice in the construction of a masochistic tableau; the vividness of the scene is in stark contrast to the featureless settings of a Sadean montage. Characters' experiences of the places they inhabit illuminate their consent to either sadistic motion or masochistic frozenness.

Brontë's characters, especially her women characters, often imagine a set correspondence between their physical bodies and the places they inhabit; they demonstrate a malleability dependent on their perceptions of their homes. Catherine the Elder more ably resists this logic than either Isabella Linton or Catherine the Younger. When Heathcliff captures Catherine the Younger, for example, she quickly finds herself fitting the role allowed her by the Heights, going so far as to bite Heathcliff almost as soon as she enters the house (206).[17] Similarly, Isabella becomes a "thorough little slattern" once she enters Heathcliff's adopted home. In fact, the only character that does not degenerate upon entering the Heights is the adult Heathcliff (115).[18] Catherine the Elder's recuperation at the Grange has a similarly drastic effect on her behavior and encourages her to shed some of her apparent wildness.[19] As the novel progresses, though, the Heights restrains women more powerfully than does the Grange. And, once Heathcliff takes possession, he embarks on a project that emphasizes feminine degradation and control.[20] Why don't Heathcliff's actions engender in Isabella and Catherine the Younger the stalwart resistance that Mr. Earnshaw's neglect and later Frances's tampering instill in Catherine the Elder? While the Heights' inhospitality to women does not limit Catherine the Elder's resiliency, the other women who move there seem incarcerated rather than freed by the place. The key point, however, is that Isabella and Catherine the Younger are introduced into the Heights as wives, while Catherine the Elder is initially introduced into the Grange as a recuperating visitor. The realignment brought about by marriage, then, encourages debasement, not willful wildness. *Wuthering Heights'* marriages imprison wives and expose them to violence. Though places have the power to alter or adjust personality, the alterations manifested in Isabella's and Catherine the Younger's cases seem more violent and more limiting. For while Catherine the Elder often seems "wild," she never seems degraded in the ways Isabella and Catherine the Younger do. Both Isabella and Catherine the Younger are exposed to more explicit physical and sexual degradation; in part, this is because they encounter Heathcliff's more aggressive energy, but this also signals these characters' major difference from Catherine the Elder—they are more comfortable with sadism's action than with masochism's frozenness.

But Catherine the Elder's power does seem somehow limited or altered by her marriage and her life at the Grange. Rachel Ablow has convincingly argued that Catherine's power (over Heathcliff, over Edgar) is illusory and that her madness is brought about by her sudden recognition of her own powerlessness: "Catherine has no real power, after all; nothing more than requests they might or might not choose to fulfill. And at the moment when Catherine recognizes this fact, she is forced, too, to recognize her insanity" (59).[21] In Ablow's account, Catherine's marriage results in her powerlessness; a wife cannot compel a husband (or anyone else for that matter) to act in a way discordant with his own inclination. Catherine's apparent power, then, develops only from the willingness of the people who surround her to accede to her wishes. This accords with the first description of Catherine's nervous illness in the novel, in which the attending doctor says that Catherine will "not bear crossing much" (70). Indeed, the combination of the doctor's orders and Catherine's narcissistic willfulness means that any power she claims for herself remains unchallenged. Ablow's account of Catherine's power ends with her madness and death; for Ablow, death follows from marriage, and both light up Catherine's failure. I claim, however, that Brontë imagines Catherine's power to be real *despite* the legal limits placed upon it by nineteenth-century marriage law. This becomes clearer if we imagine death not as a sign of Catherine's failure but as indicating her ability to think beyond death's boundaries. The differences between the types of limitation Catherine the Elder experiences after her marriage and the degradations Isabella and Catherine the Younger experience offer one basis for this kind of analysis. Catherine the Elder imagines herself as capable of attaining a kind of limitlessness; she does not imagine her personality disappears on her death. In contrast, Isabella and Catherine the Younger both imagine death as a boundary—not only do people cease to exist after death; their metaphysical selves—their souls—leave their bodies for recuperation in heaven.[22] Thus, the attention Brontë pays to Catherine after her death fully develops this difference. In Brontë's world, personal power lasts after death, but it adheres only to the personalities that imagine themselves as constituted of both physical and metaphysical facets.

As she nears the end of her life, Catherine imagines herself as capable of resisting change, specifically change brought about by death. At first, as I've indicated above, Catherine the Elder's mobility appears to be a feature of her childhood (the "scamper on the moors" being perhaps the clearest example of this), curtailed by her radical transformation after her stay at the Grange. Indeed, Gilbert and Gubar have made a compelling case that the elder Catherine's starvation and self-destruction are intimately linked to her limited mobility after her absorption into the Lintons' world, an absorption that results in her eventual marriage and the realignment of her homeplace (271–73). Instead, I want to emphasize the elder Catherine's ability to imagine her body in other spaces—even other states—toward the end of her life. When the maddened Catherine says she thinks she will "feel the same distress underground" that she does alive, she imagines a world that solders the physical body to the soul—or metaphysical self—that inhabits it. She imagines death as a premature burial, which connects physical feeling to emotional feeling. If her "shattered prison" irritates her, it also binds her to the world she inhabits with Heathcliff; it is no surprise that the consummation Heathcliff eventually imagines with Catherine depends on the blending of their bodies' physical traces (see Brontë 125, 220). Both imagine a physical afterlife that unites their bodies with their metaphysical selves, whereas the novel's other characters imagine a separate world beyond the physical one where their metaphysical selves find rest or recuperation. For both Catherine and Heathcliff, then, death is not something that separates one's body from one's soul, but the event that seals the two together unmistakably. One peculiar aspect of Brontë's cosmology is that the blended world of Catherine the Elder and Heathcliff offers more sustaining pleasure and satisfaction than does the conventional Christian world imagined by the other characters.

In this way, the physical landscapes in *Wuthering Heights* separate into the Christian physical world, organized by pain and suffering caused by violence escapable only upon death, and the blended metaphysical world, organized by states of attenuation, anticipation, and the suffering that attends these states. Masochism usefully underscores these differentiations. If the physical world is a place of mere bodily suffering, Brontë imagines Catherine's and Heathcliff's misery as the sufferings of their souls, which connects the metaphysical sphere increasingly to the realm of the sexual. Their bodily interactions, mainly limited to the sequences of erotic tableaux immediately preceding Catherine's death and to Heathcliff's necrophilic encounters with Catherine's dead body, underscore the relationship's dependence on a model of anticipatory desire. These scenes read as climaxes in part because the pair's bodies are kept separate for most of their interactions after childhood. But I want to suggest, too, that the adult pair imagines a clear division between their childhood relationship and the union that develops in adulthood. If we imagine the unity of Catherine and Heathcliff in childhood to be the novel's ideal, we ignore how Brontë's nongenital sexualization of the adult pair develops their relationship. Because the adult Catherine and Heathcliff apparently do not engage in genital sex, the impulse is to imagine their adulthood connection as an intense version of their childhood unity. This is not the case. Brontë portrays their sexual connection as one of maintained distance punctuated periodically by frozen embraces. Not only does this structure continue after Catherine's death; it mimics the model of masochistic suspense I have elucidated above.

The typical distance between the two characters enhances the emblematic quality of their encounters toward the end of Catherine's life. Brontë thematizes the movement from childhood to adulthood with Catherine's removal to the Grange. Skulker's attack means the Grange (or Frances Earnshaw's version of femininity) absorbs Catherine rapidly. As J. Hillis Miller notes, "As soon as Cathy can say, 'I *am* Heathcliff,' or 'My love for Heathcliff resembles the eternal rocks beneath,' they are already divided" (61). But Heathcliff's return troubles her realignment with the Grange not because they cannot reclaim their lost childhood unity but because it begins the sequence of frozen, suspended meetings between the pair. In fact, Heathcliff's return might be all the more disruptive because Catherine, as we later learn, is pregnant. Because of its immovability, the masochistic grasp Catherine has on Heathcliff is at odds with the reproductive world she is poised to enter.

Generative Sadism, Barren Masochism

Brontë connects sadistic sexuality to reproduction and, in doing so, connects the institutionality of marriage to sadism. In contrast, the masochism displayed in Catherine's relationship to Heathcliff is nonmarital, nongenital, nonreproductive, and, unconventionally, thus valued above the sadistic satellite relationships. While Edgar's relationship to Catherine may not be explicitly sadistic, its conventionality, as Gilbert and Gubar and also Ablow have claimed, secures his power in the marriage. Catherine's view of Edgar before their marriage, unlike her relation to Heathcliff, is a "bitter parody of a genteel romantic declaration which shows how effective her education has been in indoctrinating her with the literary romanticism deemed suitable for young ladies" (Gilbert and Gubar 277).[23] When Frances Earnshaw makes Catherine into a "lady," she instills in the younger woman a desire for a wifely *status* rather than a companionate marriage. And while Edgar is not explicitly cruel, his indifference toward Catherine as her madness increases can be read as a neglect borne from his acceptance of marriage norms that deny women agency.[24] In light of this, Isabella's marriage to Heathcliff looks almost like a perverse extension of Edgar's marriage to Catherine. Heathcliff's power over Isabella takes the form of physical, mental, and most likely sexual abuse. In both of these cases, though, the marriages are reproductive.[25]

As Georges Bataille notes, Brontë makes sadism most explicit in Heathcliff's relationship with Isabella; his interest in tormenting Edgar's sister is intensified by her "mawkish, waxen face" (84); her placidity encourages his sadism (Bataille 20).[26] This violence has a particularly sexual character; Heathcliff warns Catherine that she would "hear of odd things" should he marry her, and, once he does, Brontë explicitly ties Isabella's desire to leave him to their wedding night—"the very morrow of our wedding, she was weeping to go home" (84, 117). Here, Brontë implies a connection between genital sexuality and violence; it is unclear whether Heathcliff's intention is to secure the legitimacy of his marriage, to attempt to secure his property into later generations, or simply to offer Isabella an unmistakable indication of his brutality. But, according to Heathcliff, his project to make Isabella hate him has been a "positive labour of Hercules," because she does not respond as he would wish to his abuses. He complains about her willingness to accept his brutalities: "Can I trust your assertion, Isabella? Are you sure you hate me? If I let you alone for half a day, won't you come sighing and wheedling to me again?" (118). And, as Heathcliff continues to explain his married life to Nelly, the depths of his cruelty become clearer:

> "The first thing she saw me do, on coming out of the Grange, was to hang up her little dog; and when she pleaded for it the first words I uttered were a wish that I had the hanging of every being belonging to her, except one: possibly she took that exception for herself. But no brutality disgusted her. I suppose she has an innate admiration of it, if only her precious person were secure from injury! Now, was it not the depth of absurdity—of genuine idiocy—for that pitiful, slavish, mean-minded brach to dream that I could love her? Tell your master, Nelly, that I never in all my life, met with such an abject thing as she is. She even disgraces the name of Linton; and I've sometimes relented, from pure lack of invention, in my experiments on what she could endure, and still creep shamefully cringing back!" (118)

Here, Heathcliff suggests that Isabella may be willing, on some level, to engage with his misuse of her. Her animal behavior (she is a "slavish, mean-minded brach") links both to Heathcliff's sexual sadism (his "experiments") and to her willingness to submit to him. Further, Heathcliff's language here ("I've sometimes relented, from pure lack of invention, in my experiments on what she could endure") borrows from the pseudoscientific language of the Sadean encounter. Where Masoch's sexual tableaux stress the agreed-upon roles participants perform, the Sadean scene highlights the sadist's directions to the bodies that populate it. More Sade than Masoch, then, Heathcliff's behavior turns Isabella into a research subject, not a coconspirator. His relationship conforms to a scientific method; his assaults are tools to discover the limits of Isabella's slavish devotion. This also implies a scientific excess in Heathcliff's torture. It is not that Isabella cannot endure his brutality, it's that he lacks the "invention" to imagine new tortures. One of the disturbing possibilities raised by this scene, especially when we consider that Isabella reaches a breaking point only when Heathcliff throws a knife at her, is that she takes pleasure in her sexual subjection. Her "innate admiration" for Heathcliff's violence suggests this further; but Isabella's masochism, if that is what it is, conforms more decidedly to a Freudian model. There are no models of agreement or consent in Heathcliff's marriage, though this is precisely what orders his relationship to Catherine.

In one of the novel's most quoted passages, Catherine Earnshaw offers Nelly an account of her relationship with Heathcliff:

> "My great miseries in this world have been Heathcliff's miseries, and I watched and felt each from the beginning; my great thought in living is himself. If all else perished, and *he* remained, I should still continue to be; and, if all else remained and he were annihilated, the Universe would turn to a mighty stranger. I should not seem part of it. My love for Linton is like the foliage in the woods. Time will change it, I'm well aware, as winter changes the trees—my love for Heathcliff resembles the eternal rocks beneath—a source of little visible delight, but necessary. Nelly, I *am* Heathcliff—he's always, always in my mind—not as a pleasure, any more than I am always a pleasure to myself—but, as my own being—so, don't talk of our separation again." (64)[27]

Catherine distinguishes between her changeable love for Edgar, one focused on personal characteristics (his handsomeness, youth, and cheerfulness) and her eternal feeling for Heathcliff (he is her basis or foundation). In Catherine's account, Heathcliff is internalized and incorporated into her identity.[28] This passage constructs that identity from both her physical, waking life and "an existence . . . beyond [her]." She imagines the intransience of her feeling for Heathcliff as elemental and supportive: he is the "eternal rocks beneath" her world. But if Catherine imagines Heathcliff as foundational, Heathcliff imagines her as ghostly. The difference between these two imagined versions of relationship is the difference between the submissive and dominant partners in a masochistic dyad. In Catherine's account, Heathcliff's "annihilation" (and it is significant that she use this word rather than the perhaps more conventional "death": Brontë implies a difference between a personal death and a fuller obliteration) would mean Catherine's alienation from the world. It's important here to note that Catherine's feeling of identity with Heathcliff is not a true identity; they are not the same. Rather, what she describes here is a feeling of foundational support by and dependence on Heathcliff. Catherine's surety of Heathcliff's presence corresponds to a position of dominance; it is she who orders the masochistic scenes that form the core of their relationship. Alternately, Heathcliff's description of his life after Catherine's death as marked by a perpetual haunting corresponds to the sexualized anticipation that delivers the submissive masochist's charge.

When he admits to Nelly that he has bargained with the sexton to open his coffin into Catherine's after his death, Heathcliff tells her how he spurred himself on in his initial attempt to unearth Catherine's body immediately following her death. He recounts his graveside thoughts to Nelly: "I'll have her in my arms again! If she be cold, I'll think it is this north wind that chills *me*; and if she be motionless, it is sleep" (220). In his account of the time immediately following Catherine's death, Heathcliff imagines an embrace that allows him to pretend that she lives on, an account at odds with his later request of the sexton. It is not the pretense that Catherine lives still, though, that encourages him when he digs up the coffin again, seventeen years later. By that point, although Catherine's body remains unchanged (when Heathcliff tells Nelly his tale, he says that her face "is hers yet"), the plan Heathcliff sets into motion is one that depends on her body's eventual obliteration (220). He does not imagine an embrace in the grave, but a mingling of the pair's already disintegrating dust.

By the end of the novel, we have encountered significant evidence that implies Catherine still exists in some form (Lockwood's encounter with the ghostly Cathy, the community's insistence that Catherine and Heathcliff wander the moors, even Heathcliff's visions of Catherine's face everywhere). But the novel's commitment to realism both discredits these supernatural visitations (Lockwood's ghost appears in a dream; a small, frightened child claims he's seen Catherine and Heathcliff) and indicates a perhaps stranger notion of a self's combined physical and metaphysical existence. In its use of ghostly markers, *Wuthering Heights* develops the form of the historical novel even if it is not, strictly speaking, a historical novel. While the national framework of the novel is implied, it is not central to the novel. In some ways, the world that Brontë bodies forth resembles what Ian Duncan calls the "necromantic medium" of Walter Scott's novels (29).[29] *Wuthering Heights* bears some structural resemblances to Scott's Scottish Gothic, though the past narrated by the action of Brontë's novel is both more recent and less nationally significant than are the periods detailed in Scott's historical fictions. What remains, though, is the balance between, on the one hand, the tension between the supernatural and the real and, on the other, an investment in a historical relationship to the world described in the novel. In Duncan's reading, history works to develop "a spiritual identity with a lost past, abolishing the material differences between then and now" (62). In this view, moments that float the possibility of haunting become manifestations of both the actual social and political history of a place and a sign of an apparently teleological impulse that connects the represented, ghostly past to a manifest, real present. In *Wuthering Heights*, though, the "real present" shown in the novel's action works obsessively to close the representational gap between the novel's then and the novel's now.

Thus, death, for Catherine, does not include a metaphysical transcendence but an all too physical stasis. Her static body waits for Heathcliff's. This means that, even after his death, Heathcliff occupies a position of anticipation. As the coffins' wood decays and the bones become dust, the two bodies enter into one another in an almost impossibly slow slide. All of this implies that these two have a control beyond death. If Catherine does not turn into a ghost, her body ties itself to the world she inhabited with a hold strong enough to keep it from disintegrating before Heathcliff can join her. She maintains both her self and her relationship to him, even after death. And she must maintain this self or risk becoming like Heathcliff (that is, supportive and foundational to his existence, as he was to hers) while he remains living, a possibility the masochistic dyad works to resist. The dyad is founded on the set relationship between the two characters, not on their unity, and not the reversibility of their roles.

In distinction to Catherine's feeling of foundational identity with him, Heathcliff explains to Nelly his feelings about Catherine in the time leading up to his own death:

> "I cannot look down to this floor, but her features are shaped on the flags! In every cloud, in every tree—filling the air at night, and caught by glimpses in every object by day, I am surrounded with her image! The most ordinary faces of men and women—my own features—mock me with a resemblance. The entire world is a dreadful collection of memoranda that she did exist, and that I have lost her." (247)

This might be the closest Heathcliff gets to an identic account of the relationship; but, even though he sees Catherine in his "own features," it is not that he sees Catherine *only* in the mirror—he sees her in everything. Heathcliff's description here depends on a heightened sense of vision: he sees Catherine's image in the surrounding world, and he describes this vision in terms of a haunting. For Heathcliff, Catherine is multiple and everywhere. He admits these feelings to Nelly at a moment when he feels "a strange change approaching"; his desire for vengeance has lessened, in part because Catherine the Younger and Hareton are now united against him. As his world dissolves around him, repeating images of the dead Catherine populate it. He describes the world turning not into a "mighty stranger" but into an infinity of Catherines. It is this limitlessness that typifies Heathcliff's experience of masochism; it is painful but never ending. This is further clarified when we reexamine the central tableau in the living Catherine's relationship with Heathcliff. After Edgar forbids him entrance to the Grange, the relationship between Catherine and Heathcliff rapidly escalates in a succession of painful embraces.

Grasping

The long series of masochistic tableaux begins when Heathcliff sneaks into the Grange while Edgar is at church. Brontë renders Heathcliff's appearance in explicitly sexual language: "the open house [is] too tempting for Heathcliff to resist walking in," and with "straining eagerness" Catherine waits for him. Upon gaining the sickroom, Heathcliff has "her grasped in his arms" in the beginning of a sequence of embraces that ends with Edgar's eventual reentrance. And though Heathcliff penetrates the sanctum of the Lintons' home, it is Catherine who "kiss[es] him first" when the two finally meet:

> Heathcliff had knelt on one knee to embrace her; he attempted to rise, but she seized his hair, and kept him down.
> "I wish I could hold you," she continued, bitterly, "till we were both dead! I shouldn't care what you suffered. I care nothing for your sufferings. Why shouldn't you suffer? I do! Will you forget me—will you be happy when I am in the earth?" (123–24)

Catherine's choice to pull Heathcliff's hair might simply be a by-product of her weakened state—perhaps she can't grasp Heathcliff's arm or leg as forcefully—but it is incredibly effective as a tool of domination.[30] Controlling his head instead of his limbs, Catherine's gesture accentuates the submissive aspects of Heathcliff's character. These scenes of domination are integral to any reading of the novel that imagines Catherine and Heathcliff's relationship as sexual. And while the pair, as I've said earlier, does not seem to engage in an explicitly *genital* sexual relationship, scenes like this make it difficult to read the pair's relationship as entirely "sexless" (Bersani 213).[31] Catherine's grasp here is as effective as it is unconventional; by holding Heathcliff's hair, she implies a combination of ownership and domination enhanced by the increasingly sexualized passion they share (again, this gesture appears immediately after Nelly witnesses Heathcliff's flurry of kisses, precipitated by an apparently single kiss from Catherine). If, in their childhood, Catherine and Heathcliff imagined themselves as identical partners, indistinguishable beneath their pinned-together pinafores, this scene shows how their partnership has adjusted to accommodate a sexualized notion of difference. Catherine controls Heathcliff, and Heathcliff actively submits.

When Heathcliff finally "wrenches" his head free, the embrace tightens further:

> The two, to a cool spectator, made a strange and fearful picture. Well might Catherine deem that Heaven would be a land of exile to her, unless, with her mortal body, she cast away her mortal character also. Her present countenance had a wild vindictiveness in its white cheek, and a bloodless lip and scintillating eye; and she retained in her closed fingers a portion of the locks she had been grasping. As to her companion, while raising himself with one hand, he had taken her arm with the other; and so inadequate was his stock of gentleness to the requirements of her condition, that on his letting go, I saw four distinct impressions left blue in the colourless skin. (124)

Catherine's aspect here becomes more and more crystalline. Not only does she look drained of blood, but also her "scintillating" eye glitters under Nelly's gaze. Brontë's tactile description of the "four distinct impressions" Heathcliff leaves on Catherine's livid skin further intensifies the image. Her body appears to be hardening, continuing the process begun in her first fit.[32] But the frozenness of the pair's grasp is made all the more apparent by the "violent, unequal throbbing of [Catherine's] heart, which beat visibly and audibly" beneath her skin. Much like Masoch's Wanda, Catherine is not transformed into a statue here, though her pallor and immobility indicate otherwise. Instead, her pulse becomes so violent that Nelly, standing across the room, can see and hear her heart beat. Even at her most frozen, Catherine's body throbs with a paroxysm that seems more orgasmic than anything else. The intensity of Heathcliff's embrace agitates her while it also seals her in a "strange and fearful picture." And, repeatedly, the pair's movements begin with Catherine's actions: she kisses Heathcliff; she "springs" toward him after they have separated; she calls him to "[c]ome to [her]" from across the room (125). These advances are usually met with a more violent and extreme reaction from Heathcliff, but, nevertheless, Catherine's willfulness keeps the scene going.

The most explicit example of Catherine's power over Heathcliff comes as Edgar Linton returns from church. It is worth quoting at length to see the full arc of this particular grasp:

> "You must not go!" she answered, holding him as firmly as her strength allowed. "You shall not, I tell you."
>
> "For one hour," he pleaded, earnestly.
>
> "Not for one minute," she replied.
>
> "I *must*—Linton will be up immediately," persisted the alarmed intruder.
>
> He would have risen, and unfixed her fingers by the act—she clung fast, gasping; there was mad resolution in her face.
>
> "No!" she shrieked. "Oh don't, don't go. It is the last time! Edgar will not hurt us. Heathcliff, I shall die! I shall die!"
>
> "Damn the fool. There he is," cried Heathcliff, sinking back into his seat. "Hush, my darling! Hush, hush, Catherine! I'll stay. If he shot me so, I'd expire with a blessing on my lips."
>
> And there they were fast again. I heard my master mounting the stairs—the cold sweat ran from my forehead; I was horrified.
>
> "Are you going to listen to her ravings?" I said, passionately. "She does not know what she says. Will you ruin her because she has not wit to help herself? Get up! You could be free instantly. That is the most diabolical deed that ever you did. We are all done for—master, mistress, and servant." (127)

Again, Catherine's fixity of purpose is at odds with her weakened state; Heathcliff "would have" loosened her grasp, but he does not. Perhaps most peculiar, though, are the repeated "musts" at the scene's opening. "You must not go," says Catherine, to which Heathcliff answers "I *must*." If Catherine's order describes an action she thinks Heathcliff is obligated to perform, his

tes his insistence on respecting—even at this late
e social convention. When Heathcliff says he "*must*"
want to meet Edgar on the stairs. When Catherine
t go," she means that he is obliged to stay with her;
soul, he has no volition to move away from her. Once Heathcliff
renders to Catherine's call, the two return to their closed embrace. It is,
oddly, here that Nelly interjects that she is "horrified." The pair's refusal to
acknowledge the world beyond them both offends Nelly's moral sense ("Will
you ruin her?") and encourages her to read Catherine's behavior as utter
madness. Though she complains that this is Heathcliff's "most diabolical
deed," it's clear even to Nelly that Catherine instigates this embrace. Stranger
still is Nelly's exhortation that "[w]e are all done for—master, mistress, and
servant." While this might indicate Nelly's idea that Edgar (her "master")
will be crushed if he enters the room to find the closeted pair, it also suggests that Heathcliff, and not Edgar, is the "master" in this scene. This implies that Nelly perceives Heathcliff to be Catherine's true partner; if they
are the master and mistress, the threat in this scene is the intercession of an
outsider, Edgar.[33] If the threat of exposure troubles the dyad, the pair shores
itself up through the grasp. And, eventually, both partners develop marked
bodies—hardened and bloodless—that imply a corporeal freezing.

In the logic of masochism, Catherine's body appears to be solidifying
into a kind of statue; the danger of this, of course, is that this crystallization
ends her life and so extinguishes the pulse beneath her skin. Heathcliff's
body, too, undergoes a starvation that ends in a bodily hardening. Nelly describes his deathbed: "The lattice, flapping to and fro, had grazed one hand
that rested on the sill; no blood trickled from the broken skin, and when I
put my fingers to it, I could doubt no more—he was dead and stark!" (256).
The wound that does not bleed stresses the body's coldness, an aspect enhanced by its fixed expression. Here, a sign of death (that the wound didn't
bleed) comes to look instead like a sign of Heathcliff's frozenness (his expression remains though he is dead). Nelly continues, "I tried to close his
eyes—to extinguish, if possible, that frightful, life-like gaze of exultation,
before any one else beheld it. They would not shut; they seemed to sneer at
my attempts, and his parted lips and sharp, white teeth sneered too!" (256).
The body is so stiffened that it cannot be moved; the moment immediately
preceding death, the moment when Heathcliff's expression was fixed, remains—or remains enough to trouble Nelly. Heathcliff's "gaze of exultation"

freezes him in a posture of anticipation. Unable to "extinguish" Heat preternatural stare, Nelly must encounter his unending hopefulness a prospect of rejoining Catherine. Her attempts to sentimentalize Heathclif death (to shut the eyes "before anyone else beheld [his expression]") fail; the body still speaks its anticipation. Heathcliff ends his life in Catherine's childhood bed, frozen by the moors' wind and rain. If Catherine's frozen grasp on Heathcliff begins her decline, Heathcliff here adopts a posture of reaching—his hand rests on the sill (where, earlier, Lockwood has imagined a violent attack on the ghostly Catherine), and his eyes stare ready to "meet" the gaze of anyone who enters the bed. In this way, both Catherine and Heathcliff's deaths are described as the encroachment of an icy frozenness.

This moment marks *Wuthering Heights*' crucial difference from the masochistic model Deleuze lays out. For Deleuze, the masochist's investment in coldness is not an eroticization of frozenness per se. The masochist does not, for example, want to be dominated by a statue. Instead, the coldness hides the sensual core; the masochist's torturess, in Deleuze's account, must be warm-blooded. For Brontë, the masochistic contract is so forceful that it eventually drains people of blood. Masochism's frozen aspect overtakes its limitless potential. As their bodies freeze, what happens to Catherine and Heathcliff, then, looks like a logical extension of the masochist's project, but it actually marks the end of the contract's tenability. Instead of shoring up the masochistic dyad against an inhospitable world, the pair's bodily frozenness signals the dyad's end, though it also promises the pair an ultimate consummation in the grave.

One of the dangers of the erotic tableaux that structure the novel's masochism is this risk of death. While their eventual union is promised, the only way for Catherine and Heathcliff to reach it is to become statues, to die. By freezing their bodies in their scenes, they harden themselves to the point of death, and it is death that allows the slow decay that will end in their consummation. While Brontë's reproductive sadism is channeled into an instructive marriage, the masochistic dyad has no real heir in the novel. Reproduction is not the only way to access the future in the novel, as the final pages' possible hauntings make clear; but it is the only way to do so without imagining death as a necessary part of that futurity. Brontë shows masochism's slow slide to inaction as tending toward death, but this does not seem to obliterate the model's potential. Instead, Brontë privileges the intensity of this pairing in part because masochism allows her to imagine sexual relation as surviving death. Its potential can be found only beyond the grave; the grasping intensity of the earlier embraces transforms into an embrace that can barely assume the name. Certainly, Catherine's hold does extend over Heathcliff until they are both dead. The dissolution Heathcliff sets in motion when he bribes the sexton is the final version of relationship the two can share. And, in one sense, Heathcliff is indeed happy when Catherine is in the earth; her dissolving physical self allows him the fullest consummation of his relationship with her. By bribing the sexton, Heathcliff conceives of a literally particular embrace. This is the grasp taken to its limit point, though it is accessible only in death.[34] As we shall see, Brontë's other major tool of physical submission, the slap, does not accommodate this model of consummation.

Slapping

In one early scene, we see how Catherine the Elder uses violence to compel others' behavior. There is, however, a difference in this early version of outburst and the methodical, grasping violence with which Catherine controls Heathcliff. This scene also precipitates Edgar Linton's declaration of love, a declaration that springs from his physical misery at Catherine's hands. His misery is of a different quality than what Heathcliff feels. In the latter case, the aim of the violent outburst is to seal or freeze the couple in a tableau and to shore up the masochistic pair against the encroaching (generative, marital) world beyond them. Catherine and Heathcliff both understand the feelings that combine them, though they remain undeclared. But, in this earlier scene, Catherine's violent eruptions are more general as she finds victims in Nelly and Hareton as well as Edgar. Because the slap she gives Edgar occupies a sequential chain of physical outbursts, the sexual character he gives it seems more like a misunderstanding.

When Nelly draws attention to the pinch Catherine gives her while trying to force the servant to leave the room, Catherine responds with rage:

> "I didn't touch you, you lying creature!" cried she, her fingers tingling to repeat the act, and her ears red with rage. She never had power to conceal her passion, it always set her whole complexion in a blaze.
>
> "What's that, then?" I retorted, showing a decided purple witness to refute her.
>
> She stamped her foot, wavered a moment, and then, irresistibly impelled by the naughty spirit within her, slapped me on the cheek, a stinging blow that filled both eyes with water.

"Catherine, love! Catherine!" interposed Linton, greatly shocked at the double fault of falsehood and violence which his idol had committed.

"Leave the room, Ellen!" she repeated trembling all over.

Little Hareton, who followed me everywhere, and was sitting near me on the floor, at seeing my tears commenced crying himself, and sobbed out complaints against "wicked Aunt Cathy," which drew her fury on to his unlucky head: she seized his shoulders, and shook him till the poor child waxed livid, and Edgar thoughtlessly laid hold of her hands to deliver him. In an instant one was wrung free, and the astonished young man felt it applied over his own ear in a way that could not be mistaken for jest. (55–56)

Brontë here locates Catherine's passion in the realm of the sexual as her fingers "tingle to repeat the act," and the whole scene leaves her "trembling all over." It is at moments like these that Catherine the Elder's sexuality appears to hinge on a general application of violence. But these aspects are mitigated by her original intention in the scene: to force Nelly (and with her Hareton) to leave the room so as to prompt Edgar to more explicit declarations. Marriage, unlike the masochistic union, demands a declaration. Peculiarly, though Catherine's intention to be alone with Edgar would seem to be the best way to propel him to make his proposal, violence brings the pair into closer union. Brontë's emphasis here is on the slap's sharp delivery rather than the threat of pain implied in the masochistic raised whip or hand: "the astonished young man felt it applied over his own ear in a way that could not be mistaken for jest." The emphasis on the felt experience of the slap, and the surprise it occasions, move this image of violence outside of a masochistic logic. This scene highlights the difference between Catherine's attitude toward Heathcliff, with its focus on intense holding, and her relation to Edgar, which here is divorced from an anticipatory logic by the very slap that spurs him on to declare his love. The conventional romance between Catherine and Edgar turns on a narrative perception of Edgar as the instigator, though the most explicit version of that perception immediately follows this moment (wherein Catherine's power is extended into physical power).

Somewhat strangely, Edgar's weakness belies his viciousness when Nelly notices his strange expression after Catherine begs him to stay: "[t]he soft thing looked askance through the window: he possessed the power to depart, as much as a cat possesses the power to leave a mouse half killed or a bird half eaten" (57). Ablow comments on this passage, suggesting that Nelly's viewpoint coincides with Catherine's belief that she will be able to maintain power after her marriage: "Thus, even though the actual image she uses casts Edgar as the predator rather than the victim—the cat unable to leave until it has finished its bloody work—the overall impression the passage creates is that his unhappy fate has been sealed by powers beyond his control" (Ablow 58).[35] While it's clear that Edgar's power here aligns with the legal constraints marriage imposes on women, in my reading this image emphasizes Edgar's potential cruelty (and his conventionality by the novel's standards) by linking him with a predator which has been caught in the midst of an action but who desires that action's completion. That the imagined prey is "half-eaten" or "half-killed" implies an ongoing action that has been suspended. Were Edgar a masochistic submissive, the half-killed/half-eaten aspect of this image would have been his goal, not a problem that spurs him to further violence. As it stands, Edgar's aims with respect to Catherine the Elder focus on securing her in marriage, thus securing her in the Grange.

The other major scene that connects impending marriage to slapping occurs at the novel's end, when Lockwood revisits the Heights and spies Catherine the Younger tutoring Hareton Earnshaw:

> The male speaker began to read. He was a young man, respectably dressed, and seated at a table, having a book before him. His handsome features glowed with pleasure, and his eyes kept impatiently wandering from the page to a small white hand over his shoulder, which recalled him by a smart slap on the cheek, whenever its owner detected signs of inattention. (234)

Catherine the Younger enforces her power over Hareton with a series of "smart slap[s]." But Hareton's impatience here relates both to his desire for Catherine's attention and the slaps that signal that attention. He importantly looks back for her "small white hand" and not at the "smiting beauty" of her face. The pedagogical imperative of this scene has been remarked upon before.[36] Catherine's gesture, however, connects this scene to the other scenes of slapping in the novel. Like the earlier scene I detailed above, this slap signals Catherine's irritation and Hareton's desire. When her mother slapped Edgar out of spite, he misread the gesture as a signal of sexualized violence. In this later scene, Brontë sexualizes the slap. While Catherine the

Younger is intent on her task, this pair has already declared itself and their wedding date has been set. Furthermore, these two have a history of violent interactions that has led them to this point. Brontë actually includes an account of one of the first physical interactions between Catherine and Hareton, in which Hareton reaches out to Catherine almost as if he were in a dream: "[A]t last he proceeded from staring to touching; he put out his hand and stroked one curl, as gently as if it were a bird. He might have stuck a knife into her neck, she started round in such a taking" (226). This scene incorporates the symbolic logics of a few earlier encounters. Brontë draws a sharp distinction, for example, between Catherine the Elder's "brown ringlets" and Heathcliff's "uncombed hair" when she first returns from her recuperation at the Grange (41). And Nelly's exclamation recalls the knife Heathcliff throws at Isabella and which she actually pulls out of her own neck. Catherine the Younger's encounter with Hareton collapses under the weight of its imagistic antecedents. The sexual histories of their parents and their parents' siblings inform the pair's development even at this early stage. But, immediately, Catherine's response is violent, and she keeps her distance from Hareton until his degradation begins to interest her. Her initial forays dehumanize Hareton—she asks him whether or not he dreams and compares him to Heathcliff's dogs—although quickly her interest shifts to a pedagogical mode, as she leaves books about hoping to entice Hareton into her tutelage. What I suggest is that Catherine the Younger's switch to a pedagogical imperative dampens the eroticized connection between the two cousins and, in so doing, prepares them for their eventual marriage.

As I claimed earlier, marriage in *Wuthering Heights* is both damaging and reproductive; conversely, the energetic pairing of Catherine the Elder and Heathcliff maintains its power *through* its refusal of genital sexuality. It is significant that when he reaches out to touch her curl, Hareton significantly cannot see Catherine's face—his sexualized focus alights on only a *part* of Catherine's body. Later, as they sit pouring over their reading, Hareton *chooses* to focus on Catherine's hand—again, not her face. One possible reading of Hareton's seemingly distracted gaze might be that Brontë means to align him with an erotics built on a kind of fetishism. While Lockwood "[bites] his lip" and complains about his failure to "[do] something besides staring at [Catherine's] smiting beauty," Hareton contentedly concentrates on her hand, and the next sharp slap it might deliver. This is to say that

Hareton's distraction signals the possibility of a perverse sexuality that has been constrained or tamed by Catherine's educative project.

While the second generation's pairing *could be* a masochistic pairing, dependent on internal agreement, Brontë's move at the novel's end to enforce a marriage between the two characterological descendants of her central dyad indicates a dampening of the second pair's unconventional power. The marriage between Catherine and Linton Heathcliff remains unconsummated, and the contracting parties do not, in any clear sense of the word, consent to their marriage; both of these blocks to marital legitimacy unsettle the explicit connection between marriage and sadistic, reproductive, genital sex. Linton's sadism is a pathetic extension of his impotence; it hasn't the teeth that Heathcliff's does. In place of this connection, Brontë develops a ligature between marriage and education. As the cousins build their courage to resist Heathcliff, they start to alter their surroundings—most explicitly they dig up some of Joseph's prized currant bushes. Heathcliff's response to Joseph's complaint highlights the altered relationship between the cousins: "And who the devil gave *you* leave to touch a stick about the place?" he asks, "And who ordered *you* to obey her?" (244). Again, Brontë makes clear the power dynamic in this query: Hareton has dug up the bushes, but only at Catherine's order. The tenor of these orders, though, significantly differs from the tenor of the first generation's orders. Catherine the Elder's commands to Heathcliff tend to reduce to commands for his attention to her ("Come here and kneel down again!") while Catherine the Younger orders Hareton to alter (and improve?) her surroundings. Even though the possibility of sexualized command exists in this dyad, their energy more often than not transforms into a new kind of productive energy, the energy of self-improvement.

Thus, the novel ends with a marriage, though the institution has heretofore proved violent, disappointing, or miserable for its participants. One could read the marriage predicted in the novel's final pages as a positive compromise—that the sadistic model set out in the novel's first generation has been altered into something more companionate and more sustainable. And, indeed, Catherine the Younger and Hareton's proposed marriage has already been fruitful—the Heights has been restored not simply to its original state but to one that bids entry; Lockwood notices, "I had neither to climb the gate, nor to knock—it yielded to my hand" (234). This forward-looking marriage betters Hareton (though in another light, it simply returns him to his birthright), and it forces Catherine the Younger to direct her energies toward another (the spoiled only child must learn to think of others as well as herself).

But, in many ways, the novel's final pairing reads as a reduction—in gravity, in intensity, in meaning. Brontë, having made clear the resemblance between sadism and marriage, checks that equivalence. Having convinced the reader that the nongenerative, nongenital connection between Catherine and Heathcliff is not only more intense than marriage but more fulfilling, the novel's end relegates their consummation to the grave. But perhaps this lights up one of the most striking features of *Wuthering Heights*. While the private, masochistic world of Catherine and Heathcliff is the novel's ideal, it is entirely untenable. The hope of limitlessness leads the pair to annihilation. If one occupies a position of eternal waiting, consummation can never truly come. This is, in some ways, an example of how the masochism I've been describing tends to fail. The anticipatory logic either gives out (the whip meets its mark, and anticipation gives rise to action) or persists. But, by continuing endlessly, the difference between anticipation and death diminishes. Without action, the masochistic tableau looks more and more like the grave. Not only is Catherine and Heathcliff's masochism nongenerative, but it depends on a time frame beyond the human scale. And while Brontë implies that these two can, and do, experience that consummation, it remains beyond the scope of the novel. Again, the masochistic core of the couple's relationship is entirely private and insulated from external view; in a novel, this is a sign of relationship's failure—it cannot be read. But we can decipher, like Lockwood, the gestures and glances that bind Hareton to Catherine the Younger. Brontë's project, then, is an impossible one. Her ideal resists representation, although her novelistic project demands depiction. This ideal resides in the first generation's unreadable couple; Catherine the Younger's relationship to Hareton may be legible, but it lacks the cipher-like intensity of the earlier pairing. However, Brontë suggests that this final marriage does offer some correctives to the contract's sadistic tendencies. If Hareton doesn't have Heathcliff's, Linton's, or Edgar's sadism, he does have the patriarchal power of marriage on his side. Because of this, Catherine the Younger's pedagogical instincts (and sharp slaps) act as a needed counter to legal and social convention. With her active violence, she shores up her relationship against the sadistic tendencies of marriage. The idealized erotic grasp at the center of Catherine the Elder's relationship to Heathcliff is un-attainable. Perhaps, then, the only thing that remains—or what remains if one inhabits a generative, productive world, a world that can be read by others—is to reduce sadism's hold on marriage.

3

Buoyed Up

Trollope

In the previous chapter, I argued that Emily Brontë's *Wuthering Heights* separates sadistic from masochistic sexualities and, further, evidences an investment in the equalizing powers of the masochistic dyad. This separation aligns with Deleuze's account of masochistic sexuality, though it departs from his account insofar as I read a woman character, Catherine the Elder, as actively engaged in the creation of her masochistic dyad with Heathcliff. If Deleuze's masochistic dyads are ordered and controlled by the submissive male partner only, the dyads I am describing all feature more equitable partnerships wherein scenes of erotic suspension are constructed by active collaboration between both partners. Masochistic waiting or suspension is one of the key ways the exquisite masochism I'm describing is represented in novels. Again, while Gilles Deleuze's account of Masoch's *Venus in Furs* imagines that the submissive male masochist orders the sexual scenes he occupies, I read Masoch as presenting a form of masochism wherein scenes are constructed by ongoing negotiations between the two partners. In the following chapter, I extend this account of masochistic feminine agency to include a novelist with two competing impulses in relation to such activity—Anthony Trollope. If his plots often valorize traditional, gentlemanly paragons, their energy is often reserved for disreputable and sexually aggressive women who circulate at those plots' perimeters.

For Trollope, suspended scenes are most evident during the period of sexualized, but explicitly nongenital, suspense that he imagines forms marital engagement. Though his novelistic output was immense, his marriageable women frequently fit into one of two categories, both of which I think resonate with exquisite masochism. Nineteenth-century marriage forces unmarried women to accommodate themselves to one of these two forms: they are either sexually aggressive, and often sexually experienced, women grasping at respectable marriage, or they are modest girls for whom marriage is a necessary step they must take to secure their entry into adulthood. Trollope's novels, however, feature a number of engagements that do not follow a smooth path from declaration to marriage. Engagement, in Trollope, is a necessarily insecure state, but that insecurity does not simply mean that marriageable women must maintain their holds on prospective suitors. It also allows them the flexibility of committing to a sexualized relationship without incurring the finalizing control of marriage. Like Masoch's Wanda and Severin, then, Trollope's dominant women orchestrate scenes of suspenseful seduction in their quests for masochistic partners desirous of submission; these women are often jettisoned from the plot, as their explicit sexual aggression gives way to novel-ending marriages. I suggest that, somewhat counterintuitively, the virginal English girls who form those marriages similarly use engagement as a time to expand their control over their impending marriages.

In this chapter, I argue that in Trollope's novel *The Way We Live Now* (1874), masochistic plots at the text's periphery help to shape and frame the marriages at its conclusion. In contrast, masochistic sexuality is at the center of Trollope's earlier *Can You Forgive Her?* (1864); and its inclusion explains, in part, the peculiar development of Lady Glencora Palliser over the Palliser series.[1] Trollope's later, more self-contained novel *The Way We Live Now* banishes its masochistic women to foreign soil while *Can You Forgive Her?*, perhaps because it initiates a series, allows them to remain within Trollope's serial universe, provided they shift their emphases from sexual suspension to a new, social model. In both novels, however, Trollope's use of masochistic sexualities frames his investment in sexualized engagements as precursors to marriage. *The Way We Live Now* gives a clear example of the difficulty of contracting a sexual relationship without sexual compatibility, whereas *Can You Forgive Her?* implies that by translating sexual into social engagement, one might be able to inhabit pleasure in marriage even without a perfect alignment of desires. As I noted above, *Can You Forgive Her?* shows some ways masochistic sexuality might be partially preserved, though it must undergo radical alteration; *The Way We Live Now* instead expels its masochistic characters in a bid to secure marriage to a model of landed gentlemanliness.[2] Again, the sexualized scene is not orchestrated by the submissive male partner but, instead, by the dominant woman, so one can't read *The Way We Live Now*'s Mrs. Hurtle's dominating aspect as purely sadistic. Her insistence on scenic control and on contractual obligation place her firmly within the scope of masochism.

Unlike typical marriage plots, the plot of *Can You Forgive Her?* does not hinge on the application of Alice Vavasor's suitors, but on her inability to decide between them. And Glencora Palliser's plot in the same novel does not lead up to her marriage but begins after it she is already married. Similarly, in *The Way We Live Now*, Winifred Hurtle's plot follows from an already extant engagement and includes an already extant marriage. By evacuating these marital plots of typical momentum and by focusing on the suspended state of engagement or indecision, Trollope avoids placing emphasis on what will happen, choosing instead to focus on how scenes develop. Others have noticed that the late-nineteenth-century marriage plot focuses more on the aftereffects of family life than on the progress to the wedding, but Trollope's investments in engagements with foregone conclusions offers an importantly different model, one that diminishes investment in plot much more radically. His are novels of inertia. Admittedly, this makes some of the novels difficult to read if one focuses only on the suspense that develops from plot, but the pleasures Trollope allows, the pleasures of suspension in the scene—of luxurious house parties, fox hunts, and Continental traveling—remain.

I have chosen to begin this chapter with a popular novel and to end it with an almost comically unpopular one. To draw out the starker and more typical masochistic economy first, I begin with a discussion of *The Way We Live Now*. In that novel, masochistic women are more explicitly perverse, and they are argued out of the Trollopean world—they are either inscribed into a nonpublic domestic sphere or shipped off to America. Alternately, in *Can You Forgive Her?*, a space exists after marriage for some women that allows masochistic investment to flourish. Because of this, I read *Can You Forgive Her?* as more positively invested in the masochistic models I adduce than is *The Way We Live Now*. For example, by developing scenic displays for her activities beyond the scope of the sexual, Lady Glencora Palliser carves out a space of suspended pleasure, while Trollope removes other masochistic women once they serve their plot-level purposes. From Glencora's introduction, Trollope aligns her with a vivid model of aesthetic display; her "peculiar low voice" emanates from her fur-covered Whitechapel carriage (*CYFH* 265). But these early scenic displays seem to "burden" her with their magnificence (266). As the Palliser series continues, these early versions of scenic display give way to tableaux on a larger scale—house parties, archery tournaments, and even political campaigns. The pleasures of these scenes are similar to the initial personal pleasures in which Glencora invests energy—nighttime walks around the ruins of Matching Priory and helter-skelter cart rides with her ponies. But, by turning these scenes outward, away from the sexual self, Glencora's version of masochism undergoes a radical change. As the series progresses, the scenic displays become larger in scope; rather than the pleasure of self-display, Glencora instead finds pleasure in "sheer display," in which a commitment to scale takes the place of sexualized intensity (*Prime Minister* 230).[3] In underpinning Glencora's later political and social investments with a version of masochism, Trollope implies that one way of managing perversity is to reroute one's desire for perverse sex into a desire for perverse sociability. One of the major questions Trollope's work raises is how invested sexuality must be in sex. If Glencora survives her novel, it is only by rerouting her sexual desires into social desires. Are the masochistic women who leave their novels (because their desires are *too* explicitly sexual) thus being dismissed, or does their dismissal allow them to remain productively tethered to the sexual world? Further, if Glencora's use of masochistic waiting accounts, in part, for the unpopularity of *Can You Forgive Her?*, are the dismissals of masochistic women in *The Way We Live Now* integral to its popularity?

While *Can You Forgive Her?* was, at the moment of its publication, a source of irritation for its readers, *The Way We Live Now* (1874) has long been perceived as one of the crowning achievements of Trollope's extensive career.[4] One of the main reasons for that early irritation is the earlier novel's focus on what I call "masochistic waiting": a model of narrative delay that contradicts the plot-driven world a novel reader desires to encounter.[5] Further, Trollope's chronicles show a model of narrative delay that at times looks like Glencora's nonsexual masochistic practices of suspension; Trollope aligns this practice with the central character of his series. Trollope's apparent lack of investment in narrative suspense (his plots are not inventive; his novels' conclusions are often apparent well in advance) belies his heavy investment in his characters' suspended states (engagement, gambling, speculation). Across his body of work, Trollope often connects the masochistic suspense I am detailing with disreputable or dangerous characters. These characters are often expelled from novels and include (among others) Winifred Hurtle in *The Way We Live Now*, Madalina Demolines in *The Last Chronicle of Barset*, Signora Neroni in *Barchester Towers*, and Amelia Roper in *The Small House at Allington*. But in *Can You Forgive Her?*, Trollope places waiting at the novel's center and links it to one of his most powerful characters, Lady Glencora Palliser.

As I have been suggesting, Trollope associates sexual suspense with marriageable women, and a period of masochistic waiting, or engagement, is integral to his ideal marriage plot. During this period the organizational powers of women have free reign, and it is this period that strongly counters the aggressively genital sexuality associated with so many of Trollope's apparently unimpeachable young men. John Grey in *Can You Forgive Her?* is an excellent example of this, though Johnny Eames in both *The Small House at Allington* and *The Last Chronicle of Barset* and Paul Montague in *The Way We Live Now* offer more troubled versions. In all of these cases, young men fixate on marriage's ability to alter young women's categories and use their physical power as a "reliably persuasive" instigator of this categorical shift. And in all cases, their power over women is linked to their demand for physical contact (Ablow 138).[6] Trollope further implies that, in some cases, this state can adhere to a person *after* marriage; for example, Glencora becomes suspended between experiences of marriage and engagement because her marriage is so rushed. In her case, childbirth and not the penetrative sex of the honeymoon finalize her transition from maidenhood to wifedom. I suggest that this model of sexualized suspense has far-reaching significance for Trollope's chronicles. Engagement counters the apparent necessity of the marriage plot, and it allows couples (even if only briefly) to avoid choice; the pattern is repeated on a larger scale, in the open-ended constructions of Trollope's series.

Trollope's narrative landscapes offer a dizzying perspective on Victorian society, and their subjects include, often within the span of a single novel, cutthroat social maneuvering, church politics, gold-digging marriages, and the waning aristocracy. This vast patchwork has produced its share of critical befuddlement, most tellingly directed at the question of what, if anything, the novelist values. *The Way We Live Now* has a particularly intricate array of plots. It follows the rise of the parvenu financier Augustus Melmotte in London as he infiltrates polite society, bargains his daughter's hand for an aristocratic title, wins a seat in Parliament, and, ultimately, commits suicide as his questionable, speculative business practices finally catch up with him. Trollope balances the ostentatious, aggressive Melmotte plot with a series of plot lines organized around the traditional, landed Carbury family. In reading the plot's solution as valuing the social embeddedness that a gentleman like Roger Carbury embodies, many critics have ignored or dampened the narratological energy that swirls around the bad characters in the novel; as Trollope remarks in his autobiographical note on *The Way We Live Now*, the interest in this particular book "lies among the wicked and foolish people" who populate its pages (*Autobiography* 309).[7] By "narratological energy" I mean to light up not only the ways Trollope's "wicked" characters seem, at times, to take over the plots of their novels, but also the narrator's investments in thinking through, or trying to understand the reasons behind, their badness. Rather than attempt to locate a single place or character of value in *The Way We Live Now*, I instead want to focus on a particular kind of relationship that radiates throughout the novel, the engaged partnership of a dominant woman and submissive man.[8] For Trollope, the conflation of sexuality and domination in *The Way We Live Now* represents one of the markers of modernity, the sexualized and powerful woman. And the sexualized power relations in the text actually show how sexual suspense becomes particularly important in managing the novel's marriage plots.

Across the board, Trollope's novels offer characters remarkable for their hypocrisy, opportunism, backstabbing, and general "wickedness"; what's truly remarkable about these characters is the level of narratological interest when they appear on the scene. While the "good" and "honest" characters receive plot-level success (proper marriages, carefully scripted inheritances, comfortable living situations), the "wicked" characters propel plots along with their scheming and grasping. Trollope has often been accused of being a conservative novelist of manners, an indictment that has some truth in it on the level of plot; but in *The Way We Live Now* the ostentatious and overreaching figures of Augustus Melmotte and Winifred Hurtle linger in the reader's imagination. In a text where even a clearly villainous figure such as the financier Melmotte receives a kind of blessing, one is hard pressed to discover that plot-level resolutions (marriages, economic successes) do not reliably index narratalogical interest.[9] For Trollope, decadent characters never descend fully into Dickensian grotesques or Collins-like ogres. Instead, his project pivots on inserting these somewhat bad or downright wicked figures onto a canvas that might well bless "good" and "honest" figures, but that doesn't damn outright those who are neither good nor honest. Narratological energy in Trollope's texts is frequently reserved for characters who are "wicked," "disgraceful," "dishonest." What is peculiar about this energy, though, is the disparity between this and the intense plot-level approval of a conservative, embedded, English way of life.[10]

For characters like Winifred Hurtle, Matilda Carbury, and Marie Melmotte, the recognition of perverse sexuality (or a potential partner's lack of perversity) reveals a partnership's viability. And while I am not arguing that this novel privileges perverse sexuality per se, I do want to draw attention to the fact that the perverse sexual subplots underscore how the seemingly nonperverse sexual plots are managed. For example, the subplots of Mrs. Hurtle and Marie Melmotte demonstrate an incorporation of perverse sexuality into marriage (though these marriages are tellingly expelled from the English landscape of the novel). In contrast, both Ruby Ruggle's and Matilda Carbury's impending marriages reverse the female-dominant model of the perverse subplots. In these marriages, women attempt to carve out a dominant space for themselves but are finally relegated to marriages that cast them as submissive partners. The marriages that reinforce the English scene, then, drive out perverse models of sexuality in favor of more conventional power dynamics.

I begin with an analysis of Winifred Hurtle, an American divorcée trying to pin Paul Montague into marriage. Paul meets and becomes engaged to Mrs. Hurtle on a trip across the United States. Once he repatriates to England he meets and falls in love with Hetta Carbury—it is at this point that his story in *The Way We Live Now* begins, with his attempts to disentangle himself from Mrs. Hurtle in hopes of marrying Hetta. However, Mrs. Hurtle continues to draw out their engagement through a series of masochistically organized, aestheticized scenes. Mrs. Hurtle's particular kind of domination looks a lot like the masochism that Deleuze describes in "Coldness and Cruelty," with a twist. Where Deleuze focuses on a masculine subject's control of his feminine partner, Trollope's Hurtle impresses her dominance onto a seemingly willing Paul; and, further, this domination stops short of refusing the possibility of Paul's subjectivity. Mrs. Hurtle's powerfully sexualized subjectivity serves as a model of female-dominated sexuality for a number of other relations in the text. I single out two of these. Trollope figures Marie Melmotte's entrance into self-consciousness in terms of her increasing power over the men with whom she is involved. Matilda Carbury, in contrast, slightly alters her expectations of domination as she enters into a marriage with Mr. Broune.

Venus in Spurs

In *The Way We Live Now*, Trollope presents a clearly sexual relationship between Paul Montague and Mrs. Hurtle. The relationship, for the purposes of the novel, is all but over: by the time the reader meets Paul, he has fallen out of love with Mrs. Hurtle and in love with Hetta Carbury. However, this particular love/nonlove plotline is more complicated than my gloss indicates: Paul gravitates to Mrs. Hurtle, and her power hinges on her ability to prepare scenes for him where the outcome is explicitly sexual intimacy between the two. Apart from her artfully created scenes, there are surface similarities between Masoch's Wanda and Trollope's Winifred Hurtle: both are described as "lionesses," both have astonishing control over their appearances (both are able to either blush or fade to deathly pallor almost on command), but perhaps the most striking similarity is their use of whips, real whips in Wanda's case, imaginary ones in Mrs. Hurtle's.[11]

The story leading up to Mrs. Hurtle's imagined scene of horsewhipping is predicated on a series of scenes of attempted seduction. The narrator's description of one of the first scenes for which Mrs. Hurtle prepares, her rendezvous with Paul at the theater, indicates her artistry: "There was a scent which he had once approved, and now she bore it on her handkerchief. There was a ring which he had once given her, and she wore it on the finger with which she touched his sleeve. With his own hands he had once adjusted her curls, and each curl was as he had placed it" (*WWLN* 215). At every point in the description, Mrs. Hurtle recreates something Paul has either given her or admired in her. The scene works because Mrs. Hurtle has Paul's tacit approval in her scent, her ring, and her hairstyle. But his approval is not acknowledged as the *source* of her personal decisions; instead, the narrator notes Mrs. Hurtle's ability to renew choices for which Paul showed a past preference. The attention to material detail is not the limit of Mrs. Hurtle's artistry: "There are closenesses and sweet approaches, smiles and nods and pleasant winkings, whispers, innuendos and hints, little mutual admirations and assurances that there are things known to those two happy ones of which the world beyond is altogether ignorant. Much of this comes of nature, but something of it comes by art. Of such art there may be in it Mrs. Hurtle was a perfect master" (215). There is, then, an additional artistry to intimacy that nature alone cannot create, and Mrs. Hurtle is a "perfect master" of this art. While her art is enough to keep Paul entranced at Lowestoeffe, it is not enough to impel Paul away from his more conventional romance with Hetta Carbury. Trollope's narrator finds something missing in the relationship between Paul and Mrs. Hurtle: her artistry, while impressive, lacks a sympathetic viewer to engage with her scenes; their relationship looks more like entrancement than love.[12]

The scenes that repeat throughout the Hurtle/Montague subplot are organized around this pattern: Paul attempts to leave, tells Mrs. Hurtle of his plans to marry, and eventually Mrs. Hurtle's tableaux re-seduce him. The repetition of these scenes implies that this cycle could continue indefinitely in a version of what Deleuze calls masochism's "frozen waiting." As far as Paul is concerned, this seems to be the case. When Paul finally tells Mrs. Hurtle he has spoken to Hetta about marriage, Mrs. Hurtle decides she must resolve their relationship. She then writes a series of letters that clarify Paul's position in relation to her and that eventually make it clear that Paul, this particular "tame, sleek household animal," as the narrator calls him in a moment very close to free indirect discourse, is not tame in quite the way she wishes (*WWLN* 691).

Mrs. Hurtle's recourse to letters is particularly telling: they offer her yet another version of suspended relationship after Paul relegates the couple's face-to-face relationship to the past. After Paul leaves Mrs. Hurtle at Lowestoeffe, she writes a letter (that she does not send) that imagines a scene in which she generously withdraws from the engagement. However, when she arrives back in London, she receives a letter from Paul asking her to relieve him of his promise to visit her in Islington, which spurs her to write a furious second letter threatening to whip him for the ill treatment she has suffered. Before sending that second letter, though, Mrs. Hurtle reconsiders and sends a cryptic third letter requesting that Paul visit her after all. When he arrives in Islington, she shows him all three and asks him to choose among them.

Mrs. Hurtle writes three letters, sends the least substantive, and later shows the other two to their nonrecipient.[13] But, in her shifting responses after receiving Paul's letter, one sees her attempts to create in Paul the formal version of masochistic waiting: at first, in her anger, she writes a letter that threatens to "whip [Paul] until [she has] not a breath in [her] body" (*WWLN* 368). Second, she reconsiders sending the note she wrote while they were at Lowestoeffe, capitulating to Paul's desire to break off the engagement (368). Finally, she sends an ambiguous, brief note "Yes. Come" (392). Mrs. Hurtle addresses her conciliatory letter "Dear Paul"; the letter threatening violence, "Paul Montague." But her final note, the one she actually sends, has no salutation. The first greeting marks Mrs. Hurtle's ability and desire to comfort or soothe, the second is aggressive, like a call for a duel, and the third unaddressed letter relies on an assumption about both the sender and receiver of the cryptic note. "Yes. Come." indicates that there is an agreed-upon relationship, as though this assumption works as the underpinning of a masochistic, contractual relationship. In these letters, Mrs. Hurtle manages her behavior through a practice of writing by refusing to negate either the letter written in anger or the letter written "bidding [Paul] adieu, sending him her fondest love, and telling him that he was right" (368).

To concentrate on the differences among these letters—ameliorative, aggressive, or briefly intimate—misses Mrs. Hurtle's important use of them all as weaponry. Her use of them demonstrates her strategy. When Paul later arrives at Mrs. Hurtle's home, we see the "weapons" of her written-and-not-sent letters pulled out for a face-to-face combat that works much more painfully than would any battle in correspondence (WWLN 368). Paul imagines Mrs. Hurtle's "Yes. Come." letter to be "all [she] had to say," but Mrs. Hurtle counters by showing Paul the letter containing the threat of her whip: Paul's response—that he does not "think that under any provocation a woman should use a horsewhip"—underlines Mrs. Hurtle's violent response as unladylike (395). His recourse to the term "unladylike" highlights the violence of Mrs. Hurtle's imagined gesture as out of keeping with his own views of womanly behavior; Paul may be willing to suffer Mrs. Hurtle's emotional scenes, but he will not suffer physically for love, as his refusal of her imagined whip demonstrates.[14] Mrs. Hurtle, though, answers this with a call to arms: "It is certainly more comfortable for gentlemen . . . that women should have that opinion. . . . As long as there are men to fight for women, it may be well to leave the fighting to the men. But when a woman has no one to help her, is she to bear everything without turning upon those who ill-use her? Shall a woman be flayed alive because it is unfeminine for her to fight for her own skin? . . . If she be treated as prey, shall she not fight as a beast of prey!" (395). Here, she imagines herself the victim of an imagined whip, the dominant partner's worst nightmare. Paul refuses to accept the validity of her whip letter because its kind of violence reverses the gendered lines of masochism and asks that he be willing to suffer physically for love. Again, Paul will engage with Mrs. Hurtle's emotional masochism (particularly, he will engage in her scenes), but he cannot understand her move to physical violence, even when the "physical" in this case refers to the threat of an imaginary whip. This is especially striking as the couple considers the three letters as a group, and Mrs. Hurtle asks Paul to choose which of them he believes: "Sometimes I feel that I could tear you limb from limb, so great is my disappointment, so ungovernable my rage! Why—why should I be such a victim? . . . There, you have seen them all. Which will you have?" Given that Mrs. Hurtle builds into this question the very violence Paul decides is not "an expression of [her] mind," one must read the violent, whip letter as more closely aligned with the kind of response Mrs. Hurtle wants to enact (395). But there remains the complacent letter, the letter Mrs. Hurtle wrote when Paul initially leaves her at Lowestoeffe.

The complacent letter, of course, was written before either of the others. Mrs. Hurtle pens it after Paul makes his intentions to marry Hetta clearly known. But, as she writes it, the narrator strangely comments, "The reader may judge with what feeling she wrote the following words." The narrator's refusal to pin down Mrs. Hurtle's emotions here allows one to read her "feeling" not as pity or humble acceptance of Paul's marriage but as a canny manipulation. More interesting, the letter is written after Mrs. Hurtle decides to "play her game with such weapons as she possessed." Her note agrees that "[o]ur marriage would not have been fitting," and, further, she writes, "I attracted you when we were together, but you have learned, and I have learned truly, that you should not give up your life for such attractions. If I have been violent with you, forgive me" (*WWLN* 368). The "attractions" Mrs. Hurtle refers to here seem to operate fairly well for Paul, right up until his last meeting with the widow. However, there is an implication that these "attractions" are, in fact, one of the main reasons the two do not "fit" together: Mrs. Hurtle's "violence," here so clearly linked in her mind to her "attractions," is too much for Paul.

Mrs. Hurtle puts the "generous" letter aside and later, when she receives Paul's reassertion of his intention *not* to marry her, contemplates her course of action:

> Those words, fairly transcribed on a sheet of note paper, would be the most generous and the fittest answer she could give. And she longed to be generous. She had all a woman's natural desire to sacrifice herself. But the sacrifice which would have been most to her taste would have been of another kind. Had she found him ruined and penniless, she would have delighted to share with him

all that she possessed. Had she found him a cripple, or blind, or miserably struck with some disease, she would have stayed by him and have nursed him and given him comfort. Even had he been disgraced, she would have fled with him to some far country and have pardoned all his faults. No sacrifice would have been too much for her that would have been accompanied by a feeling that he appreciated all that she was doing for him, and that she was loved in return. But to sacrifice herself by going away and never more being heard of, was too much for her! What woman can endure such sacrifice as that? To give up not only her love, but her wrath also—that was too much for her! The idea of being tame was terrible to her. (*WWLN* 391)

Mrs. Hurtle is said to have "all a woman's natural desire to sacrifice herself," but the sacrifice for which she seems most keen is Paul's, whether he is crippled, blinded, or diseased. Like a good masochist, the sacrifice Mrs. Hurtle refuses is that of her scenes—she wants to prolong the relationship and its condition of frozen waiting until she figures out whether Paul ever could be the masochistic partner she imagines him to be.[15] Her generosity here is linked to her ability to care for Paul in an imagined hour of need, and she imagines this in a series of scenes wherein she plays a comforting nurturer to a weakened, submissive Paul. The images link Mrs. Hurtle to a dominance that does not depend on total domination but rather offers comfort tinged with domination.

Mrs. Hurtle continues:

Her life had not been very prosperous, but she was what she was because she had dared to protect herself by her own spirit. Now, at last, should she succumb and be trodden on like a worm? Should she be weaker even than an English girl? Should she allow him to have amused himself with her love, to have had "a good time," and then to roam away like a bee, while she was so dreadfully scorched, so mutilated and punished? (*WWLN* 391)

The images of Paul's submission to her as comforter are transformed into images of her own submission to two figures. In the first image, Mrs. Hurtle is "weaker even than an English girl," Hetta Carbury, implying that the Hurtle/Montague love affair has been broken by the intrusion of a third party.[16] The second image, of Mrs. Hurtle being trodden on like a worm, links more closely to her insectivorous metaphor for Paul's departure ("like a bee"). In this final set of images, Mrs. Hurtle is not only "trodden" upon, she is also "scorched," "mutilated," and "punished" by Paul's departure. She is, then, intent on not "sacrificing" herself by removing herself from the story. She imagines that to be "tame" is to be "punished," and to be punished by Paul would be out of keeping with her dominant position. Mrs. Hurtle's chastening image, of an obliviously dominant Paul injuring her not by any act of violence but by his absence, feels like violence to her. In this version of masochistic sexuality, roles cannot be reversed and dominant positions are not interchangeable.[17]

Ultimately, Mrs. Hurtle's attempts to involve Paul in a sympathetic masochistic relationship fail. And, interestingly, her slippery movement from dominant torturess to trodden-upon submissive mimics that of other dominant women in the text. We are made to understand that Matilda Carbury and Ruby Ruggles will become good, submissive wives even though both seemed to indicate a desire for domination and self-control. Mrs. Hurtle's fate, in the marriage-laden plotting of the novel's end, is more striking. Because Paul is not sympathetic to her image of the whip, the violence with which she threatens him ends up looking like simple violence instead of the sexualized, suspended scenes that dominate their relationship earlier in the novel. Her engagement with Paul must end. The narrator, then, blesses her for her "goodness" but also carts her off to America, where her sometimes-dead, sometimes-divorced husband, Caridoc Hurtle, still seems to be both alive and married to her. This strange removal points to how her (imagined) continued existence outside of the novel is in keeping with the masochistic suspension she has attempted to engineer throughout. Mr. Hurtle, a character whose shadowy status has been unclear throughout—at one point it is suggested that he may even have been killed by Mrs. Hurtle's own hand—reappears on the horizon of the text. Where the narrative has previously indicated that Mrs. Hurtle's marriage was problematic because of its violence, one now finds, after her disappointment with the imagined whip, that her marriage to Caridoc might be possible precisely because of that violence.

Before moving to *Can You Forgive Her?*, I want briefly to examine two other characters in *The Way We Live Now* who organize their sexual relationships with scenes of domination and submission, Matilda Carbury and Marie Melmotte. These two characters offer two very different examples: Lady Carbury opens the novel with a series of letters that pit her sexual desirability against three of London's elite editors, while Marie Melmotte begins the novel in the shadow of her financially powerful father, Augustus Melmotte.

Lady Carbury's trajectory involves the exchange of dominant sexual power for dominant domestic power as her influence moves from the literary to the domestic sphere, whereas Marie Melmotte demonstrates an emergence from an imaginary, romance-tinged sexual scene to an embodied and equitable one. If Lady Carbury's involvement in the literary world inflects her sexuality, finance inflects Marie Melmotte's. These investments in worlds outside of the purely sexual are one of the key differences between these two characters and Winifred Hurtle. And while, in *The Way We Live Now*, this difference helps shape these characters' integration into marriageable stability, it is this kind of investment, one that borrows from the sexual but is not synonymous with it, that explains Lady Glencora's decidedly more sustainable success in the Palliser series.

Lady Carbury presents a thwarted version of masochism. Where Mrs. Hurtle's aggressive machinations produce her as a torturess without a submissive and finally relegate her to the American horizon of the novel, Lady Carbury's attempts at playing the dominant woman leave her grasping for something else. In her story, attempts to torture produce an overabundance of anticipation. Finally, Lady Carbury finds that a sympathetic relationship to the hardened Mr. Broune—a man whose proposal she refuses earlier in the novel—offers her the most possible happiness. In this relationship, Lady Carbury plays a submissive role: where she previously had congratulated herself on her masterful handling of the editor, she now imagines herself prostrate before him. Trollope writes, "It did not occur to her to rebel against him. After what he had said, of course there would be no more praise in the *Breakfast Table*—and, equally of course, no novel of hers could succeed without that. The more she thought of him, the more omnipotent he seemed to be" (*CYFH* 757).[18] In Lady Carbury's plot, the masochistic form allows for characters to try on dominant or submissive power positions but, further, stresses that the character must assess his or her affinity for the role he or she plays. Lady Carbury discovers, at the end of the novel, that she has been stuck playing the wrong part for far too long.

Alternately, Trollope makes it clear that one should read Marie Melmotte as a quickly changing character. At the novel's opening, she is described by Felix Carbury as neither pretty nor plain, neither clever nor stupid, and neither saint not sinner. To Felix, this description marks Marie's mediocrity, but there is a strange strength in her even at the Melmottes' ball. Though her "destiny had no doubt been explained to her" (much as had Glencora's before her marriage to Plantagenet in the Palliser series), she blocks the young aristocrats vying for her hand (*WWLN* 32). And although at first Marie appears to be a pawn in her father's speculations, offering him a convenient tool to bargain his way into a British title, she develops over the course of the novel into a woman focused on maintaining self-sufficiency, at first in the face of physical threats from her father and finally in response to Hamilton J. Fisker's zealous pursuit.

Marie temporarily inhabits both the position of masochist and that of torturess. While overshadowed by her alternately aggressive and generous father, Marie acts the part of a docile submissive, living in a strange state suspended between "knocks and knick-knacks" (*WWLN* 706). In her engagement to Sir Felix, and in the elopement she masterminds, Marie begins to demonstrate the orchestral powers of a dominant masochistic partner. Her management of the affair tends toward scenes of storybook romance, and she finds herself a lonely actress in the scenes she constructs. After her father's death, Marie is wooed by Hamilton Fisker, whose attempts to romance Marie fall on deaf ears. However, when Fisker begins to weave legalistic and financial details into his romance, Marie listens. The result is a masochistic exchange wherein Fisker is Marie's "servant," at her disposal both sexually and financially. In Marie Melmotte's case, the masochistic battleground of the body is indistinguishable from the bank.

In this novel, these masochistic dyads resolve themselves into dyads of two wills; the masochist's will, with its overwhelming desire for subjection, and the torturess's will, with its desire to subject and to control the aesthetics of the scene. The powerful aspects of these speculative torturesses are problematically positioned in the novel; if they are powerful, they are also threatening. Thus, Hamilton Fisker's submission counters Marie Melmotte's ascendancy, and they are removed to America. Because of this, too, Mrs. Hurtle must be pushed beyond the borders of the text, back to her husband and the hints of a sympathetic masochistic bond, while Paul Montague, whose desires for domination stop short of a desire for subjection, marries Hetta Carbury and maintains landed embeddedness as a value for one more generation. That Paul and Hetta offer the only thread of this value in the novel hints at the direction in which Trollope felt society to be moving. *The Way We Live Now*, then, manages the boundaries between a newer world of abundant speculation and sexual reciprocity and an older world of landed embeddedness and social order in part by jettisoning the speculators from the novel. Instead of destroying it completely, a hint of Mrs. Hurtle's possible satisfaction endures, but only in America.

In contrast to Mrs. Hurtle, in *Can You Forgive Her?* Lady Glencora occupies a high status that allows her to simultaneously occupy stable marriage and never-ending suspense. Unlike the American, she is not pushed overseas but reigns over the course of six novels. America is, of course, on the periphery of Trollope's *Can You Forgive Her?*, but only as a holding tank for the explicitly sadistic—and explicitly expelled—George Vavasor. *Can You Forgive Her?* presents masochistic power differently than does *The Way We Live Now*. Lucinda Roanoke in *The Eustace Diamonds* offers a more pathological version of American danger. These two antiheroines' Americanness binds them to one another conceptually, though their versions of sexual aggression are slightly different. Americanness marks them within their respective texts. While the characters have some astonishing similarities, they cannot be seen as copies of or versions of one another: Mrs. Hurtle's kind of rapacious, other-directed sexuality is at odds with Lucinda's embodied virginity, her defining feature. What unites their sexualities, both so evident in their respective novels, under the umbrella of "Americanness" is an insistence on self-control that other characters, and the narratalogical voices, call "wild."[19] In his earlier novel, Trollope develops a model of masochism that does not seem at odds with marital success, in part because this earlier model does not seem as securely tied to the sexual world; somewhat counterintuitively, Glencora's social position means she is more solidly tied to marriage and family than *The Way We Live Now*'s social climbers are, but these ties are flexible enough to allow her pleasurable absorption elsewhere. Glencora's eventual project, unlike Mrs. Hurtle's, is the domination not of a single man but of a social order.

Incident and Event

Can You Forgive Her? introduces Trollope's multinovel heroine, Lady Glencora, shortly after her marriage to the upwardly rising politician Plantagenet Palliser and during a moment when Glencora considers leaving her husband to attach herself to her rakish former lover, Burgo Fitzgerald.[20] In the Palliser marriage, Glencora is the bright spark that propels her husband to soften his political stoicism, and in *Can You Forgive Her?* we see the first indications of her power. Glencora's flirtation with leaving Plantagenet in some ways explains her centrality in the remainder of the series.[21]

In this first of the Palliser series, Trollope attributes masochistic waiting to three women—one, a vulgar widow (Mrs. Greenow); another, a good English girl (Alice Vavasor); and the last, Lady Glencora Palliser, a multinovel character who, over the course of her story, combines aspects of vulgarity with a moral centrality.[22] Alice Vavasor's desire to suspend herself indefinitely in engagement fails when faced with her cousin's active sadism and John Grey's moral force. Mrs. Greenow's investment in masochistic scenes is pragmatic inasmuch as it allows her to choose the suitor most likely to let her have her own way. But Glencora, slightly differently, shifts from a wish to elope—to physically leave her husband—to a capacity for imaginatively inhabiting her desire for Burgo and thus for inhabiting a suspended desire as a personal principle.

As I have noted, Can You Forgive Her? is an unpopular novel. Much of the critical dissatisfaction, both at the time of the novel's publication and today, comes from its apparent stasis: the women all end up happily committed (or recommitted in Glencora's case) to married life, and the plots' convolutions end with two new marriages and one new son. Whatever their sins, all three women are "forgiven" in readily apparent ways. But Can You Forgive Her? more fundamentally centers on these women's engagements—by which I mean their suspension between two states of being. And, as I have suggested, it is engagement (in various guises) that is the subject of much of Trollope's fiction. Like Winifred Hurtle, both Alice Vavasor and Mrs. Greenow occupy engagement problematically, but Lady Glencora's flirtation with Burgo Fitzgerald is, in the terms of the novel, inexcusable. By the time the novel opens, Glencora has already married Plantagenet, and Burgo is her former fiancé, one who has been spurned by her relations as undeserving of her because of his "worthlessness," a worthlessness countered only by his astonishing beauty (CYFH 358). Glencora occupies the space of engagement because she cannot yet fully inhabit the space of the wife; she still loves Burgo, and, perhaps more importantly, she has not yet borne Palliser an heir.[23] For Glencora, familial reproduction has the same effect (tamping down possible feminine self-will) as weddings do in the novel's other plots.[24] But although Trollope ends Can You Forgive Her? with conservative gestures to wedded and familial futurity, the novel's plots inhabit these not-quite-sustainable spaces of engagement, revealing an investment in these "incidents," and not in the "events" that end the novel. Furthermore, these "incidents" spill over the novel's end and propel Glencora into her position as a central figure in subsequent novels.

My use of these terms ("incident" and "event") are drawn from, and point to a problem in, Henry James's 1865 review of the novel in the *Nation*. James's critique of the novel emphasizes the, as he perceives it, unfulfilled promise of its plots. Why, he asks, could not Alice Vavasor be made to stay away from John Grey, mulling over her mistakes? Or why could not Lady Glencora have been driven from her husband and "vulgarly disposed of"? Finally, James petitions for the rightful death of another character consigned to a life outside the novel's frame:

> Another case in which Mr. Trollope has burdened himself, as he proceeded, with the obligation to go further, is that of George Vavasor. Upon him, as upon Lady Glencora, there hangs a faint reflection of poetry. In both these cases, Mr. Trollope, dealing with an unfamiliar substance, seems to have evoked a ghost which he cannot exorcise. As the reader follows George Vavasor deeper into his troubles—all of which are very well described—his excited imagination hankers for—what shall we say? Nothing less positive than Vavasor's death. . . . But for Mr. Trollope anything is preferable to a sensation; an incident is ever preferable to an event. George Vavasor simply takes ship to America (252).[25]

By positioning "incident" against its seeming cognate, "event," James highlights the difference between the two. An incident is a momentary (scenic) pause in the flow of an action, while an event, typified in James's account as Vavasor's "death," is more final. Events are the things that typically end novels: births, deaths, marriages.[26] If Trollope's novel ends with scenes that appear to be events (birth and marriage), his progress toward these events is made up of a concatenation of incidents, scenes that link together in an episodic, but not necessarily linear, plot. Furthermore, in Trollope's world, these end-of-novel events do not signal an "end" to his characters' lives; Trollope's form is famously the chronicle and not the novel. Thus, the "exorcism" James points to is fulfilled by exchanging incident for event. Instead of sending George Vavasor beyond the novel's margins, James wishes the character's "life" coterminous with the novel's ending.

James's complaint gets at a few of the major characteristics that distinguish Trollope's chronicles from other Victorian novels. Trollope's penchant for eking out characters' stories over a number of novels means that James's review is partial: his major criticism of Glencora's treatment is that it's skimpy, which is not a criticism that can hold once the Palliser series is concluded.[27] As I noted earlier in my account of Winifred Hurtle, Trollope's characters often do not meet "novelistic" ends and instead are summarily dismissed from novels with brief sentences.[28] By drawing attention to these exits, I mean to light up how James's recommendation for Alice Vavasor's ending looks very much like a perversion of Isabel Archer's decision to live with her choice in James's later *The Portrait of a Lady*.[29] According to James's advice, a more telling (and perhaps more compelling) ending to *Can You Forgive Her?* would leave Alice, because unable to grant herself forgiveness, unable to reattach herself to Grey; she would be forced to live with her choice. And while Isabel's refusal to separate herself from Osmond looks very much like a refutation of a comedic novelistic ending (there is no "happily ever after" in *Portrait*, not even in Henrietta Stackpole's "Just you wait!"), in another way, James's antinomian ending is conventional. Isabel's story ends.[30] One difficulty of Trollope's novel is that although she does not forgive herself (as the narrator frequently reminds us), Alice Vavasor does indeed become Alice Grey. For a variety of reasons, the absolute (moral) choice over her fate available to Isabel Archer is unavailable to Alice Vavasor.[31] Isabel's choice gets to the core of her character's independence from oversight, while women in Trollope's novel make choices of a different kind—they are not necessarily forced to live out their choices because, in Trollope's world, their "choices" are always limited. If James makes it clear that Isabel's choice is her own, Trollope's women never fully own choice. At the crisis in her marriage, Glencora is offered a "choice" between remaining with Plantagenet and eloping with Burgo Fitzgerald, but in many ways neither of these choices is tenable. If she elopes, she will enter the liminal world of a fallen woman; if she remains as she is with Plantagenet, she will be folded into conventional married life. By refusing to fully choose, Glencora discovers a route out of these limiting subject positions. In Glencora's case, she rejoins her husband, but remains always a "woman who doubted" (*CYFH* 354). All of this points to the key way in which Trollope refuses to exchange incident (or episode, or scene) for event (or conclusion, or ending). This means that characters' choices are never fully available as choices—to make a choice would be to assume one has some kind of control over the outcome. And, crucially, Glencora's plot strains beyond the novel's edge—an expansion contingent on her peculiar ability to find pleasure in suspension. If a character has self-will, or free choice, there can be an outcome to that choice. Mrs. Greenow gets as close as one of these female characters can to having a true choice, but both Alice's and Glencora's choices are constrained. The broadest way of saying this is that Trollope's formal strangeness (and open-endedness) has a direct relation to his characters' limited autonomy. And that willfulness has an inverse relationship to open-endedness. In the sexualized suspension that Trollopean women inhabit, particularly in engagement, we see a possible way of forestalling choice. However, Trollope alters this radical possibility, available to Glencora in the novel's middle section, by rerouting her sexualized suspension into a general principle of sensual suspension. This rerouting does not entirely obliterate the sexual from Glencora's character, though it is remarkably changed. To further illuminate these ideas, I will address in turn each of the separate subplots of the novel, beginning with the least successful, and perhaps also the most unforgivable, woman in *Can You Forgive Her?*: Alice Vavasor.

Alice's status as an unmarried woman compromises her ability to put off decision. She refuses to explicitly choose a husband, a behavior that confuses almost every other character in the novel. Her cousin Kate, for example, complains when Alice claims indecision over her possible reengagement to George, Kate's brother. When Kate asserts that surely Alice made up her mind as soon as she received George's reproposal, Alice responds, "I have not made up my mind as to what answer I will give him; but I have shown you his letter in order that I might have some one with whom I might speak openly. I knew well how it would be, and that you would strive to hurry me into an immediate promise" (*CYFH* 346).[32] Eventually, Alice is conscripted into a marriage that the narrator tells us is loving but that seems in various ways oppressive. This oppressiveness follows not only from John Grey's sinister bodily power but also from Alice's apparent prudishness. It is possible to reconcile Alice's eventual sexual submission to John Grey with her desire to control her fate by refusing to choose between her suitors.

Beyond her inability to commit to a *single* engagement, Alice typifies a refusal to choose in her repeated threat to "leave the room" or "part" from those who cross her.[33] Alice threatens Kate and George Vavasor, Lady Glencora, Plantagenet Palliser, and John Grey (among others) with her removal from their sight. Alice's selection of this particular threat indicates a notion of her own exceptionality, but it also points to her desire to remove herself from the surrounding social action should it disagree with her, to disentangle her body from the marriage market in which it is implicated. Alice's desire for punishment alongside this desire to suspend choice marks her as a

peculiar blending of Freud's idea of moral masochism and Deleuzean masochism. In Freud's account, moral masochism is both unconscious and apparently separated from sexuality: "[t]he suffering itself is what matters"
(19:165).[34] Freud's version of moral masochism separates suffering from its
sexual root, and general punishment is the masochist's aim; moral masochism crucially "[dispenses] with the need for an external object" (Silverman
196).[35] On the contrary, Deleuzean masochism is necessarily sexualized. For
Alice, this blending causes, in part, critical dissatisfaction with her character:
while she refuses to choose, she also feels guilty for any perceived infraction
she commits. Alice's moral masochism links to her position as an unmarried,
and thus virginal, woman. Her encounter with the two sadistic male suitors
(Vavasor is physically sadistic, threatening physical violence, while Grey is
morally sadistic, denying her consent to marriage) marks Alice as incapable
of fully inhabiting her own dominant impulses. Although Alice frequently
tries to control or limit other characters' behaviors (these repeated threats
to "leave the room at once" when faced with something antagonistic to her
become almost comical by the novel's end), her attempts eventually fail. And
Grey's physical efforts at the novel's end destroy Alice's disembodied efforts
to carve out a space of resistance to the marriage market.

For example, Grey's "proposal" evidences so much mastery that it produces anxiety about his embodied authority in the narrator (who often
agrees with Grey's moral authority):

> He was so imperious in his tranquility, he argued his question of love with such
> a manifest preponderance of right on his side, that she had always felt that to
> yield to him would be to confess the omnipotence of his power. She knew now
> that she must yield to him,—that his power over her was omnipotent. She was
> pressed by him as in some countries the prisoner is pressed by the judge,—so
> pressed that she acknowledged to herself silently that any further antagonism
> to him was impossible. Nevertheless, the word which she had to speak still
> remained unspoken, and he stood over her, waiting for her answer. Then
> slowly he sat down beside her, and gradually he put his arm round her waist.
> She shrank from him, back against the stonework of the embrasure, but she
> could not shrink away from his grasp. She put up her hand to impede his, but
> his hand, like his character and his words, was full of power. It would not be
> impeded. "Alice," he said, as he pressed her close with his arm, "the battle is
> over now, and I have won it."

"You win everything,—always," she said, whispering to him, as she still shrank from his embrace.

"In winning you I have won everything." Then he put his face over her and pressed his lips to hers. (*CYFH* 772)

Other than Alice's desire to distance herself physically from Grey (she tries to, but cannot, "shrink away"), two things are particularly striking about this passage. First, Alice's "acceptance" of his proposal looks more like an acceptance of his physical domination. The word that Alice "had to speak" remains unspoken even after Grey claims his prize. Instead of accepting the proposal, Alice cedes that Grey "wins everything." Her ability to consent is compromised by Grey's absolute omnipotence. If he "wins everything," her ability to agree to marry him is a nonissue. Grey's sheer strength of will excludes Alice from what is ostensibly her own decision. Second, Grey's kiss is violently aggressive. He "puts his face over" Alice's, physically subjugating her. And instead of offering a model of responsive sexual communication, Trollope simply says that Grey's lips "pressed" Alice's. Grey's imposition here does not seem drastically distinct from George Vavasor's earlier desire to compel Alice to kiss him, and it is difficult to imagine the difference between these two suitors as being the categorical difference the narrator claims (*CYFH* 381).[36] Given, too, that the novel's focus is ostensibly Alice's marital choice, it's bizarre that her consent is so narratalogically limited in this crucial scene. The foreclosure of Alice's choice implies, among other things, that this decision is not the true focus of the novel. This decision has, Trollope suggests, been a foregone conclusion, both because of Alice's virginity and Grey's extreme physical and moral power.

Alice's attempt to avoid Grey's aggressive advance (an avoidance built on playing one engagement off another) backfires once George Vavasor's explicit violence forces her to end their engagement. Had George been less openly sadistic, or had he not pressured Alice to submit to his own advances, Alice might have occupied her engagements indefinitely. But part of the problem with this desire to occupy engagement appears to be the novel's refusal to accept Alice's nongenital sexuality as sexuality. Her virginity complicates her sexual investments in suspension; the novel's end implies that she must be introduced to the world of genital sexuality before she can decide to resist it. And, unfortunately, Alice's investments in sexualized suspension do not survive her marriage. Alice attempts to avoid the event-focused system of the novel by suspending herself in engagement. Her failure to do so points to the system's inescapability for someone, like Alice, poised to swap maidenhood for wifedom. Both Greenow's widowhood and Glencora's marriage allow them to shift for themselves in ways unavailable to Alice.

When the reader meets Arabella Greenow, Alice Vavasor's paternal aunt, she has recently lost her wealthy, but patently not aristocratic, husband. Her plot follows her process of deciding between two suitors, and much of the criticism treating her character focuses on her vulgarity. Mrs. Greenow's eventual marriage to shifty Captain Bellfield may well be the most successful marriage in the novel, especially in relation to her maintained authority over her husband. Her marriage does not dampen her power; in fact, she chooses her mate in part because he is easier to rule than his counterpart, the aggressive Mr. Cheesacre. Although she rules Cheesacre as a friend, his wealth means that the money the widow would bring to the partnership would be absorbed into an already substantial income. By choosing the impoverished Bellfield, and by training him beforehand, Mrs. Greenow maintains her power over both her money and herself after her marriage.[37] The widow achieves this maintenance, in part, by her ability to produce and control dramatic scenes that inscribe her suitors as devoted lovers and that allow her to observe how comfortable each is with that position. By presenting herself ostentatiously as a widow, she puts off choosing a suitor until she can properly read their potential for supplication.[38]

Her need for supremacy is made clear from her first introduction; her "taste for masterdom" reveals itself on the train ride from London to Yarmouth, when the widow orders the railway's employees about in an ostentatious display of wealth (*CYFH* 101). Similarly, after she arrives in Yarmouth, she makes a scene at church: "Mrs. Greenow's entry into church made quite a sensation. There was a thoughtfulness about her which alone showed that she was a woman of no ordinary power" (103). Almost as soon as she hits the Yarmouth sands, Mrs. Greenow constructs an identity for herself as a rich, and beautiful, widow. This identity is in some ways fixed in her character's physical and financial qualities, but the narrator makes it clear that these scenes, and her constructed appearance, require some work. Perhaps the most striking aspect of Mrs. Greenow's scenes is their display of both opulence and frugality.

The widow's talent for constructing scenes on the cheap filters through her plot: when she cosponsors a dance on the Yarmouth sands with financial assistance from Cheesacre, the party considers her the founder of the feast and she compels Cheesacre to behave like a "head servant" (*CYFH* 119–20). At another moment, Mrs. Greenow both adamantly refuses to accept a delicacy-filled basket Cheesacre attempts to deliver and proceeds to return the basket emptied of its luxuries.[39] These scenes depend on an illusion of privacy—she often seems to be alone with her suitors, but her maid Jeannette lurks in the background, as it were, to help her mistress manage her props. Jeannette's investments in and assistance to Mrs. Greenow's scenes further highlight their constructed, artificial character.[40] Given Mrs. Greenow's desire to dominate through these performances, and Cheesacre's apparent willingness to submit to her rule, her decision to marry Bellfield might seem counterintuitive. But Mrs. Greenow recognizes early on that Cheesacre's investment relates to her wealth. His two anxieties are that the widow will throw her money away by marrying Bellfield or that she will throw it away on luxury goods. Cheesacre's resistance to the trappings of Mrs. Greenow's scenes (in this case, her carriage with a liveried attendant) indicates a deeper resistance to her power.[41]

This becomes even clearer when we turn to Greenow's superintendence of Charlie Fairstairs's marriage to Cheesacre. Mrs. Greenow's advice is integral to Cheesacre's mushrooming desire for Charlie. Because of Charlie's familiarity to the farmer (Charlie has "been on the sands of Yarmouth for the last twelve years"), the widow recommends a tactic designed to obscure Charlie's ordinariness—avoidance, a tactic that produces a spectacle: "At one time Mr. Cheesacre did get close up to her [Charlie] and spoke some word, some very indifferent word. He knew that he was being cut and wanted to avoid the appearance of a scene. 'I don't know, sir,' said Charlie, again moving away with excellent dignity" (*CYFH* 805). Instead of backing away from this kind of performed avoidance (Charlie's "excellent"—or excellently acted—dignity), Cheesacre is intrigued. When Charlie finally entices him away from the group, into the woods, the kiss that seals their engagement is observed by Mrs. Greenow herself: "He gave one glance around him to see that he was not observed, and then he did kiss Charlie Fairstairs under the trees. 'Oh, Mr. Cheesacre,' said Charlie. 'Oh, Mr. Cheesacre,' echoed a laughing voice; and poor Cheesacre, looking round, saw that Mrs. Greenow, who ought to have been inside the house looking after the boiling water, was moving about for some unknown reason within sight of the spot which he had chosen for his dalliance" (812). Here, Mrs. Greenow, who has spent much of her plot con-

structing closed-off scenes to further entice her suitors, acts as a stage man-
ager for Charlie's scene. Charlie is, in Trollope's terms, "the bait," and her
freshly ironed muslin, her slow, deliberate movement away from the group,
and her retirement into the apparently secluded woods beyond the party's
boundaries appear to evince a desire to separate Cheesacre from the social
system by inducting him into a private sexual world. Instead, Mrs. Greenow
inserts herself into this supposedly private scene and exposes the relationship to the social world. Although Cheesacre tries to worm out of his implied
contract with Charlie, Mrs. Greenow's presence "fixes" the wedding day: "It
would be too long to tell now . . . how Cheesacre strove to escape, and with
what skill Mrs. Greenow kept him to his bargain" (813). Her recognition of
Cheesacre as a possible suitor for someone uninterested in scenes—or, in
Charlie's case, someone who must be coached in those scenes—lights up her
own need to delay her sexual choice as long as possible. Because Mrs. Greenow's status as a widow necessitates some delay before she reenters the marriage market, this is easier for her to do than it is for Alice Vavasor. Further,
her ability to control her own mourning—that is, to pointedly misremember
and misrecognize both the time that has passed since her husband's death
and the motivations of her two suitors—gives her the time she needs to make
her own remarriage.

While Mrs. Greenow's marriage might be *Can You Forgive Her?*'s most
explicitly masochistic model, Glencora Palliser's career allows her to inhabit
suspended pleasures alongside her marital duties. In *Can You Forgive Her?*,
Glencora roots herself in anxiety about her marriage—she seriously debates
leaving Plantaganet for Burgo Fitzgerald. Throughout her crisis, Trollope
uses descriptions of her absorption in this problem to characterize her.[42] A
letter she receives from Burgo at Matching Priory becomes a fetishistic reminder in her paralytic deliberations and brings about the crisis. As soon as
the letter appears, it immobilizes Glencora. She is unable to perceive her
feelings let alone to act upon them: "She could not analyse her own wishes,"
Trollope writes. "She sent no answer to his letter. She made no preparation
for going with him. . . . She was as one who, in madness, was resolute to
throw herself from a precipice, but to whom some remnant of sanity remained which forced her to seek those who would save her from herself"
(453). Glencora's position as a woman on the edge is linked to her incapacity to fully exchange single life for married life. Consequently, for Glencora,
these first years of marriage are like an extended engagement.

Without a child, without an ability to move herself where she would like, without access to friends beyond those of her husband's choosing, Glencora is indeed frozen, but not by her own agency. The two ponies the Duke of Omnium has given his young niece-in-law are indicative of Glencora's arrested development; Dandy and Flirt offer mobility, but only as long as that mobility leads from Matching Priory to Matching Station. So circumscribed is Glencora's movement that she must ask her groom to reharness Dandy to keep him from "pulling at the bar" when she diverges from her typical path by driving Alice through the priory's grounds instead of through the front gate (*CYFH* 246). Thus, when Burgo's letter proposing elopement arrives, it is so outside of Glencora's ordinary life that she immediately latches onto it as a significant object and carries it with her at all times, a reminder of the abnormality of her current position. In fact, Glencora often "grasps" the letter in her pocket as though its very fact stabilizes her intention to consider the elopement (461, 526).

After Burgo's proposal, Glencora inhabits intrigue with an absorption that finds its fullest demonstration in her waltz with him at Lady Monk's. At first she does not notice that all eyes are upon her, and she revels in the moment: "[i]t was all very sweet, that dancing . . . as they used to dance, without any question as to the reason why it was so; that sudden falling into the old habits, as though everything between this night and the former nights had been a dream" (*CYFH* 534). But when Burgo actually questions Glencora about leaving with him, Glencora's dream dissipates: "The words [Burgo's "old days"] roused her from her sleep at once, and dissipated her dream. The facts all rushed upon her in an instant; the letter in her pocket" (534). This marks a switch in the letter's use in the novel. Heretofore, it had allowed Glencora a physical reminder of a possible future (as she repeatedly touched the letter while it rested in her pocket); here its presence (it is a "fact") reminds her that these possibilities actually present her with decisions to be made. Burgo alters Glencora's desire, her indefinite indecision, with a phrase that reminds her of their history and of their physical contact in the moment, both of which offer possible routes to a very real future: "Does it put you back in mind of old days?" (534). In this passage, "old days" is repeated four times—twice in Glenocra's head, twice by Burgo. However, the second time Burgo repeats this, Trollope embeds it in quotation marks: "Does it put you back in mind of 'old days?'" (534).

In this moment, Glencora recognizes that her physical movements have consequences and that these consequences stand to "dissipate" the dream world she has constructed for herself. The dream world would be shattered by a real one should Glencora choose to elope with Burgo—her control over her absorption would vanish.

This marks a shift in Glencora's interest in the elopement scheme, but it does not evaporate it completely. An ongoing sexual danger threatens her. After the scene at Lady Monk's, Plantagenet Palliser relinquishes his own driving ambition and consents to take Glencora (and Alice) to the Continent for the winter. Burgo visits Glencora at her home, surprising her. She refuses to listen to his entreaties and threatens to leave: "[w]e [Glencora and Alice] will leave Mr. Fitzgerald here, since he drives us from the room." Trollope's narrator continues, "In such contests, a woman has ever the best of it at all points. The man plays with a button to his foil, while the woman uses a weapon that can really wound" (CYFH 699). Glencora's adherence to social niceties is a "weapon" that not only drives Burgo from the room but also has the ability to "wound." As he is leaving, however, Glencora cries back to him: "He was on the threshold of the door before Glencora's voice recalled him. 'Oh my God!' she said, 'I am hard,—harder than flint. I am cruel. Burgo!'" (699). Burgo's position here, on the threshold leaving Glencora's room, signals the pull her voice can have on him; it compels him back to her, though at this point it's clear (Alice is there, watching them) that the situation cannot change. Glencora's assessment of herself here, that she is "cruel" and "hard," connects to the more general masochistic system I have been delineating. The scene ends with a tableaux, Burgo holds her waist and, "stopping over her, kisse[s] her lips" (700). This moment epitomizes the pair's suffering. While Burgo's superficiality limits his ability to fully enter into a dialogic relation with Glencora, his theatricality allows him to embody the suffering lover almost perfectly. Burgo simply repeats back to Glencora that she is "hard and cruel," but he cannot produce such a characterization without her lead. Glencora's reentry into married life appears to be a compromise, but if it is so, it strangely does not change much about her: "As for running away with him, I have not the courage to do it. I can think of it, scheme for it, wish for it;—but as for doing it, that is beyond me" (701). The thinking, scheming, wishing in which she has indulged can continue and do continue in some ways unabated.

It is on the Continent that Glencora begins to imagine models of suspension unrelated to her possible elopement. When Glencora hears Burgo's voice at Lady Monk's, she realizes that he is not, as she thought, an ideal interlocutor for her desires; he encourages her to act. Burgo presses his point about old days because the absorption Glencora feels is not enough to "further his views" (*CYFH* 534). From this moment on, Glencora sets out on what looks like a single-subject search for absorption and suspension. By relinquishing an investment in a possible dyadic model, Glencora becomes more like the Deleuzean masochist I described at the beginning of this chapter. But instead of suspenseful scenes organized by a submissive partner, Trollope's novel presents a powerful Glencora transforming her interests in sexual suspension into something tenable. Her imaginative constructions depend not only on Burgo: when Plantagenet proposes their removal from London, away from politics, he signals a willingness to engage more fully in his wife's masochistic scenes.[43]

One of the key places the danger of Glencora's displaced investments in suspension becomes clear is in her combination of political life with social life. While Plantagenet's irritation at this marks him as a good Liberal, Glencora imagines (dangerously at times) a world in which political right is linked to social right. The danger in this way of thinking is perhaps most evident in Glencora's social *position*. In *The Prime Minister*, for example, her squandering parties are brought about through the hard work of an assemblage of invisible workers. In *Can You Forgive Her?*, she pettishly complains when she must leave her "things" to be inspected by customs (706). While Glencora is politically liberal, more liberal than her husband, she is consigned to a social position of extreme power. Thus, his resistance to her investments in suspension come to look like proper Liberalism while there remains an implicit criticism in Plantagenet's resistance to more radical political positions (like the hidden ballot). Plantagenet's resistance to some of Glencora's scheming takes aggressive form at certain points in the series, but the discordant dialogue that Trollope sets up in *Can You Forgive Her?* allows the couple to move ever forward without subjecting themselves to the aggressive script of the companionate marriage at any turn. Following on recent work by Rachel Ablow, I argue that the companionate sympathy so insistent in certain Victorian novels is, in *Can You Forgive Her?*, transformed into the less agreeable, but more politically productive, form of companionship, epitomized in the Palliser model. This model, unlike the pairing in *He Knew He Was Right*, offers a *sustainable* version of the "pleasures of alienation," pleasures secured by Glencora's attention and desire to immobilize herself in scenes of delay and suspension.[44] Her relationship with Plantagenet depends on, and is not jeopardized by, her sexualized investments beyond marriage. Glencora lives, as it were, in a state of perpetual engagement. Her willingness to give herself over to suspension is perhaps seen most clearly in the scene at the edge of the Rhine.

For Glencora to remain a central figure, that is, if she is not to desert her husband or disappear into the demimonde, Trollope must transform her sexual investments into something else. Her squandering parties, her matchmaking, her archery codes, even her investment in Mary Palliser's engagement to Frank Tregear, all point to a model of absorption and suspension that is, in the end, pleasurable to her though it is not explicitly sexual.[45] This transfer apparently paves the way for her continued narration in Trollope's world. She has been "saved" from shipwreck by the end of *Can You Forgive Her?*, but the possibility shipwreck offered is never erased. Instead, Trollope's narrator reminds us of it again and again, and, even after her death, Glencora is always a woman who doubted her marriage and, in doubting, buoyed herself up. Whether this is enough remains a question.

Going Abroad

As Mary Hamer has noticed, Trollope uses the Rhine as a metaphor for both Alice's and Glencora's desire for self-shattering sexuality. The river first makes an appearance during the Vavasors' Continental journey, after Alice has decided to give up John Grey, and it signals Alice's grudging reacceptance of George Vavasor's proposals.[46] The Rhine image repeats much later in the novel, as the now-rescued Glencora sits overlooking the same spot: "Suddenly, there shot down before them in the swift running stream the heads of many swimmers in the river, and with the swimmers came boats carrying their clothes. They went by almost like a glance of light upon the waters, so rapid was the course of the current" (*CYFH* 723). The river's seductive aspect is glimpsed in the bodies of the swimmers and in the rapidity of their movement down the river: they move faster than they can swim, propelled by a current outside of themselves. Glencora's response, given that she is supposedly "out of danger" (because pregnant), is striking:

"Oh, how I wish I could do that!" said Lady Glencora.

"It seems to be very dangerous," said Mr. Palliser. "I don't know how they can stop themselves."

"Why should they want to stop themselves?" said Lady Glencora. "Think how cool the water must be; and how beautiful to be carried along so quickly; and to go on, and on, and on! I suppose we couldn't try it?" (723)

Glencora's response ("Why should they want to stop") reminds the reader that her sexual desires are not stopped by the fact of her pregnancy or by the fact of her marriage. Glencora's susceptibility to Burgo might be lessening, but her susceptibility to the opportunity signified by the Rhine swimmers ("to go on, and on, and on!") cannot end.

Her desire for Burgo is not a desire that needs fulfillment: she does not need to leave her husband or her fortune to experience the thrill that comes from such a desire. In fact, impossibility situates this desire. Glencora occupies it in suspense, and although it is outside the daily activities of her life with Plantagenet, it inflects their relationship at key moments in the rest of the series.[47] When, later in *Can You Forgive Her?*, she sees Burgo in a gambling salon, in dire straits, without money, and contemplating his own destruction, she implores her husband to keep him afloat so that she may continue to inhabit her imaginative desire for him. Glencora's experience of Burgo more often than not exposes her suspended self: she is in a dream as she dances with him at Lady Monk's; she imagines herself in a watercolor with him, enthroned in ivy while he kneels at her feet; even in her cold ramble through the Priory ruins, Glencora admits to Alice she would "throw herself into Burgo's arms" if she could (534, 457, 306). But in the final gambling scene at Baden, when Glencora sees Burgo heading to dissolution, they do not interact at all *because* he has shown he wants her to act. On the contrary, her desire for him is not a desire for action—is not a desire for event, to use James's term—instead, it is a desire that can live alongside her familial and wifely duties. The danger, then, of "shipwreck," that particularly Trollopean term for sexual misadventure, is not only the threat of being stranded in an unfamiliar country or even the threat of destruction per se. It might also be the threat of being kept from the sea, the absorbing medium that buoys you up at the same time as it moves you along.

Can You Forgive Her?'s trio of heroines exposes how engagement allows women the appearance of choice but also lights up how little choice is actually available to them. And though Glencora is the only heroine whose character develops beyond this novel, the other women demonstrate different uses of the masochistic waiting I've been describing above. The question I have been gesturing toward remains: Does Glencora's plot success over the remainder of the series imply that her transition from explicitly sexual masochism to a model of suspended pleasure is Trollope's recommendation of how women can manage sexual perversity within the world of his novels? Or does Trollope suggest instead that the women dismissed from the plot—the ones who maintain sexual masochism—remain interesting to the narrator by virtue of their dismissal, that they are somehow valorized at the very moment when Trollope's narrator ceases to observe them? Is success in Trollope's world dependent on a character's further representation or on the suggestion of its life beyond the novel's boundaries? I suggested earlier that Trollopean narration often drops off when a character's purpose has been served; George Vavasor and Burgo Fitzgerald are thus expelled, as are, in slightly different ways, Mrs. Greenow and Alice Vavasor. These differences among these various narratalogical dismissals, though, shed some light on Trollope's views of these women. If Trollope's ungentlemanly men are summarily dismissed, these women require a little more narratalogical finesse; we see a glimpse of their possible futures in the few brief sentences that signal their escape from the narratalogical eye. In *Can You Forgive Her?*, the dismissed women suffer drastically different fates: the vulgar widow, Mrs. Greenow, remains invested in suspense, while Alice Vavasor, the typical English girl, is reassimilated into the world of aggressive marital sexuality at the novel's end.

Of them, Mrs. Greenow alone has a free choice in her marriage. She knows she likes to dominate, and while Cheesacre assumes the position, she quickly realizes he is not a submissive. This is made clearer when Alice and her cousin Kate speak of Charlie Fairstairs's possible future as Mrs. Cheesacre: "He'll be rough with her once a month or so, and perhaps tell her that she brought no money with her; but that won't break any bones, and Charlie knows how to fight her own battles" (*CYFH* 803). Mrs. Greenow understands Cheesacre's interests, both his mercenary interest in her wealth and his interest in a masculine domination within the domestic sphere. He can only masquerade as a masochist in public. Mrs. Greenow's plot settles the connection between money and sexual servitude. Like Masoch's Wanda, Greenow makes Bellfield economically dependent on her before the marriage, doling out cash in five pound increments. And while Bellfield's financial investments in the widow are more obvious than are Cheesacre's, his poverty aligns with a submission that guarantees the widow leverage. At the novel's end, the reader believes that the widow has merrily beaten the marriage market by entering it on her own financial and sexual terms. Mrs. Greenow's success makes Alice Vavasor's ending rather more problematic.

While the novel-long emphasis on Alice Vavasor's indecision and her refusal to give a suitor any clear-cut consent to marriage offers a possible escape route from the marriage market's plodding focus on the sale of women as sexual commodities, John Grey's oppressive force shuts this down for good. There is in her plot something very like Stockholm syndrome—we are told that she loves John Grey, often by Alice herself, but we see very little evidence of this love other than a willingness to submit herself to his advances. Alice's plot of delay and suspense actually conditions John for the moment when he fully captures her. Her bid to refuse marriage by accepting engagement, and thus her bid for sexual dominance, collapses when faced with the sheer might of Grey's impassive body. The moment when John Grey "claims his prize" is quite different from Glencora's tableau with Burgo, predicated by her call to him as he crosses the threshold (*CYFH* 772). Alice's end (and it is an end, even for Trollope, as she disappears from the remaining Palliser novels almost at once, though Grey reappears as an incumbent MP) shuts down the possibility that seems to open up with her refusals to commit; marriage absorbs her, revealing her new identity as Mrs. Grey (827). But Lady Glencora's investments in possibility extend well beyond the end of this novel. She is the lively spirit of the Palliser series, and even the novel that famously begins with her death is pervaded by her wit and rebelliousness. While Burgo disappears into the margins of the series, his shadow lingers, frequently reminding the reader that, for a long moment early in her life, Glencora considered an escape from marriage, an escape that, for her, remains an escape to a blissful (but imaginary) shipwreck.[48]

This is indeed a lesser model of freedom than either one in which Glencora escapes from her husband's world or one that allows her to feel the physical thrill the letter brings throughout the remainder of her story. Her suspension, after all, is only imaginative, and the Palliser pregnancy checks her physical desire for Burgo. Glencora no longer has the freedom to act on her whims. By transferring her investments in suspense into the social world, Trollope reduces Glencora's eccentricity and subdues her power. But I want instead to draw some attention to the peculiarity of Glencora's position in the Palliser novels, or even in Trollope's body of work more generally. As I argued earlier, Glencora's masochistic waiting is transformed into a less sexual, more attenuated suspense. Trollope's other masochistic women (Mrs. Hurtle, as I have argued, but also Lily Dale and Madalina Demolines) are written out of the novelistic world. For these other women, going abroad or making a clear decision about marriage signals their story's end, while, for Glencora, marriage ushers her onto the series's scene and Continental travel redefines her masochism.

One of the reasons *The Way We Live Now* enjoys more eager critical acclaim than *Can You Forgive Her?* is that it is more heavily plotted than many of Trollope's novels. The financially speculative energies of Augustus Melmotte drive the plot forward in a way that the marital plots other novels do not. And, as I have argued, the peripheral masochistic plots are so energetic that the final, conservative resolution of Hetta Carbury's acceptance of Paul Montague diminishes in importance. Similarly, Roger Carbury's version of gentlemanly embeddedness quickly becomes anachronistic in the speculative world represented in the novel. However, the solely marital speculation that motivates *Can You Forgive Her?* dampens critical investment because it eradicates suspense even from the novel's opening. The Palliser series, like the Chronicles of Barset, does not catalog clear rises and falls as much as it does gentle modulations; the climactic scene of Melmotte's fall in Parliament does not find its match in any of the chronicle novels. Instead, Glencora's climactic moment in *Can You Forgive Her?*—when she chooses between Burgo and married life—is internalized and imagined rather than literalized and performed. But this—in contrast to Winifred Hurtle—paves the way for her grand performances throughout the series. Because Mrs. Hurtle's sexual scenes have one focus and because Paul Montague cannot fully engage with the violence her desire brings, she loses her place in Trollope's fictional world. While the pairings in *The Way We Live Now* hinge on sexual sympathy (and Mrs. Hurtle relinquishes her claim to Paul when she sees he cannot engage in her scenes as fully as she would like), *Can You Forgive Her?* offers a marriage wherein Glencora's desires are bolstered and enhanced by her willingness to allow pleasurable absorption beyond the scope of the sexual. Her remodeled masochistic investments—first in an easily removable "idol" (her new baby), later in her political parties at Gatherum Castle—allow her to continue through the series (*CYFH* 828). While it's true that Glencora's sexual perversity—her desire to run off with Burgo—is dampened, Trollope's narrator never lets the reader forget that her early doubts have aftereffects; Glencora's ambitions are never fully satisfied, but neither is she fully defined by her husband. And Glencora's dissatisfaction complicates the novels that include her. Because her pleasure is internalized, Trollope implies that one needs a kind of sexual self-mastery to access something like agency. The problem with this, of course, is that self-mastery looks a lot like repression, and this model might exclude any model of sexuality that's clearly relational.

Trollope's uses of masochistic women point to three possibilities, two of which offer some space for feminine agency. For Glencora, nonsexual masochism affords narrative presence; her story doesn't end because she transforms her potentially destabilizing investments in masochistic waiting into her social life. Her success over the course of the Palliser series can be imagined only in terms of representation. Trollope continually reshapes her over the series, and while he never allows her full satisfaction, her pleasure in setting scenes shields her from complete obliteration. Her reordered sexual desires allow her to remain in Trollope's world. In contrast, Trollope allows Mrs. Hurtle, Marie Melmotte, Mrs. Greenow, and the other women who refuse to reshape their masochisms no further narration. Yet, by consigning the continuations of their stories beyond the novels' edges, Trollope allows these women both greater freedom and the possibility of satisfaction. These are two versions of limited agency, but they are agency is some form. Furthermore, both of these character types are informed by Trollope's particular brand of narrative delay: Glencora's story develops over a series of novels, Winifred Hurtle's develops beyond the scope of narrative entirely. But, in any account, it's clear that Alice's transformation at her novel's end, her inscription in a marriage defined by John Grey's oppressive, genital sexuality, all but makes her disappear. While Alice Vavasor becomes Alice Grey, Lady Glencora never loses her title; it is hers by birth, and not by marriage. And while Mrs. Hurtle's name is linked to her husband, that husband's shadow presence throughout the novel signals her prominence. When Alice Vavasor marries, she ceases to exist. Glencora, then, remains the only married woman whose masochism is represented; while that masochism is altered, her investments in suspension are not.

4

Hideously Multiplied

Jude the Obscure

This chapter hinges on two claims about Thomas Hardy's 1895 novel *Jude the Obscure*. First, his depiction of Sue Bridehead is not that of a frigid or sexually unavailable woman.[1] Second, more importantly, the novel's final quarter does not represent a mournful turn away from the explicitly sexual logics that motivate the first three quarters. Instead, I read the final movements in Hardy's pessimistic plot as presenting readers with a tentative, though ultimately failed, attempt on Sue Bridehead's part to reclaim the novel's earlier erotic tensions. The difficulty, of course, is that the final fourth of the novel is stretched across the most apparent trauma in the plot—the deaths, at the hands of Little Father Time, of Sue's two children, Little Father Time himself, and the unborn child Sue carries. In my view, Hardy's trick—and the most painful question that the novel poses to its readers—is that the story continues after this event. Are we to read these pages as anything *but* a dénouement? In other words, can anything of affection live beyond such cataclysmic, damning death?

My first point is rather simple, but it's also one that has caused problems for the novel's critics throughout its reception history.[2] The violence of Sue's married refusal of Richard Phillotson, and her subsequently tortured acceptance of his suffocating affection, make the case for her sexual frigidity. But, in my reading, this sexual relationship stands in stark contrast to the sexual connection Sue develops with Jude. Sue's battle for much of the first three-quarters of the novel is to develop, and then act on, her sexual desire for her cousin Jude. One of the issues here, of course, is that a contemporary reader might find it difficult to parse the distance between Sue's chaste—but clearly sexualized—interest in Jude and her revulsion at Phillotson's advances.

Hardy's focalization, a sympathetic third-person omniscience, never reaches an explicit level of intimacy, but it should be clear that Sue's reaction to Phillotson's absent-minded, if wholly unpleasant, approach is an antiseptic response. What I'm marking out here, then, is the difference between Sue's somatic, pathological unwillingness to sleep with Phillotson and her initial, principled resistance to sleeping with Jude. Sue's lack of desire for Phillotson is both principled and visceral. By the time that Sue Bridehead realizes her error in marrying Richard Phillotson, she produces a critique of her status, that of a woman who is unhappily married but not mistreated:

> "What tortures me so much is the necessity of being responsive to this man whenever he wishes, good as he is morally!—the dreadful contract to feel in a particular way, in a matter whose essence is its voluntariness! . . . I wish he would beat me, or be faithless to me, or do some open thing that I could take about as a justification for feeling as I do!" (212)[3]

Sue complains that, should she leave her husband, as she later does, she will receive no public approval for her separation, because no cruelty has forced her from her home. She also argues that the marriage contract, by virtue of its writtenness and unchangeability, enjoins husband and wife to "feel a particular way," something Sue finds oppressive, given her investment in behavior guided by impulse and personal experience instead of socially ordered codes. After Sue leaves Phillotson, she develops a relationship with Jude that is structured by a different system. Instead of a written contract, Jude and Sue's union is organized by a constant reassessment of the relationship's value. In what follows, I examine the formal significance of Sue and Jude's romantic union, which consistently rejects written contract in favor of an unwritten one, and consider the conditions that lead to this unconventional relationship's failure. In *Jude*, sexual connection develops from earlier expectations of relationship, especially familial relationship. What will become clear over the course of this essay is how sexual relationship's fragility exposes some of the ways other social relationships, specifically family relationships, remain fragile even though they are naturalized. Because all relationship depends on contract or agreement, sexual relationship exposes the contractual nature of human relationship as such. Each union carries with it the tangible possibility of failure, a possibility from which familial relationships often exempt themselves. Again, this becomes evident in the crucible of sexual desire, but it ripples out across all kinds of interaction in Hardy.

In some ways, what I explain about this, Hardy's most significant contribution to the novel of ideas, is its dependence, negative though it may be, on embodied character. This chapter goes some steps toward explaining why the body is a crucial aspect of character—one readers tend to ignore as we hunt for evidence of psychological or emotional truth. It's my contention that the nineteenth-century novel marks out the sexual body as a characterological baseline. In *Jude*, though, we discover that the body both tells too much about and asks too much of character—it has the capacity to make one's private life public, but it's also the field upon which that private life unfolds.

Critics often read *Jude* as a polemic against the sacramental idea of marriage prevalent in the late nineteenth century, one that positions its central characters, Jude Fawley and Sue Bridehead, as martyrs for legal divorce. Even Hardy's postscript to the novel's 1912 edition indicates such a reading; he notes that his "opinion at that time . . . was what it is now, that a marriage should be dissolvable as soon as it becomes a cruelty to either of the parties—being then essentially and morally no marriage" (467). Hardy's concern is that an obligation that should be purely consensual and temporal is mistaken for one that is sacramental and elemental, and it is this aspect that blocks marriage's free dissolution. What I am drawing attention to here is that while Hardy links his novel explicitly to divorce laws, a more general investment in contract and mutual consent underpins the narrative threads in *Jude the Obscure*.[4] At points, Hardy values Jude and Sue's free union, especially in relation to the written and legally binding contracts of both Sue and Phillotson and Jude and Arabella; but, eventually, the free union's failure at the novel's end mimics the legal or written contract's failure. Scripted relationships are of great importance to *Jude*'s formal investments.

In *Harm's Way*, for example, Sandra Macpherson suggests that the novel form depends on causal plotting, not character.[5] In terms of Hardy's novel, Macpherson's model of emplotment, in which characters are tragic if their novels recognize them as causes and not subjects, would seem to offer a strong account of narrative progression (the children's murder could be seen as "caused" by the first fateful meeting between Arabella and Jude) (96). But, as I hope to show, Hardy's novel makes it quite clear that this is not the best way to read his apparently causal plot. Instead, Hardy's plotting points to causality to dismiss it, as it points to heredity to deny its power to order lives; the twinned problems of choice and will, represented at the novel's every turn by written and unwritten contracts (marriage, sexual union, parenthood, etc.) mean that narrative development is not linked to any logical chain, causal or otherwise. In other words, while it may seem to be the case that the novel oscillates between poles of plotted determinism and characterological choice, it actually groups determinism and choice together as conceptual blockages to the real problem of the novel: that no security, relational or otherwise, can be found. An explicitly masochistic union might appear to avoid this problem in part because its unwrittenness allows it flexibility; however, it remains vulnerable in several key respects.

Hardy's novel holds this union as potentially valuable, but the couple remains beset with interrelated problems that stem from masochism's dependence, like that of marriage's, on a contractual model; the public exposure of private life, the introduction of children, and the failure to renew commitment all harm the relationship. What's striking about these problems is that they are all typically (unthinkingly) adopted into the larger framework of marriage. Marriage forces a public recognition of a sexual relationship, and its status as a privileged space for reproduction and child rearing—even its status as following from a singular avowal, not one to be repeated periodically—highlight its difference from masochistic sexual relations, which are secretive, nonreproductive, and in constant negotiation and recapitulation. The mixed conditions of the masochistic dyad—it's apparent structural relationship *to* marriage alongside its exposure of marriage's tendency to expand and absorb other kinds of relatedness into its purview—mark its significance in describing the limits of imagining human interaction contractually.

In *Jude*, these are negative aspects of three different models of change: temporality, social change, and reproduction.[6] But, for all these negative aspects, Hardy's novel presents a varied account of change. If Jude's interest in self-development seems linked to a progressive view of educational change, it is also telling that these interests follow from Jude's desire to enter into the closed-off and delimited world of the university. Jude doesn't want to alter the patterns and hierarchies of Christminster radically; instead, he simply wants entrance. Sexually, though, the novel imagines total unchangeability as the ideal form of sexual relation. And this in turn points to one of the major difficulties for the novel as a form in representing relation: at the moment the novel ends with Jude's death, the relation is necessarily fixed if it was not fixed before. This appears in Hardy's examination of the rapidly apparent difficulties in Jude's early marriage to Arabella: sexual feelings initially unite them but quickly change, underscoring their unsuitability. Seen in this light, it is the static nature of Jude's desire for Sue that gives that pairing the best chance of success within the world of the novel. And this relation's representational dominance over the second half of the novel suggests that the prime focus of Hardy's protagonist is his sexual, and not his academic, struggle.

But even though *Jude*'s most valued principle is a kind of stasis, such stasis, the novel makes clear, is impossible. Because generative systems necessitate change, there is no such system in the novel that is not doomed to failure. This highlights the connections between the educational and romantic plots in the novel: in both, the passage of time brings with it constitutional change. In the case of Jude and Sue's relationship, the social world beyond the dyad threatens it from the first, and public exposure of the sexual relationship at the core of the masochistic system destroys the system. Moreover, the introduction of the child into the dyadic structure forces a reevaluation of contract's applicability to relationships that include children. Little Father Time thus becomes both a symbol of Jude and *Sue's*, not Arabella's, sexuality, one that cannot be hidden from public view, and a reminder that contract and agreement cannot account for all human interaction. Masochism's emphasis on the insular, unchanging couple offers a useful lens through which to observe the warping effects of any social interaction on dyadic sexual connection. By the novel's end, Jude's refusal to recontract with Sue on her terms, his turn away from the promise the masochistic contract holds, marks the masochistic dyad as a complete impossibility.

In constructing his martyred couple, Hardy uses the power conventions of masochism to insist that sexual and romantic connections must be consistently reexamined. This relates to a more general masochistic focus on suspended action throughout Hardy's career. Hardy never sets the masochistic union in stone. It is not written down, but neither is it sacramental— the partners want their union to maintain flexibility.[7] As I've suggested, suspense is a categorical necessity for masochistic literature: it provides both the structure of the relationship and is its sexual charge. The images we associate with masochistic sexuality (a raised whip, hand, or boot) hinge on a delayed gratification, delayed to the point that the delay itself produces sexual sensation. In turning away from Sue at the novel's end, Jude relinquishes his investment in such sexuality, the desire that, for the course of the novel, has motivated his development even more than has his scholastic ambition.

Suspending Sex

In *Jude*, Sue has a habit of refusing the genitally focused sexual advances of all of her male admirers, from Jude to Phillotson to the nameless undergraduate who dies—she says—in part from her "cruelty" (148). These sexual refusals and her constant ability to transform herself highlight unassimilable portions of her character, those aspects unavailable for domination or control. And these are the aspects that, in many ways, most attract Jude.[8] In *Jude*, the masochistic dyad depends on two wills that collude in a performative (some might say creative) act that culminates in complex, symbolically charged sexual scenes. Sue desires management and organization, while Jude desires sexual domination. The novel's critique of conventional marriage hinges not only on Sue's assumption of power and will within the dyad but also on Jude's denial of conventional ideas of masculinity and marital power. And while the problem of marriage at first seems to be simply a problem with ordering relationship, on further analysis, it includes a concern about the family's ability to destroy the closed system of the dyad. Once the couple becomes a publicly recognized *family*, that is, once a child appears, the secret dyad breaks, and the masochistic union is unsustainable, both inside and outside the home.

In Hardy, the infiltration of (and observation by) the social order breaks the masochistic sexual union, again, based on an implicit rather than written contract; further, the fruits of genital sexuality mark the masochists as sexual agents in a way that their masochistic sexualities do not. *Jude* demonstrates the social world's ability to dislodge fantasy's purchase and unravels the couple's dream of a frozen, hermetically sealed world of purely dyadic relation. When relationship passes from the nonnormative to the normative, that is, when it becomes socially reproductive, the union contains within it the seeds of its own destruction. The child breaks the couple's unwritten union in two ways. By fully refusing contract's applicability to relationship— by the very fact of his unsolicited appearance—Little Father Time's infiltration of Sue and Jude's sexual union intensifies their own line of argument against contracting love. Additionally, and perhaps more dangerously, the child draws public attention to the sexual relationship between the partners.

A question emerging from this analysis, then, is whether Hardy valorizes an isolationist view of nonreproductive marriage insofar as the dyadic system breaks down when the couple enters the social world as a family. Society's ability to apprehend the family, specifically the sexual relationship of the "parents," leads to the novel's grim ending. Considered in this light, Sue and Jude might be an exemplary case of a heterosexual refusal of what Lee Edelman has called reproductive futurism.[9] Edelman's term seems uncannily applicable to this novel's bleak view of futural familial bliss: the child's entrance into the novel begins a dénouement that ends with Jude's death and Sue's reentry into claustrophobic bourgeois life. Indeed, the deaths of Jude and Sue's children seem less a reassertion of the primacy of reproductive futurism than a claim for the dyad's preeminence as the primary system of value in Hardy's novel, and perhaps in the novel as such.[10] In many readings, the pathos of the children's deaths overwhelms the novel's major investment in easily dissolvable marriages. If we read Sue's refusal to see Jude after the children's deaths not as a repression of sexual hopefulness but instead as a recommitment to an exquisite, suspended, masochistic version of sexuality, we might see the struggle in the final quarter of the novel as a struggle against family-building, genital sexuality.

This view accounts both for the novel's final turn, where the apparent conventionality of Sue's ideas obscures her reemergence as an engine of ideation, and also for the minimal space accorded the children as characters within the novel.[11] Reading *Jude* this way allows us to see the children for what they are, a site of unearned, pathetic cathexis within a novel that imagines its major loss as that of the close compact between Jude and Sue. Crucially, where Edelman locates this struggle solely in queer resistances to reproductive futurity, Hardy's novel presents an apparently normative heterosexual partnership as a source of antireproductive energy.

If, as I've been suggesting, the gender standards of the period tended to involve masculine domination and feminine subordination, in Hardy's hands, the reversals of these elements are unmistakably suggestive. Indeed, as a sexual system organized around dominance and submission, the masochistic union rivals the written marriage contract. But by reversing the assumed gender roles, Hardy's dyad calls into question not only Victorian ideals of bourgeois, domestic order but also the links between, on the one hand, docility and femininity and, on the other, dominance and masculinity. Most importantly, this union's refusal of an entirely genital sexuality underscores a strong tension between the novel's bourgeois family circle and the self-contained, romantic couple. This lights up a major tension in the nineteenth-century novel: the romantic couple is both self-sustaining and inviolate, but, at the same time, it is necessary that the couple reproduce itself in a family to fur-

ther the authority of embedded British domesticity. To this end, the romantic core is broken by the development of a family. In *Jude*, we see these two
imperatives conflict. While the children's deaths might seem, in the breach
they produce between Jude and Sue, to indicate the family's value, Sue's
impulse to reconstitute the masochistic dyad indicates that the couple, and
not the family, is the relationship with primary value in Hardy's novel.[12]

After Jude Fawley leaves his home and travels to Christminster to further his education, he imagines his cousin Sue Bridehead as a companion
before he meets her: "Jude, a ridiculously affectionate fellow . . . put the photograph on the mantelpiece, kissed it—he did not know why—and felt more
at home. She seemed to look down and preside over his tea" much like the
divinity he later imagines her to be (85). Sue enjoys power over Jude even
before she physically enters the action, and her dominance appears as one
of the novel's major concerns.[13] In Christminster, Jude shadows her, and at
one moment he experiences something like divine intervention as she appears near him while he works:

> All of a sudden . . . his cousin stood close by his elbow, pausing a moment on
> the bend of her foot till the obstructing object should have been removed. She
> looked right into his face with liquid, untranslatable eyes, that combined, or
> seemed to him to combine, keenness with tenderness, and mystery with both,
> their expression, as well as that of her lips, taking its life from some words just
> spoken to a companion, and being carried on into his face quite unconsciously.
> She no more observed his presence than that of the dust-motes which his ma-
> nipulations raised into the sunbeams.
>
> His closeness to her was so suggestive that he trembled, and turned his face
> away with a shy instinct to prevent her recognizing him, though as she had
> never once seen him she could not possibly do so; and might very well never
> have heard even his name. (89–90)

In this moment, Jude becomes almost a Pygmalion, the close, dense atmosphere of the stone yard struck by sunlight imparting to these proceedings
a feeling of magical incarnation, as though Jude has conjured Sue's lithe
body from the photograph itself. If Jude indeed projects his desires onto the
blank slate that is Sue, one might further this reading in the Deleuzean
framework, describing Jude as the sole source of this assessment of Sue. But
one might also produce an account of Sue's expressivity unmoored from
Jude's authorship: while we are told that her eyes seem to Jude to produce

the kind of complex articulation above, we are also told that even this "translation" of the expression, for all its fineness, is inexact.

The inexactitude in Jude's appraisals of Sue etches out the nascent masochistic system in the novel. Sue, trembling and quivering, rebels violently against Jude's readings of her, offering up instead an account of herself as something of a supersensualist, evidenced by her "pagan" identification and her resistance to genital sexuality throughout the novel.[14] When Jude mistakes Sue for "modern," for example, she counters, "I am more ancient than mediævalism, if you only knew" (135). Consistently, Sue defines herself against Jude's reading. In the novel's final movement, for example, as Jude has become both increasingly "modern" and increasingly pagan, Sue pushes against his expectations once again, reinventing herself as a mourning, devout, explicitly Christian wife. It's important to remember that Sue's performance of these attributes is just that—a performance. If we think of her character as neither deeply pagan nor deeply Christian, but instead as deeply conditional, her transformation at the end of the novel is clearer. Sue's ability to devote herself fully to her transformations distinguishes her from Arabella and her more formulaic, and more superficial, renovations. It is this self-definition against expectation that marks Sue throughout the novel and that folds her into the masochistic system of suspension. As soon as Jude "catches up" philosophically, Sue transforms and offers a new philosophical system for Jude to incorporate. These shifts drive the plot, and it is this distance (between Sue as she is and Jude's readings of her) that compels him toward her.

The precision of her gaze's penetration into Jude, before she actually meets him, commingling "keenness with tenderness" and "mystery with both," further demonstrates a supplementary notion of Sue's power of expression. Sue incorporates all expression while at the same time seeming distant and excepted from analysis. Hardy differentiates Sue from his other progressive heroines primarily though a pattern of uneasy narration, exemplified in this moment. First, Sue's progressive, protofeminist politics are fully formed before we are introduced to her in the novel. Unlike vaguely politicized heroines like Eustacia Vye and Bathsheba Everdene, Sue's politics do not seem to be responsive to social oppression. In fact, Hardy charts a different course, with Sue's return to ritualistic Christianity as a response to social opprobrium.

Somewhat similarly, Hardy initially introduces Sue to the reader as a virulent pagan; her resistance to contemporary Christianity (and her interest in Hellenistic rather than Druidical paganism) separates her from a more benighted form of pagan heroine like Tess Durbeyfield. Where Tess's paganism is blinkered, Sue's is aware. Hardy unmoors these two attributes, her politics and religion, from her narrated behaviors. Both qualities are fully developed before the narrator has access to them and, unlike Eustacia, Bathsheba, or Tess, these attributes seem more beholden to Sue's self-development than to her characterological development.

To put this more bluntly, Sue is a character who seems, through Hardy's sleight of hand, to have developed outside of or beyond the grasp of his narrator's control. If Eustacia and Bathsheba are politicized, and if Tess is paganized, it is the work of Hardy's narrator. Not so with Sue. Finally, Hardy's physical descriptions of Sue mark her peculiar status. While most of Hardy's heroines are women of "amplitudes," in his last novel, Hardy introduces a "complete and substantial female human" (39) as an antiheroine rather than a heroine. Sue's minuteness, her diminutive physique and quicksilver temperament, set her apart from Hardy's other English heroines. In some ways, her closest double is Lucetta Templeman in *The Mayor of Casterbridge*, a character whose nervousness leads to her eventual death. But where Lucetta is vain and showily performative, Sue's anxious performances (and I suggest that they are, indeed, performances) do not link to a native theatricality. Instead, Hardy marks out Sue as a serious character prompting sympathy rather than pity. If Lucetta's undoing is linked to her desire for conspicuous display and Michael Henchard's own virulent ambition, Sue's downfall is, I suggest, fully a product of her own action. Even after the children's deaths, Hardy leaves a space in the novel for reconciliation between Sue and Jude, but Sue's reentrenchment in her masochistic plotting prevents this cincture.

Thus, Sue is not a New Woman, a figure designed to showcase the effects of protofeminism on a contemporary woman, any more than she is a saintly Christian: her modernism lies in her chameleonlike ability to reflect the expectations of her observers back on them. These constant reinventions conceal her steely commitment to whatever position she happens to inhabit. In this way, Sue's initial encounters with Jude are quite different from his encounters with her: she oscillates between a frank and generous flirting and a worry that Jude has become too attached to her. Jude, on the other hand, maintains his strong compulsion Sue-ward. And although Hardy's narrator acknowledges Sue's "colossal inconsistency" as a problem in the novel, it is impossible to deny that her vacillations, and her peculiar stubbornness, drive the plot (175). In fact, Sue's obstinate commitment to her adopted positions marks her as strangely similar to Arabella Donn, Jude's first wife, against whom Sue is defined for much of the novel.[15]

Indeed, most discussions of Sue read her in relation to Arabella.[16] The relationship between these two central characters clarifies the peculiarity of Sue's masochism and explains further what is lost to Jude and Sue when Little Father Time enters the novel. Sue is cerebral, Arabella earthy; Sue focuses on rationality and philosophy, Arabella, on immediacy and satisfaction; Sue is unconventional, Arabella, deeply conventional. These distinctions hold some water, but there is a basic connection between Sue and Arabella that these comparisons obscure. The real separation between Arabella and Sue is not a dividing line between the spiritual and the earthly, or between the esoteric and the fleshly, but is instead produced by Jude's (and the narrator's) elevation of Sue's version of self-cultivation over Arabella's. For Jude, the initial appeal of both Arabella and Sue is masochistic—he imagines power as constitutive of his relation to both women, but the women are separated within the novel by their commitments to use such power sexually. Both initially interest him by displaying versions of power—Arabella, physical power, and Sue, intellectual power—but Arabella's physical strength (emblematized in the pig's pizzle) diminishes when the pair marries, while Sue's intellectual strength transforms over time, producing a sequence of scenes wherein Jude is continually reengaged by her.[17] Arabella's display of power is a lure, not her habitual mode of being. Put another way, Arabella's false hair hanging on her dressing table before bed and her false dimples that vanish without a trace disgust Jude because they show her power to be fully superficial—registered on the body's surface. Arabella simply wears her sexual power, while Sue's manifests internally. Sue's flushing and quivering, her ability to completely transform herself from an undergraduate's kept woman to a nunlike student teacher compels him.[18] This difference might be a function of the two women's abilities to commit to changeability as a character trait. While Arabella's falseness is sartorial or superficial, Sue's transformations emanate from within; she flushes where Arabella makes dimples. Seen in this light, it is not that Arabella is Sue's opposite but more that she's a kind of grotesque double, an ineffectual actress where Sue is a prodigy.[19]

While Jude and Arabella's relationship develops from a combination of opportunistic coincidences in her view (Jude happens to be walking by as she's cleaning a pig's carcass, and she is in the market for a husband) and misprision in Jude's (he mistakes her summoning via pig's pizzle as an explicitly sexual gesture of dominance), Jude and Sue's relationship unfolds in a drastically different way. At first, Sue is the "ultimate impulse" that urges Jude to Christminster, a "pretty, girlish face, in a broad hat, with radiating folds under the brim like the rays of a halo" (78). Sue's angelic appearance persists after Jude first sees her, working in the "sweet, saintly business" of the relic shop, and she becomes "more or less an ideal character, about whose form [Jude begins] to weave curious and fantastic day-dreams" (89). But while Jude has envisioned Sue as a protective, saintly talisman in Christminster, the real Sue's unconventionality surprises him.[20] Similarly, Masoch constructs his Venus in marble before Wanda actually enters the action of *Venus in Furs*: the idealized figure of the woman resembles the living companion-to-be, but her lack of life, of pulsing blood, is remarkable only when the living figure enters the scene. Masoch writes:

> But what is this? The goddess is draped in fur: a dark sable cloak flows from her marble shoulders down to her feet. I stand bewildered, transfixed; again I am gripped by an indescribable panic. I take flight. In my hurry I take the wrong path and just as I am about to turn off into one of the leafy avenues, there before me, seated on a bench—is Venus; not the marble beauty of a moment ago, but the goddess of Love in person, with warm blood and a beating heart! (156)

What Masoch describes, the sudden shift from a stable, statuesque image to a living woman, occurs in Hardy's novel both as Jude first encounters Arabella, when her "marble" arms come to life, and when Jude first sees Sue outside of her workplace (40). In Sue's case, however, Jude's foreknowledge of her image points to the kind of transformation that Masoch outlines in his novella: it is precisely the difference between the image and the actual living woman that propels the masochistic supersensualist to pursue his ideal. Said another way, Jude's mental shaping of Sue's body primes him for a sensual experience like the one I'm describing here. The movement from the representation to the real catalyzes sexual desire in a way that Arabella's unprompted entrance into the scene of Jude's life cannot.

At the moment when Jude first sees the original of his photographic copy he realizes: "There was nothing statuesque in her; all was nervous motion. She was mobile, living, yet a painter might not have called her hand-

some or beautiful. But the much that she was surprised him" (90). This supplementary thing (the "muchness") that marks Sue throughout the novel is
motility, her anxious pulsing. The drastic change from statuary to an embodied ideal is marked by the changeability of a body pulsing with life. And
it is changeable suspense that comes to be the defining characteristic of the
fully formed masochistic dyad. By "changeable suspense," too, I mean the
uncannily motile aspect of the suspense or frozenness in the masochistic
dyad—Sue is a *living* statue. Jude imagines her not as a simple divinity but
as a divinity that "buzzes" with life. The pulse of blood under the skin's surface is not simply an indication of life but also a reminder of the possibility
of change—a possibility collapsed by Deleuze's single-subject model of masochism. This possibility, of suspension's failure, of the freeze's thaw, is the
threat of masochistic sexuality succumbing to genital sexuality.

In both of his relationships, Jude wants to be dominated, but it is Sue's
ability to maintain this masochistic suspension—figured especially by the
borders she places between herself and Jude—that maintains his investment. From the first moment when Jude sees Sue's photograph to his secret visit to her workplace to his visit to the teacher's college at Melchester,
Jude's interactions with Sue are delimited by window frames, doorways, and
other thresholds.[21] While his interaction with Arabella very quickly moves
from image to action (her "marble" arm has already thrown the pig's pizzle
and she has engaged him physically before he clearly sees her), his interactions with Sue always hold off physical contact. J. Hillis Miller has rightly
observed that the barriers between Jude and Sue are almost always of Sue's
creation, and although Jude begins the relationship imaginatively, it is Sue
who propels it further with these constant suspensions of companionship.[22]
It is these same suspensions that rear up again as a possibility at the novel's
end. Unfortunately for Sue, in the intervening years, she and Jude have re-
placed their masochistic suspension with a genital sexuality, which has produced children. In *Jude*, the masochistic system cannot fully reassert itself
in the wake of their children's arrival, in part because the children open the
couple up to public scrutiny.

Sordid Contracts and Public Houses

Just as Arabella and Jude's marriage reaches its nadir when Arabella
strips in the public street, reminding Jude of the fleshy world of the bedroom, the interference of public critique signals the end of Jude and Sue's

relationship. Arabella's behavior is unsettling to Jude in part because it makes knowledge of the couple's sexual relationship accessible to the community: her unraveling hair and dress hint to the passing churchgoers the couple's sexual connectedness. Later in the novel, Little Father Time's entrance and the births of Jude and Sue's subsequent children mark another version of this accessibility. The children's presence blurs the assumed boundary between the public world of street life and the private world of the home by their very presence. Until Little Father Time appears, Sue appears to the surrounding community to be only Jude's cousin and housekeeper. The cousins are able to obscure clear readings of their sexual relationship in part through their consanguinity.[23] When the child enters the novel, he is a reminder of Jude's sexual connection to Arabella, a marker of Jude and Sue's developing genital, rather than masochistic, sexuality, and, additionally, a crucial sign of their relationship's sexual basis, heretofore thought of as familial or platonic by neighbors. And, when the couple begins reproducing socially, they can be socially excluded, as is the case when Jude and Sue are barred from the church where they are working.

The scene of Jude and Sue's expulsion also serves to highlight the danger with which church work is inscribed throughout the novel. It's dangerous not only because the bourgeois public desires a moral fit between the people who work *on* the church and the church itself but also because the church operates in a public place that often *seems* private. While it seems initially a public space (for example, banns must be read before a couple can marry: a public announcement foretells the private contract of marriage), church in *Jude* offers a certain amount of privacy, especially when the building is separated from its sacramental use. But things that seem private (marriage, the home) are made public by causes beyond the couple's control, either because what appears to be private is in fact public (marriage) or because what is private is made public by evidence that cannot be hidden (the couple's home life is seen clearly only after the children appear).

In their search for more private places, Jude and Sue try to cut themselves off from public life, but their attempts fail. Sue particularly cannot bear scrutiny. Before the children appear, she tries to turn public space private, but once the evidence of the couple's relationship exists, any attempt to do so is pointless.[24] By comparing the scene of the couple quietly painting (where the church becomes a place of work) to the scene of Jude and Sue walking up the aisle before her marriage to Phillotson (where the church becomes a place for intimate conversation), we see that the momentary possibilities of privatizing public space are completely evaporated by the children.

Sue's desire to be walked up the aisle by Jude immediately before her first marriage to Phillotson lights up the complications of the space in which the scene takes place: Jude and Sue have a private, sacrilegious conversation in a room that is soon to be made legal, both sacred *and* public (see 172). The church stands in as a metaphor for marriage within the novel: it is a place that seems to offer a privacy that evaporates once the space is opened for its intended purpose: just as marriage dissolves into a public system once children appear, the church's privacy dissolves once parishioners arrive. Earlier in the novel, Arabella's ability to move easily in the seemingly "pure" economic landscape of the public house frustrated and worried Jude, though here Jude and Sue do something similar. Jude assumes that the public and economic space of the church is purely private, or capable of being closed, at least temporarily, from the social and the sacred.

The couple partially succeeds in privatizing the church, but their conversation's irreligious bent is interrupted when Phillotson enters the scene. Hardy writes, "The too suggestive incident, entirely of [Sue's] making, nearly broke down Jude," and even Sue knows their behavior is somewhat problematic as she withdraws her hand quickly from Jude's arm when Phillotson appears—Jude's touch is a piece of evidence easily removed in a way the children are not (173). Sue erases the impropriety of her feelings for Jude, leaving no trace of their tempting conversation, in a way that she cannot erase the later evidence (i.e., Little Father Time's presence, Sue's pregnancies) of their genital sexuality. This is not to say that the *religious* power of the church causes these fluctuations in Jude and Sue's antinomian principles but, rather, that the church's status as a public place, or a place that reduces the possibility of truly private interaction, unsettles the pair.

Later, as the pair discusses marrying, they have a hard time finding a place suitable for their ideas of union. Sue's main problem with marrying in the registrar's office is that it is gaudily public, and she asks to move to the church in hopes that it will be more sheltered public space. Of course, the church's version of the wedding "frightens" her as much as the registry's, and both seem unsettling to her mainly because of their lack of privacy and their inability to capture the "awful solemnity" of marriage (286). Sue's ideas about marriage are at odds with the sordid techniques of the only two institutions capable of offering marriage services. Her complaint is that marriage, in both the registry and the church, is as "sordid" as a "business contract," again reiterating the idea that the private (dyadic) relationship is poorly ordered by the economically minded public sphere (209, 259, 286).[25] The contract Sue wants would refuse engagement with the public, economic sphere entirely: in this way, the contract she "makes" with Jude, a private verbal contract that is *not* an "irrevocable oath," is the only one that would suffice (287).

While various communities offer criticism of Jude and Sue's behaviors throughout the novel, it is a clear public exposure of their sexual relationship that precipitates their inability to keep house. Throughout the novel, the public world is made to seem both economically motivated and also bogged down in gossip. This version of public life is provoked by gossip, especially by gossip that compares characters' individual lived experience to "standard" practice.[26] After Sue capitulates to Jude's sexual advances, they attempt to work in a church's nave, repainting the Ten Commandments. The parish's gossips come out of the woodwork, almost literally, and push the sexton to fire the couple. It is in this moment that the dangers of public critique come into greatest clarity: it is necessary that people work for money, but, in *Jude*, this necessity puts them at the mercy of the gossip-laden social world (301). Jude and Sue's eventual expulsion from economic life is linked to gossip about their indiscretions—now read as clearly sexual. The signs of children—both Little Father Time's body and Sue's pregnancy—offer the couple up for dissection by the people around them. Privacy, then, is only accorded a couple if they bare no traces of genital sexuality, if they bear no children.

As I said at the outset of this chapter, the novel's turning point does not happen at the point when Little Father Time kills himself and the children of Sue and Jude's companionship. Rather, it happens just as Little Father Time enters the text. His appearance marks a turn away from an isolated, verbally contracted, privatized relationship—that of the couple—to a receptive, contractless, public relationship—that of the family. And while the family's lack of contractual order seems positively valued in some ways (Sue's attentions to her children are touching to the narrator and even to Arabella Donn), it exposes the couple to public scrutiny. When Little Father Time appears, he introduces a character for whom Jude and Sue feel responsible but with whom neither Jude nor Sue can contract. His introduction marks both the limits of a sexualized understanding of sociability and the inevitable failure of contract to account for every contingency.

Little Father Time appears as an indication of Jude and Arabella's various sexual histories in the novel, but he also stands in as a specter of Jude and Sue's sexual relationship, entering the text immediately after Sue "gives in" sexually to Jude (267). He is indeed an indication of the erotic connection between Jude and Arabella, a withered emblem of their genital sexuality and, further, of that connection's inability to sustain anything like companionate marriage. But he is also a symbol of genital sexuality's inability to sustain Jude and Sue's relationship in the final movement of the novel and, thus, of their masochistic system's failure. An "enslaved and dwarfed Divinity" (278), his very being mirrors what is elsewhere called the enslavement of marriage: his cowed and creeping manner insinuates itself into Sue and Jude's relationship, a reversal of Eros. And it is Little Father Time who offers a final warning to the couple before they attempt to marry, "If I was you, mother, I wouldn't marry father!" even as he simultaneously reasserts their appearance of sexual coupledom: they are "mother," and "father" (283). In fact, Little Father Time takes to calling Sue "mother" almost as soon as he sees her; and his "mothering" of Sue hints at her sexual relationship with his father immediately after their genital sexual relationship begins, before any "obvious" indicator of that relationship has appeared.[27] Little Father Time is thus both a sign of an unrecoverable past for Sue and Jude and their first spouses, and a totem of their own slide toward a conventionally sexual relationship.

While other readers have recognized Sue's impulse toward religion after the children's deaths as a failure in the novel's depiction of a New Woman, I claim instead that Sue attempts, and fails, in these scenes, to reproduce the couple's masochistic cycle.[28] Instead of reading the novel's dénouement as a failure in its depiction of Sue, I would rather highlight the child's antagonism to a masochistic, coupled sexuality. In a crucial way, the family, an unmistakably public union, and the private couple are incompatible. What the social sphere had been, heretofore, willing to ignore is now obvious and thus problematic. Local rumors about the couple are at a fever pitch at the very moment Sue and Jude fail to marry, which is simultaneous with Little Father Time's entry into the novel. Hardy writes:

> The unnoticed lives that the pair had hitherto led began, from the day of the
> suspended wedding onwards, to be observed and discussed by other persons

than Arabella. The society of Spring Street and the neighborhood generally did not understand, and probably could not have been made to understand, Sue and Jude's private minds, emotions, positions, and fears. The curious fact of a child coming to them unexpectedly, who called Jude father, and Sue mother, and a hitch in a marriage ceremony intended for quietness to be performed at a registrar's office, together with rumours of the undefended cases in the law-courts, bore only one translation to plain minds. (298)

Little Father Time's transformation of the couple into the family tells the social world around them that a specifically genital sexual relationship exists, and the social world pressures the couple to conform. Once the outside pressures beg for a sacramental contract in place of Jude and Sue's verbal, changeable union, the masochistic system falters. Even within the dyad, the masochistic system of entreaty and repulsion that had until now ordered Jude and Sue's private life breaks down; their union is on shaky ground by being fixed. Furthermore, Little Father Time's strangeness, his withered adulthood, does not only signify the genital relationship of Jude and Arabella, nor does it simply enforce the movement into genital relation of Sue and Jude, but his strangeness also positions him as a member of an adult chorus, the social world, that worries about Jude and Sue's living arrangement.

Little Father Time, a peculiarly adult homunculus, is both a child and a man. His critiques of Sue and Jude's union develop in part from his childlike anxiety about the impending birth of another child but also from his overly mature mannerisms. His most open criticisms ("If I were you mother, I wouldn't marry father") position him as a dependent child, but its subjunctive mood marks him as belonging to an adult world of social critique, wherein critique takes the form of a wish that one's actions might be different. Later, his criticism of Sue's pregnancy spurs him to kill himself and the other children. While his very presence seems symbolic of reproductive futurism (he is in many ways a copy of Jude as a child), his adult mannerisms allow him to critique and check Sue and Jude's descent into procreation. Indeed, it is Little Father Time's commentary that allows us to read Jude and Sue's procreation as damaging rather than sustaining. The difficulty Sue has in re-establishing a masochistic order after the children's deaths stems from the residue of this kind of reproductive futurism: the couple cannot erase, even from the inside out, the fact that they were a family.

Beyond the Dead

Perhaps one of the most striking scenes of the novel occurs when Little Father Time questions Sue on the place of children in the world:

> "Then if children make so much trouble, why do people have 'em?"
>
> "O—because it is a law of nature."
>
> "But we don't ask to be born?"
>
> "No indeed."
>
> "And what makes it worse with me is that you are not my real mother, and you needn't have had me unless you liked. I oughtn't to have come to 'ee—that's the real truth! I troubled 'em in Australia, and I trouble folk here. I wish I hadn't been born!"
>
> "You couldn't help it, my dear."
>
> "I think that whenever children be born that are not wanted they should be killed directly, before their souls come to 'em, and not be allowed to grow big and walk about!"
>
> Sue did not reply. She was doubtfully pondering how to treat this too reflective child. (333)

This outburst further secures Little Father Time as a critic of genital sexuality. Of course, it produces pathos, more so when the children's eventual fate is revealed, but one might ask what it would mean to take the child's arguments seriously. When Sue tells him that there will soon be another baby, he berates her wildly: "How *ever* could you, mother, be so wicked and cruel as this, when you needn't have done it till we was better off, and father well!" Sue claims that ". . . it—is not quite on purpose—[that they] can't help it!" But he continues, "Yes it is—it must be! For nobody would interfere with us, like that, unless you agreed! I won't forgive you, ever, ever!" (334, emphasis Hardy's). Given Sue and Jude's history, Little Father Time is closer to the truth than he seems at first glance. This couple, after all, has been involved in a nongenital, but erotic, relationship. This reveals the peculiar power of the children: they are evidence of Jude and Sue's sexual relationship, and they are the cause of Jude and Sue's nomadic married life. The children illuminate the couple's failure because they are so unmoored from the couple's verbal contract. Little Father Time's questions point to his recognition of an unwritten and nonconsensual quasicontract between parents and children. The familial relationship is dissimilar to the unwritten, but consensual, contract that organizes the couple; but it's also drastically asymmetrical, as was Sue's initial assessment of her marriage to Phillotson. Here, partly because his entrance into his parents' lives is nonconsensual, Little Father Time exposes the child's inability to consent to enter a familial relationship.

The problem of the dead children hangs over the novel's remainder not as loss exactly but as something that directs us to what I'd argue is the novel's most radical loss: that of Jude and Sue's dyad. Doubling onto the worrisome complaints of Sue and Jude's family's expansion is the idea that perhaps Little Father Time is right. What about the children's deaths produces the strangely disintegrated Sue and the stonelike, dead Jude at the novel's end? While the pathos of Jude and Sue's situation is palpable, one is left with a residual fear that the couple somehow deserved their fate, but the novel's structure argues more strongly that the couple, if they fixed themselves again as a couple, could be saved. It is the couple's inability to recuperate itself as itself following the destruction of the family that leads to the loss at the novel's end. After the children's deaths, Sue refuses to live with Jude and returns to Phillotson, but she still attempts to rescaffold her relationship with Jude via masochistic suspension. When an ill Jude visits Sue in Marygreen, Sue produces a scene of refusal and acquiescence that seems to hint at her desire to reorder their relationship along masochistic lines:

> "You crush me, almost insult me, Jude! Go away from me!" She turned off quickly.
> "I will. I would never come to see you again, even if I had the strength to come, which I shall not have anymore. Sue, Sue, you are not worth a man's love!"
> Her bosom began to go up and down. "I can't endure you to say that!" she burst out, and her eye resting on him a moment, she turned back impulsively. "Don't, don't scorn me! Kiss me, O kiss me lots of times, and say I am not a coward and a contemptible humbug—I can't bear it!" (389)

Sue's refusal of Jude is immediate: she turns "off quickly," but Jude's response surprises her. He acquiesces to her demand and, further, says she is not worth any man's love. The underpinning notion of the masochistic dyad is that given a refusal or a threatened abandonment, the masculine partner recommits in stronger language to the couple; here, Jude disowns her. Sue repositions herself, though, and her quivering body evidences her desire to retrench in a masochistic form of scene making, since she asks Jude to recommit

again to the relationship (saying she has refused to become sexually intimate with Phillotson), only to scorn him a moment later. Jude's response
takes the form of "bruising" kisses, and, again, the relationship is ordered
with an arc of seduction and resistance. When Jude offers her a kiss—not as
a memorial for their coupledom but instead as a memorial for their "dead
little children"—Sue recoils (389). She resists Jude's turn to family as their
primary relationship, pressing instead for a return to their earlier, suspended,
masochistic state. This is the limit of Jude's progression as Sue's protégé.

And while Jude's refusal seems at first to be tied to the children's deaths,
it is instead linked to Sue's desire to widen the distance between the two as
she rearranges the relationship. Jude begins to think of himself as a "se-
ducer," saying that he never should have pressed Sue into a genital sexual
relationship. He hopes to stabilize their relationship as nongenital—an erotic
but unconsummated state—but also to keep Sue close by in his own version
of "marriage" even though she presses to return to Phillotson (343). The novel
positions Sue's desire to retreat to a masochistic form organized by physical
separation against Jude's final hope, a version that is nongenital but intimate. But Jude's claim that Sue is his wife even without the sacramental
ceremony is too similar to true contract for her (346). She wants to maintain
her connection to Jude but to evaporate it of nonconsensual obligation, of
even the need for physical proximity.[29]

Sue returns to her first husband, but not to submit to heteronormative
marriage as such. The children gone, she attempts to reorder her masochistic union with Jude by returning to Phillotson. But it is Sue's wincing decision to have sex with Phillotson that secures this: this decision blocks a continuing sexual relationship with Jude, and it is perhaps the only blockage
that, within the world of the novel, can't be ignored. One of the major problems of sexual connection within *Jude* is its ongoingness. When it comes to
sex, characters can't stop once they've started. As Sue complains about impending childbirth to Little Father Time, "But it—is not quite on purpose—I
can't help it!" (334). The children's deaths and her subsequent return to
Phillotson allow Sue to recommit to a suspense that hinges on physical separation from Jude. This is also a reassertion of her character's primary attitude: expectation's refusal—though by this point, Sue secures refusal through
sexual submission to another. Her performance of motherhood over, she
reinvents herself as another man's wife. When Jude finally comes to see her
in her new home, she attempts to remake the same system of catch and re-

lease that sustained them earlier in the novel: "Don't, don't scorn me" (389). Instead of recommitting to the system of suspended pleasure, however, Jude returns to Christminster, where he subsequently dies while in Arabella's care (388–90). Even Arabella recognizes that Jude and Sue's relationship centers on a suspended series of communications: she offers to send word to Sue that Jude is dying, but he refuses. The differences between Jude's and Sue's masochisms become too great to ignore, and what united them as perverts now separates them.

While the perverts of the masochistic dyad may appear heteronormative in their sexual pairings, the failure of such a couple to biologically reproduce marks them as "perversely" refusing procreative sexuality. Hardy's novel, however, does not feature any procreative system to counter Sue and Jude's failed masochistic one. Of all the characters we meet over the course of the novel, only Jude and Sue end up with what could be called a family. Arabella has her shadowy London husband; Phillotson his students and his friend Gillingham; the Widow Edlin her long-lost husband. Even Jude and Sue lack living parents—the cast of the novel is constructed of individuals, with little but the chosen companionship of friend or mate to sustain them. This is an aspect of Hardy's Wessex more generally; it is a world populated by people who cannot or will not reproduce and with pairs whose reproductions doom them to misery. When children are born in Hardy's novels, they either die shortly after they expose the sexual connection of their parents, or they live to produce anxiety about the truths of their parentage. Children enter the novels as signs of families' degenerations and disintegrations, and as markers of the dangers of sexual hypocrisy and secrecy.[30]

In *Jude* we find a literalization of what, in Hardy's other novels, is made thematic; the child's arrival destroys the couple's hopes of happiness. In Hardy's oeuvre, the sexual body is at odds with the generative body. And *Jude* in particular offers us no future. Little Father Time's murder/suicide erases the evidence of the pair's genital sexuality, but the violence of that erasure makes it so that no one in the novel, save Sue, can forget the children. Before the child appears, there is nothing to mark Sue and Jude as different from any of the other discrete bodies in the text. Sue's peculiarity and her singularity are earlier linked to her power over Jude, but with the arrival of Little Father Time this changes. The child, uncontrollable and uncontainable, subverts and exceeds the masochistic contract. Coincident with Little Father Time's entrance into the text, Sue is penetrated by Jude. This inducts her statue-like person, heretofore inviolate, into the world of the family. While they had been able to keep from public view a masochistic sexual engagement, once the pair relinquishes their scene building for family life, the social world reassesses their relationship and sees the truth of their ever-present sexual connection.

While the social world around Jude and Sue willingly suspends judgment without "proof" of sex, it begins to shame the pair once Little Father Time appears. Again, one must ask why Jude pressures Sue to commit to him genitally. Genital sexuality leads to pregnancies and children, and the pair becomes less and less recognizable as a pair, while at the same time becoming more recognizable as a couple to the social world around them. Hardy does not limit himself to either a comment on normative marriage conventions or to an appeal for simplified divorce proceedings. By incorporating facets of exquisite masochism, he instead critiques a social order wherein supposedly inviolate, self-sufficient couples act as a unified community. While *Jude* is sometimes read as a novel that values Jude and Sue's esoteric, dialogic relation above the coarse physicality of Jude's connection to Arabella, I've tried to suggest that Jude's and Sue's bodies as much as their minds form the basis of the attraction in the novel. It is not, then, that the body drops out but that the body becomes the major battleground for framing the novel's larger problem: Can there be such a thing as an intimate, private relation between two people? Or, put another way, *Jude* explores one of the major questions of the novel as a genre: How does embodiment complicate ideal communication? How do we navigate between the intimate connections we forge through conversation and dialogue and those that play out over the geography of the body? The cousinly telepathy that Jude and Sue share showcases the problem with imagining relationship—especially marriage— as sealed by a communion of interiors: their mental connectivity does not obliterate the need to traverse the distance between their bodies; and sex, within the world of the novel, is dangerous precisely because it has the "natural" tendency to multiply the bodies within a relationship. The couple, given enough time, becomes a trio.

Hardy draws the tension between companionate marriage and familial or productive marriage into sharp relief; social reproduction tends to destroy the creative, dialogic union of the masochistic pair. Hardy's is a world where broader community, instead of supporting dialogue and intellectual engagement, destroys them. Infiltration—by community, by family history, by children—destroys the dyad, and happiness, dependent on an impossible, insulating solitude, is unattainable. Exquisite masochism, above all else, builds on the notion of the union's soundness: much like a sacramental idea of marriage, the masochistic dyad breaks down once a third party enters the scene, and, in *Jude the Obscure*, the most damaging third party is the child.

5

Dead Gems

Lawrence

D. H. Lawrence has fallen out of the academic favor his work enjoyed in the decades immediately after his death in 1930. Many of the most vitriolic responses to his work are more rightly responses to the paternalistic aspects of earlier critical moments, moments that held up Lawrence as a savant, here to save us from falsity, hypocrisy, and grinding respectability. In that more distant past, cultural critics elevated his work, connecting it to the rise to the middle class and to the difficulties faced by the social climbers who dare to leave their natal classes behind.[1] Current readers also object to the many political and social problems evident in Lawrence's writings (fascism, racism, misogyny, a weedy nationalism), though, to be fair, these are problems we (comfortably or not) tackle with almost every writer from the past. Our current critical discourse can expand to comment cogently on ideologically objectionable texts (and Lawrence's fall well within this circle), but it cannot countenance the embarrassing excesses of Lawrentian style. Lawrence's style has been read as an offshoot of the writer's autodidacticism or as evidence of his investment in the erotic as the central sphere of modern life. But while the lives—professional, moveable, *modern*—described in Lawrence's novels are captured squarely within industrial process, their plots are stuck in models made in the crucible of the nineteenth century social-realist novel (Williams 202).

For most of its generic life, the novel has depended on marriage and childbirth as signs of sexual relationship, and it has had a difficulty representing sexual life beyond marriage and childbirth without the assistance of figurative language. Lawrence's novels are striking for just how explicitly they represent sexual life. In the following pages, I train attention on the logic of sexualized interaction in Lawrence's novels (specifically the paired Brangwen novels) and argue that, Lawrence actively reframes Victorian strategies for the representation of sex and marriage. Lawrence writes and revises the Brangwen novels in the period during and just after the Great War. In the two novels, Lawrence follows the fortunes of the Brangwen family, an aesthetically ambitious middle-class family in the midlands, with special emphasis on the lives of the Brangwen women over three generations. From the moment of her introduction into the text, Lydia Lensky is an anomaly. A German immigrant, recently widowed, she appeals strongly to Tom Brangwen's erotic desires. In the second generation, Lydia's daughter, Anna, borrows much from her stoic mother, but she develops a robust relationship with her English stepfather before her early marriage to Will Brangwen, Tom's nephew. By teasing together the biological strains of the Brangwen family with the exogamous Lenskys, Lawrence allows the final generation of the Brangwen family to be a blend of German aestheticism and emotional distance and warm-tempered English practicality. Anna's eldest daughters, Ursula and Gudrun, are the focus of the second half of *The Rainbow* and all of *Women in Love*.[2] Taken together, the novels show the rapidly changing social positions of women—by the time we get to the third generation, the stories follow Ursula and Gudrun as they develop careers and political views as well as familial and romantic ties. In Lawrence, the masochistic pair has lost its sexual charge, and the dominant woman, her narrative power and interest.

Across a range of his texts, but in these two novels in particular, it's clear that Lawrence digested the Victorian novel. The bones upon which he hangs his explicitly modern plots are drawn from earlier iterations of the marriage plot. One way Lawrence shifts the novel's terms comes from the adjustments he makes to what I understand to be the capitalist regime of the marriage plot. In Lawrence's hands, the rationale for marriage is not economic, nor does romantic love have to work to accommodate economic compatibility. The ground of marital connection—like most connections in Lawrence—is the body. For instance, in *The Rainbow*, Ursula Brangwen's affair with the wealthy Anton Skrebensky resolves with her simultaneous realization that they are not sexually compatible and that their relationship must, therefore, end. For readers of the Victorian novel, the Lawrentian difference is made immediately evident in the shocking fact that sexual incompatibility could be a middle-class woman's reason to break an engagement. But Lawrence's work is full of women who believe there is a significant connection between sexual compatibility and relationship's continuance. What's more, Lawrence gives these characters access to many kinds of sexual knowledge: no longer must decisions be made on attraction's pull. Instead, the sexual act gives knowledge that mere desire cannot reveal.

Lawrence criticism marks out the heiress Hermione Roddice, a tightly wound New Woman based in large part on the progressive heiress Ottoline Morrell, as a sign of Lawrence's dismissal of certain kinds of womanly self-development. Hermione is a significant figure for me. She operates as a kind of exquisitely masochistic heroine in a novel world that no longer comprehends that figure's form of sexual power. Leo Bersani's influential essay, "Lawrentian Stillness," makes the point that frictional, self-gratifying sex works, throughout Lawrence's oeuvre, to signal psychological (and perhaps cultural) complacency or contagion. *Women in Love*'s best example of this is Hermione, a rasping personality with cultural ambitions who has been romantically involved with Rupert Birkin, a striking physical and philosophical double for Lawrence, even before the period of the novel's action. Lawrence implies that Hermione's sexual expression revolts Birkin, which in large part accounts for their separation. For Lawrence, both Bertha Coutts's rapacious frottage in *Lady Chatterley* and Hermione's intellectually aspirational, icy disinterest produce diminished, miserable sexual lives. In *Women in Love*, this view is made clear early in the novel, when Hermione attacks Birkin with a lapis lazuli paperweight in her rooms. By describing this violent outburst with language elsewhere used for pleasure, Lawrence underscores the connection between the two for Hermione. If much of the novel focuses on the characters' development and cultivation of their sexual selves, this early moment shows what happens when ideologically bound self-development routes sex through violence. Because her aim is (political *and* social) domination and not exchange or negotiation, Hermione's sexual self, tinged as it is with her broader, ideological desire for self-promotion, disgusts the Lawrentian narrator. This episode, in which Hermione's sexualized "convulsion" becomes synonymous with mere violence, shows what happens when dyadic exchange is given up in favor of singular passion.

As we shall see, in Hermione's view, she responds to Birkin's disdain when she brings down the lapis lazuli on Birkin's bent head. Furthermore, this is, in her account of herself, a reasonable response when faced with resistance. Afterward, we get the most explicit (and explicitly sexualized) account of her character's intense perversity:

Then swiftly, in a flame that drenched down her body like fluid lightening, and gave her a perfect, unutterable consummation, unutterable satisfaction, she brought down the ball of jewel stone with all her force, crash on his head. But her fingers were in the way, and deadened the blow. Nevertheless down went his head on the table on which his book lay, the stone slid aside and over his ear, it was one convulsion of pure bliss for her, lit up by the crushed pain of her fingers. (*Women* 105)

In no uncertain terms, Lawrence here suggests that Hermione feels a sexual thrill from her attack. Faced with disagreement, she responds with violence, and this, in turn, turns her on. Hermione feels compelled to continue her attack, "A thousand lives, a thousand deaths mattered nothing now, only the fulfillment of this perfect ecstasy." But Birkin stops her hand: "No you don't, Hermione," he said in a low voice. "I don't let you" (*Women* 105–06). Crucially, Lawrence draws the metaphors mobilizing this scene's violence from novelistic descriptions of the sex act, descriptive strategies that he plays a large part in ordering. Hermione is "like fluid lightening," she experiences "unutterable consummation," and, in her final attempt, Hermione experiences a "convulsion of pure bliss." In most literary scenes, a "convulsion of pure bliss" can only mean one thing, and before the twentieth century such orgasmic energy could only be depicted in disreputable novels. But here the violence underscores the perversity of Hermione's character. If, in the nineteenth-century novels I've discussed so far, novelists have used depictions of cruelty and pain to stand in for depictions of sexual life, Lawrence's scene here alters those representational systems. Hermione has, it seems, been able to experience sexual life. But because she experiences sex as a political act, her understanding of sex is poor. In Lawrence's world, Hermione does not have the capacity to embrace sexual life simply because she sees having sex as a political stance. The lapis lazuli episode marks a moment when Hermione conceives of the faults in her sexual knowledge. Her frustration at Birkin's sexual disinterest becomes too powerful for her to manage with her awkward, distant affect, and she short-circuits. Lawrence represents this moment strangely. Her self-concept disrupted, Hermione's actions become disordered, as though her reasonable mind leaves her body over to passionate feeling, and she collapses after her attack.

To put this in exquisitely masochistic terms, Hermione attempts to produce a masochistic scene, but, when the stasis doesn't come, she breaks down. Masochism, in this moment, becomes active. Stasis becomes violence. By resorting to a physical attack, Lawrence suggests a connection between her sexual frustration (which can as easily be attached to a misunderstood sexual act as it can to frigidity or virginity) and active violence. Lawrence emphasizes the incompatibility between this character's view of sex's importance to life and the view the novel more broadly endorses. In this moment, he marks out a character, Hermione, at odds with her surroundings. It's no mistake that the difference between the two develops from differing views on sex. Hermione's sexual life is so closely connected to her desire for power and domination that, in this moment, the two become hopelessly entangled.

As in this scene, many of the passages I examine in this chapter conform, in some way, to the models I've set up: these are dynamic scenes of sexual pain, in which the female participant dominates the male. Lawrence litters his fiction with such passages. But it is the sexualized scenes in two novels— *The Rainbow* (1915) and *Women in Love* (1920)—that are most pertinent to my project; these two novels chart a relationship between women's emerging political power and a drastic alteration in novelistic representations of sexual power. There is a historical connection between the two. Like Trollope, Lawrence tends to move explicitly domineering women to his novels' periphery; but, unlike Trollope, Lawrence's central romances also feature scenes dependent on negotiation and delay. In other words, for Lawrence, there is a place for powerful tension at the heart of the novel's sexual plots— the two are deeply imbricated. But aggressive violence develops when characters manage that tension, the give and take of negotiated life, into complacency. The central outlet for the spring of such sexual tension is an exchange of power; if that dynamism stalls (or if one party tries to game that dynamic system), violence erupts. In addition, Lawrence imagines a world in which this dynamic sexual system can be worked into marriage. No longer is marriage a legitimating tool for sex as such; instead, the importance of deep sexual compatibility in marriage strikes Lawrence as the only way to imagine a future for the institution. Once sex can happen beyond marriage, it becomes more important to imagine the kind or quality of sex happening within marriage. What shifts, then, is the necessity that alluring sexual power resists the patriarchal structure of companionate marriage. In Lawrence, dialogic negotiation is a matter of course; power structures have become dynamic, and thus unmoored from patriarchal power.

Real Lawrence

Lawrence's meditative, circular prose tips out of situated, realist representation as often as he tethers his novels to real social or political crises. In other words, the tentative, rhapsodic language developed by, for example, *Kangaroo*'s (1923) narrator resembles the language of the narrator in *Women in Love*, despite the novels' dramatically different slices of life, despite their different political and social aims. More strangely still, Kangaroo's screeds on fascism and Australia's promise often sound like Birkin's monologues on British aesthetics and marriage. But, unlike the practitioners of the nineteenth-century social problem novel, Lawrence's ruminations on sexual repression, class warfare, or native peoples hardly seem like explicit sociopolitical engagements, even when his narratives call attention to ostensibly real political and social problems. In other words, the uncanny sameness of his attack in the novels is the most striking aspect of Lawrence's work. His fictional medium looks the same whether he's discussing a formidable horse or an Australian fascist. This is not to say that what counts as descriptive clarity in Lawrence doesn't change over his career. If Lawrence's explicit description of sex became most linguistically explicit in his last completed novel, *Lady Chatterley's Lover* (1928), sex and its depiction are central in much of his work. Of sex's immediacy in Lawrence, Bersani says, "Interpretation is immediate, and tends to bypass the mediating and distorting vehicle of language. There are flashes of recognition instead of an interpretive process" (164).[3] In Lawrence, desire often produces total surety; Lawrence's characters rarely fret over the possibility of reciprocation. Sexuality, like much affiliation in Lawrence, bypasses rational concept or social order. This becomes especially clear in the initial moments of sexual connectedness, such as an encounter, in *The Rainbow*, between Anton Skrebensky and Ursula Brangwen. The pair, as yet undeclared lovers, returns home in a horse cart:

> As they drove home, he sat near to her. And when he swayed to the cart, he swayed in a voluptuous, lingering way, against her, lingering as he swung away to recover balance. Without speaking, he took her hand across, under the wrap, and with his unseeing face lifted to the road, his soul intent, he began with his one hand to unfasten the buttons of her glove, to push back her glove from her hand, carefully, laying bare her hand. And the close-working, instinctive subtlety of his fingers upon her hand sent the young girl mad with voluptuous delight. His hand was so wonderful, intent as a living creature skillfully push-

ing and manipulating in the dark underworld, removing her glove and laying
bare her palm, her fingers. Then his hand closed over hers, so firm, so close, as
if the flesh knitted to one thing, his hand over hers. Meanwhile his face
watched the road and the ears of the horse, he drove with steady attention
through the villages, and she sat beside him, rapt, glowing, blinded with a new
light. Neither of them spoke. In outward attention they were entirely separate.
But between them was the compact of his flesh with hers, in the handclasp.
(*Rainbow* 275–76)

It is impossible to minimize this scene's effect on Ursula's developing erotic
life. The close, physical sensations that Lawrence here describes are only
part of the picture. That any onlookers, whoever they may be, would not recognize the erotic connection here is, likely, part of the erotic charge. This
scene presents us with a masochistic moment: Ursula's "voluptuous delight"
responds not only to the "skillful" pressure of Anton Skrebensky's fingers on
her hand but also to the contact's veiled quality. Further, the pair is at once
"knitted" together and "entirely separate"; sexual experience forms a union
that feels like identity while at the same time holding apart individual bodies
as participants. This equivocal balance develops Lawrence's typical tension,
which is pushed further as he describes the fleshly "compact" that acts both
as emblem of that tension and its tender, sweaty cause.

"Compact"—the word is peculiar. It registers an adjectival sense of the
word (small, tightly knit), the somatic real of the hand compressed into another hand, and the strange way a touch like this, in Lawrence, can seem to
be a kind of contract. Given, too, the mysteriously marital (and also masochistic) overtones of Skrebensky's "flesh" in compact "with hers," the passage
illuminates the ways that Lawrentian attention to minor bodily moments
can, in fact, link back up with the novel's larger project of a multigenerational
plot centered on genetically linked women. For Lawrence, the family plot
develops from these moments of connection—connected because flesh is
pressed to flesh and connected, too, because the fact of their touch bolsters
the pair against the wider world. If touch helps makes clearer the indetermi-
nacies of sexual attraction, the solitary Lawrentian body can manifest sense
in such a way as to explain an emotional state. The finest example of this
happens at the end of *The Rainbow*, as the multigenerational plot resolves
with Ursula's emergence into adulthood.

By this climactic point, Ursula has been abandoned by Skrebensky but finds herself pregnant with his child. The novel's denouement follows her as she attempts to explain her situation to her lover, wanders about near her home on Willey Green, and, in the osmotic ways of Lawrence, suffers a miscarriage after meeting some stampeding horses. Lawrence does not suggest a clear connection between the animals and Ursula's miscarriage; rather, the imbalance the horses represents works its way inward, like a miasma, to Ursula's womb. The animals' chaos produces a response within her body:

> Then suddenly, in a flame of agony, she darted, seized the rugged knots of the oak-tree and began to climb. Her body was weak but her hands were as hard as steel. She knew she was strong. She struggled in a great effort till she hung on the bough. The horses were loosening their knot, stirring, trying to realize. She was working her way round to the other side of the tree. As they started to canter towards her, she fell in a heap on the other side of the hedge.
>
> For some moments she could not move. Then she saw through the rabbit-cleared bottom of the hedge the great, working hoofs of the horses as they cantered near. She could not bear it. She rose and walked swiftly, diagonally across the field. The horses galloped along the other side of the hedge to the corner, where they were held up. She could feel them there in their huddled group all the while she hastened across the bare field. They were almost pathetic, now. Her will alone carried her, till, trembling, she climbed the fence under a leaning thorn-tree that overhung the grass by the high-road. The use went from her, she sat on the fence leaning back against the trunk of the thorn-tree, motionless. (*Rainbow* 454)

After this encounter, Lawrence turns our attention to Ursula's anxiety over her pregnancy. The child is, in her view, the only remaining node of attachment with Skrebensky, and she wants to break with him fully. Magically enough, the very next page explains to us that this ligature has failed: "[t]here would be no child: she was glad." Further, "[i]f here had been a child, it would have made little difference, however. She would have kept the child and herself, she would not have gone to Skrebensky" (457). What forces does Lawrence imply prompted this miscarriage? Lawrence argues for a connection to the encounter with the horses but also keeps the horses' chaos from working as the reason for the miscarriage.

This kind of vitalist exchange highlights the strangeness of Lawrentian crisis. Through her encounter with the horses, Ursula's pregnancy ends. But, more, Lawrence insists that even if this had not happened, her stance in relation to Skrebensky would have remained the same. Not only do we see an almost magical connection between Ursula's willful climb and her miscarriage; we also discover a frighteningly secure connection between self-will and plot development. Even if a counterfactual pregnancy continued, Ursula's unfolding plot would have remained identical. The point here might seem to be focused on the unreal personal power of Lawrence's characters—decisions once made in Lawrence's world maintain a security even when circumstances alter.[4] But this is not entirely accurate. Character undergoes a radical alteration when we compare this purposive Ursula to the Ursula in *Women in Love*, the Ursula that Kate Millett suggests has lost her power: "Ursula looked out of the window. In her soul she began to wrestle, and she was frightened. She was always frightened of words, because she knew that mere word-force could always make her believe what she did not believe" (*Women* 437). This is especially damning; Lawrence directly connects Ursula's anxiety to her desire to leave the snow, and Gudrun questions her sister carefully about whether the decision to leave could properly be called her own. Ursula objects inwardly to Gudrun's ridicule by claiming a desire to avoid further connection with the people in the Alps. And, a few pages later, Ursula offers a clear assessment of Gudrun's apparently solicitous, but actually vicious, care:

> "No," said Ursula, "[love] isn't [the supreme thing on earth]. Love is too human and little. I believe in something inhuman, of which love is only a little part. I believe what we must fulfill comes out of the Unknown to us, and it is something infinitely more than love. It isn't so merely *human*."
>
> Gudrun looked at Ursula with steady, balancing eyes. She admired and despised her sister so much, both. Then suddenly she averted her face, saying coldly, uglily:
>
> "Well, I've got no further than love, yet."
>
> Over Ursula's mind flashed the thought: "Because you never *have* loved, you can't get beyond it."
>
> Gudrun rose, came over to Ursula and put her arm round her neck.
>
> "Go and find your new world, dear," she said, her voice clanging with false benignity. "After all, the happiest voyage is the quest of Rupert's Blessed Isles" (*Women* 438, emphasis Lawrence's).

And this aggressive conversation comes right after a rhapsodic exchange between the sisters. Gudrun gives Ursula some of her fanciful stockings: "thick silk stockings, vermilion, cornflower blue, and grey, bought in Paris." The exchange seems almost insipid: "'*Aren't* they jewels!' cried Gudrun, eyeing her gifts with an envious eye. '*Aren't* they real lambs!'" (*Women* 436, emphasis Lawrence's). By pressing these two moments together and by papering this small, sensory vignette with the sisters' volatile argument, Lawrence creates a relational system that cannot rely on mere plot to develop its contours. Mild, sensory experience can, in Lawrence's world, pave the way for violent exchange. And, once that exchange is over, habit steps in to ease the strife it may have caused. By suturing together the angry and the sweet, Lawrence asks us to embrace his characters as flexibly related to the plots they inhabit. And that flexibility remains in spite of the apparently self-altering experiences (marriage, family death, childbirth, etc.) his characters undergo.

In other words, Lawrence is a realist through and through, though his realism is unlike that of his Victorian antecedents. The real he narrates is not the social or political real, nor even the real of the mind. Lawrence's real is the real of the body, specifically the desiring body in all of its instances. But the bodies Lawrence describes cause a kind of cognitive friction with the contemporary reader. The two things readers tend to do with bodies in narrative—uncover hidden desires or describe the represented ones—fail to capture the strangeness of the Lawrentian body. As I've already suggested, Bersani's major intervention points to some of that body's finer features— its oscillation, its desire not for action but for quiet, intense absorption. Lawrence writes a pulsing body, one that doesn't progressively feel one way or another; character development is not his objective. This pulsation defines Lawrence's characters' form. It's built into the manuscripts and typescripts. It's his characters' DNA.

Lawrence's literary form mirrors the way he draws characters. His fictional prose writes through multiple versions of the same thing in the hopes of landing not on the thing itself but on the malleable verbal pap that can describe and animate things. For Leavis, this element develops most clearly in relation to character: "it is only by way of the most delicate and complex responsive relations with others that the individual can achieve fulfillment" (118). Lawrentian character never rests. In fact, we never get a version of a Lawrentian character defined by a character's place in the story or an action. Instead, we get suspended possibilities: ongoing variations that never reduce or boil down into one variety, one type. A difficult aspect of this kind of narrative is that it both inserts readers into its represented social world and, with its odd narrative distance, encourages them to examine their own daily habits as though they have become a Lawrentian narrator. There is no way to live life at a Lawrentian pitch. Each effort toward such a life forces an encounter with your failure—failures of generosity, of discourse, of feeling, of vitriol. It is this way within the novels, too. Critics accuse Lawrence of writing his own avatars into positions of great narrative power and privilege.[5] But, in truth, almost all of Lawrence's characters have the capacity to wrest power from his apparent protagonists. Power's fungibility is the ground of Lawrentian life.

Bloody-Minded Togetherness

Lawrence's greatest cheerleader, F. R. Leavis, comments on the conceptual necessity of Lawrence's apparently discursive form:

> It is not merely that George Eliot doesn't write this kind of prose. Lawrence is not indulging in descriptive "lyricism" or writing poetically in order to generate atmosphere. Words here are used in the way, not of eloquence, but of creative poetry (a wholly different way, that is, from that of "O may I join the choir invisible"): they establish as an actual presence—create as part of the substance of the book—something that is essential to Lawrence's theme. The kind of intense apprehension of the unity of life that they evidence is as decidedly not in George Eliot's genius as it is *of* Lawrence's. It goes with his ability to talk about—to evoke—"blood-intimacy" and "blood-togetherness." It belongs, in short, to that aspect of his genius which has made him in general repute (however absurdly) the prophet of the Dark Gods—the partisan of instinct against intelligence, the humane, and the civilized. (113)

Leavis's point here puts "descriptive 'lyricism'" at odds with Lawrence's thematic "essence," but in my reading these are not entirely distinct elements. The implication is that "mere" lyricism has no place in novelistic prose and that, therefore, any interjection of the lyrical mode into the form is at odds with the novel's aim. Further, undergirding this set of claims is an assumption about the work of the novel as opposed to, and distinct from, the work of the lyric. This is, in part, because lyricism here gets figured as something that overlays, or ornaments, descriptive prose. And, in many nineteenth-century novelists, this seems to be the case. But, as Elisha Cohn has suggested, passages of sustained lyricism contribute much to the argumentative work the novel does.[6] By demonstrating reverie or lyrical detachment as a part of subjective development and by manifesting reverie in just these "lyrical" terms, novelists show how periods of lyricism help develop those stable, but examining, subjects that develop as a major starting point for social change. Unlike most major nineteenth-century novelists, though, reverie—the element that Leavis here describes as "creative poetry"—lets Lawrence carve out small places in novelistic discourse for subjective contemplation. What is unusual about the Lawrentian reverie is that it expands to take up huge amounts of novelistic space and that it doesn't focus primarily on subjective development.

To turn to a potent example, in Lawrence's strange 1925 novella *St. Mawr*, the narrator lays bare reverie as a fact of life: "The seething caldron of lower life, seething on the very tissue of the higher life, seething the soul away, seething at the marrow. The vast and unrelenting will of the swarming lower life, working forever against man's attempt at a higher life, a further created being" (170). The novella charts Lou's search not for "higher life," not for "deeper consciousness," and not for "intimacy" (151) but for "burning life" (81), which she associates with the stallion St. Mawr. Lawrence connects this capacity to animal vitality (one major subplot focuses on an attempt to geld the stallion), but desiring vital life is only the best example of the ideal Lou seeks. In fact, by developing the horse as the proper avatar of this vital power, Lawrence keeps us from reading his wishes solely in relation to sexual desire. While Lou's borderline erotic connection to the horse develops the novella's plot, the major form of her fascination seems to be in the horse's unmistakable distance from her own life:

> The wild, brilliant, alert head of St. Mawr seemed to look at her out of another world. It was as if she had had a vision, as if the walls of her own world had suddenly melted away, leaving her in a great darkness, in the midst of which the large, brilliant eyes of that horse looked at her with demonish question, while his naked ears stood up like daggers from the naked lines of his inhuman head, and his great body glowed red with power. (50–51)

By mingling the erotic ("naked lines") with the distanced ("inhuman head"), Lawrence makes a case for Lou's desire to access St. Mawr's creaturely vitality. More, by emphasizing the woman's cataloging interest in the stallion's body, Lawrence connects her meditation on his form not to a progressive personal development but to her half-lit recognition of a wider, irrational, inhuman truth. Lou's experience here doesn't change her, per se. Instead, St.

Mawr's presence thrusts itself into her line of sight: his embodiment shuts down her capacity to conceptualize (her mental structures "[melt] away"). Thus, Lawrence gives his narrator access to a reverie that moves neither plot nor character forward. The aim of these passages is to freeze the novella's action, to model the contemplation that so troubles Lou.

Reverie, in these ways, is neither limited to Lawrence's narrator nor to specific characters. Leavis's major point on this aspect of Lawrence's work, that the rhapsodic language produces the "essence" of Lawrentian prose, makes a case for discursive prose as novelistic form as such. For Leavis, Lawrence's repetitions produce the frame upon which his themes hang. And, as he goes on to explain, it is not that Lawrence is the "partisan of instinct" against these enlightenment principles but that Lawrence hopes for an ideal enlightenment responsive to instinct. The lives most hoped for by Lawrentian characters are not lives divorced from art and culture; instead, they are lives that incorporate art and culture into daily routine. In *Women in Love*, even Birkin's grumbling social and political complaints diminish once his habits become more embedded in a daily routine, that is, after he marries Ursula and embarks on a domestic, if uprooted, life. In other words, the problem of the Pompadour is not that its art is barren per se but that its art is barren because it divorces itself from general London life; the artistic community in which the demimondaine Pussum and Halliday make sense purposively distances itself from the other institutions that ballast modern life, the school, the village, even the business of the mines. In Lawrence, the route to a world that permits mind to speak to mind is blood-togetherness—the somatic thread between people, common daily life, is the way to foster rational understanding. More than this, any attempt to reason without recognizing the centrality of the vital—that is, the changeable—ultimately fails.

The trouble critics have in deciphering the weight of different relationships as they ebb and flow in the Brangwen novels is an example of a larger problem in reading Lawrence. In part because of the rapidity with which characters change, it is, as I've said, difficult to account for value in his novels. While certain characters get marked out for the narrator's or author's approval (and the narrator's approval often looks like authorial approval, if only because Lawrence's characters so often look like Lawrence), these same characters can easily be condemned. For example, even as valued a character as Rupert Birkin espouses an often difficult-to-swallow politics. This makes the critic's project, of aligning such narratological or authorial value with value as such, challenging at best. It also leads to perplexity when actually parsing Lawrence's politics: Are all the bad opinions his own? More than this, would having bad opinions mean Lawrence was unworthy of critical engagement? Strangely, Lawrence draws attention to his heroes' failings even when they are failings he himself seemed to share; more, he often connects those failings to the character's apparent allegiance to "Lawrentian" principles. Birkin's assertion of his need for manly love, at the end of *Women in Love*, fails not because it is overly risqué but because it cannot overcome the twinned critiques leveled by Gerald's disinterest and Ursula's complaint that Birkin's imagined love is rooted in political fantasy, not desire.[7]

Since John Middleton Murry, Lawrence's critics have divided the heterosexual romances of the novel into the potentially generative marriage of Birkin and Ursula and the doomed violence of Gerald's love for Gudrun. In an illuminating essay about the narrative connections between the sodomy that structures "Excurse" and the homosexual exchange of "Gladiatorial," Christopher Craft explains how limited Birkin's view of homosexual connection is in *Women in Love*.[8] Given the emphasis on penetration in the two central heterosexual plots, it is curious that the friendship Birkin holds out to Gerald includes love but not physical contact or interpenetration.[9] The "bonding" that Birkin proposes is purely ideal. In "Excurse," Lawrence represents a mutually beneficial version of sexual act:

> She had her desire of him, she touched, she received the maximums of unspeakable communication in touch, dark, subtle, positively silent, a magnificent gift and give again, a perfect acceptance and yielding, a mystery, the reality of that which can never be known, vital, sensual reality that can never be transmuted into mind content, but remains outside, living body of darkness and silence and subtlety, the mystic body of reality. She had her desire fulfilled, he had his desire fulfilled. For she was to him what he was to her, the immemorial magnificence of mystic, palpable, real otherness. (*Women* 320)

The intensity of the experience here described causes some confusion: Does Lawrence's keyword, "vital," here, as elsewhere, describe sodomy? The "living body of darkness and silence" implies this. But could this be a vaginally penetrative, but not "frictional," sex act? Ursula's "fulfillment" here (since it does not seem to be the disturbed version we find in Lawrence's description of Connie Chatterley's central sexual scene) might be a version of the frictionless orgasm Bersani argues marks the most beneficial version of sexual life accessible to women in Lawrence. True, there is an implied connection, throughout Lawrence criticism, between deeply penetrative sodomy and frictionless sex, but it's not clear that sodomy is the only route to beneficial, "vital" sex in Lawrence's world. Lawrence's depictions of generative (fulfilling, not reproductive) sex often connect very closely to his depictions of disruptive or unpleasant sexual acts. Much of this has to do with Lawrence's attempts to represent, in third-person narration, the variable experiences of a sex act. For example, in the "Death and Love" chapter of *Women in Love*, Lawrence represents the strangely unsatisfying connection between Gudrun and Gerald. I say strangely because, in many ways, this connection looks like Ursula and Birkin's encounter in Sherwood Forest:

> He found in her an infinite relief. Into her he poured all his pent-up darkness and corrosive death, and he was whole again. It was wonderful, marvelous, it was a miracle. This was the ever-recurrent miracle of his life, at the knowledge of which he was lost in an ecstasy of relief and wonder. And she, subject, received him as a vessel filled with his bitter portion of death. She had no power at this crisis to resist. The terrible frictional violence of death filled her, and she received it in an ecstasy of subjection, in throws of acute, violent sensation. (*Women* 344)

In one case, this act sustains. For Gerald, "[i]t was wonderful, marvelous, it was a miracle." Gerald's apparent aggression, in his view, is sustaining and unifying. This sexual encounter bereaves Gudrun. The oscillation between the distant third-person narrator and free indirect discourse makes the representation of this single act incredibly difficult to parse. It becomes more complex as the narration continues to describe Gudrun's experience of Gerald after the sex act. Gerald "cleaves" to Gudrun, "like a child at breast," but Gudrun remains aloof, "destroyed into perfect consciousness." As the night continues, though, Gudrun's relationship to Gerald becomes even stranger: "[s]he felt an overwhelming tenderness for him, and a dark unstirring of jealous hatred, that he should lie so perfect and immune" (*Women* 345–46).

The narrator's peculiar mode here comes not only from depicting the variance between Gudrun's and Gerald's experience of their assignation but also from Lawrence's attempt to manage a single character's internalized narrative of a sexual experience. Lawrence's narrator strikes a cautious balance in these passages. We get the sense that Gudrun and Gerald feel different about the sexual encounter, but, more than that, we also get the sense that these characters' views about the event can change. And this change of perspective is not teleological. In other words, in this passage, Gudrun's view of Gerald's sexual aggression ("ecstasy of subjection") feels in one moment like force, in the next, like something that can be borne, in the next, something that cannot be borne.

For all their maddening detail, Lawrentian scenes feel portable, as though he constructs plot by stitching together various iterations: scene with a horse, scene with art, scene with a picnic, and so on. As Bersani claims, "There is no scene of desire which is not an elaboration, a kind of visual interpretation, of other scenes. In the same way that literary works are always critical revisions of other literary works, our desires reformulate both other desires and the pleasures which are at the source of all desire" (10). The Lawrentian language of desire, "root," "darkness," "torment," point to something subterranean, something only few people can access. This element clearly opens Lawrence up to scorching critique: his version of desire is both misogynistic and fascistic. This is the most unpleasant aspect of Lawrence. His obsessed narrators catalogue characters into those who can experience "dark," true, Lawrentian pleasure and those who cannot. But, in practice, Lawrence allows most of his characters access to this version of desire, even if their access to that desire is obscure to his narrators. Further, he makes it very clear that those few who cannot experience the thrills of "breaking down" the self through desire are limited not by their gender or their politics but instead by their own need to rule others. Characters like Hermione Roddice, Winifred Inger, Kangaroo, and Clifford Chatterley are oppressive not because of their sexual inadequacies but because they want to rule, because they want to stabilize their authority over the text's other characters. In Lawrence, exquisite masochism lands on the aesthetic side of its divide: by emphasizing these characters' devotion to an exquisitely aesthetic social and intellectual life, Lawrence separates them from the vitalist energy that his more valued characters exhibit. The authority conferred by aestheticism limits or tamps down the evocative oscillation in masochistic dynamics and leaves only true stasis: death.[10]

Alternately, an oscillating core is the ground zero of character value in Lawrence's fiction. What can change about character can also change back. Although the narrator has the capacity to dip, delicately, into each character's consciousness, there is little transparency between characters. These twinned elements—immediate sexual reciprocity and total characterological opacity—make the motor that drives the Lawrentian life. So, while we, as readers, navigate the developments in Gudrun's views of Gerald's sexual dominance, Gerald never, through the entirety of his interaction with Gudrun, fully perceives them. In other words, in moments of concord, like the encounter between Ursula and Birkin I detailed above, the reader should not get the sense that the characters experiencing acts fully interpenetrate one another's consciousnesses. Instead, we understand that their senses of one another align only within their separate experiences. Lawrence's characters populate a world in which, try as they might to structure their lives with ideas—fascism, homoerotic (but, in Birkin's case, explicitly not homosexual) love, aestheticism—all such efforts fall short. The main difficulty in parsing Lawrentian character comes from the structural misalignment between characters' views of themselves, in worlds ordered by social and political affiliation, and the experiential lives they lead. Lawrence demonstrates that what we might think of as intersubjectivity—that moment of interaction where characters achieve sub- or unconscious concord—is accidental, not epiphanic.

To secure this claim, I want to turn to two scenes in *Women in Love* that, in combination, can be read as an endorsement of Birkin's apparent need for a homoerotic romance in concert with his heterosexual union with Ursula. In my view, this point, one made by critics as diverse as Leo Bersani, Christopher Craft, and Kate Millett, disregards what I see as a central difficulty in describing Lawrentian character. If, in most realist fiction, we can parse characters' views by analyzing either their discourse or their thinking, in Lawrence's fiction, we are repeatedly presented with characters whose views—both views thought and spoken and views subconscious—are unstable over time. Character is not teleological, and moments of recognition, self-assertion, and insight are just that: momentary.

Birkin's problem, for the last third of the novel, centers on Gerald and Gerald's incapacity (or unwillingness) to commit to the strongly erotic friendship Birkin holds out to him. At the end of "Gladiatorial," for example, Birkin asserts his love for Ursula at the same time as he clarifies his appraisal of Gerald's physical beauty. The passage is worth quoting in full, as it clarifies the failure of conceptual interpenetration that I describe above. Gerald complains:

> "—I begin to doubt it."
>
> "That you will ever love a woman?"

"Well—yes—what you would truly call *love*—"

"You doubt it?"

"Well—I begin to."

There was a long pause.

"Life has all kinds of things," said Birkin. "There isn't only one road."

"Yes, I believe that too. I believe it.—And, mind you, I don't care how it is with me—I don't care how it is—so long as I don't feel—" he paused, and a blank, barren look passed over his face, to express his feeling—"so long as I feel I've *lived*, somehow—and I don't care how it is—but I want to feel that—"

"Fulfilled," said Birkin.

"We-ell, perhaps it is, fulfilled;—I don't use the same words as you."

"It is the same." (*Women* 276)

There are a number of things to hang on in this passage, such as Lawrence's typical depiction of hesitance in Gerald's speech, marked by dashes and, in the last instance, that drawn out, hesitant "We-ell." But what we see here is, centrally, a miscommunication. Gerald's acknowledgement of his inability (incapacity?) to love a woman is not the same thing as acknowledging a latent homosexuality. And, as we have learned in "Gladiatorial," Birkin's vision of homoerotic connection is not entirely certain of how to accommodate physical love. The language that Birkin chooses to describe the feeling Gerald hopes to have, "fulfilled," is repeated in Gerald's response. But Lawrence carefully builds hesitation into even this apparent agreement. Birkin's response, "It is the same," ends the chapter, but we should not read this as Gerald's agreement to Birkin's terms any more than we should read this as endorsing Birkin's position of authority in the novel.

The critical tendency to read Lawrentian characters as wholesale avatars of the writer becomes especially noticeable in the passages where characters become unhinged: in the evocative, rhapsodic conversations that are present primarily as tools of persuasion within the novel worlds. One reason for this slippage is that these discussions mimic Lawrence's habit, as narrator and essayist, of drawing out conversation into looping, meditative rants. "Gladiatorial" is a key example of this in *Women in Love*: Birkin's call to Gerald to enter into a strong, dyadic male friendship with him patterns much of the novel's denouement.

Another version of this strategy appears at the novel's end, in "Exeunt." After Gerald's death on the mountaintop, Ursula and Birkin discuss what his death means. Birkin argues that he "needed" Gerald for fulfillment: he "might have lived with his friend, a further life" (*Women* 480). But Ursula resists:

> "Why aren't I enough?" she said. "You are enough for me. I don't want anybody else by you. Why isn't it the same with you?"
>
> "Having you, I can live all my life without anybody else, any other sheer intimacy. But to make it complete, really happy, I wanted eternal union with a man too: another kind of love," he said.
>
> "I don't believe it," she said. "It's an obstinacy, a theory, a perversity."
>
> "Well—" he said.
>
> "You can't have two kinds of love. Why should you!"
>
> "It seems as if I can't," he said. "Yet I wanted it."
>
> "You can't have that, because it's false, impossible," she said.
>
> "I don't believe that," he answered. (*Women* 481)

Christopher Craft expands on this ending's insufficiency: "*Women in Love* thus expires upon the posthumous instantiation of a disgruntled heterosexuality whose terminal oscillations ('You can't have it' / 'I don't believe that') dialogically rehearse the catastrophic homosexual loss that both founds this heterosexuality and confounds its powers of satisfaction and completion" (189). For Craft, this passage signals Lawrence's "chilling cathexis between homosexual desire and death," that Lawrence allows Birkin's plaintive pleas for Gerald's love to find full voice only after Gerald's icy death (190). And, there is much in Lawrence's work and in his biography to secure this reading. However, by placing this passage into closer conversation with the similarly open-ended passage I've quoted from "Gladiatorial" above, we might see the formal logic at work in these moments of close, interpersonal communication. In Craft's reading, Birkin's plea for Gerald takes precedence over Ursula's refusal of his need. This has to do more with the primacy contemporary readers give Lawrentian descriptions of homosexual or homoerotic desire over the (often borderline misogynistic) expressions of heterosexual desire. Does the ending of the novel imply that Ursula's incapacity to understand Birkin's needs remains in place? Or that Birkin's refusal to believe in male love's possibility counteracts Ursula's heterosexist viewpoint? The pathos Craft sees comes not from Birkin's last, resistant line but from Birkin's recognition that the love he had hoped for is now, following Gerald's death, a sad impossibility. This careful balancing, of homoerotic value with cultural, social, or personal impossibility, gives us a Lawrentian sexual politics that we can stomach. But, as I've been suggesting, Craft's account may not be accurate to the sexual lives Lawrence describes.

Alternately, in Millett's view, scenes like this one float the possibility of female critique only to shut it down entirely. Millett explains that, for women characters, "Lawrence's peculiar solution seems to marry and smother them (curiously related gestures here) and then to fare 'beyond women' to homosexual attachments, forming sexual-political alliances with other males" (257).[11] Further, Lawrence apparently excommunicates any characters who seem to criticize this sexual world; he depicts them as frigid or, worse, lesbians. But characters like *The Rainbow*'s Winifred Inger and Hermione Roddice in *Women in Love* are not simply totems for the women's movement, as Millett would read them. These characters connect more securely to the dominating woman character type I've been tracing throughout this book. And what's startling about their inclusion in Lawrence's "psychic narratives" is their apparent powerlessness in this new world. Rather than read this as a result of these women's association with nascent feminism, I read their narrative failures as developing from their desires to dominate. In this way, Winifred and Hermoine become avatars for Anton and Gerald: they are the feminine versions of the unresponsive, ideological strongmen who are clearly objects of Lawrence's repugnance. The "big want" Ursula feels is for free exchange, not masculine domination. By reading Birkin's relationship to her as purely dominant, Millett ignores the ways the pair develops their connection through ongoing, dialogic negotiation. The savagery of Lawrence's depiction of Hermione becomes the keystone in Millett's critique. We can read this depiction as negatively as does Millett only if we imagine Hermoine to be a potentially successful feminist. Hermoine, like Gerald Crich, stands as a sign of the progress-minded nineteenth century's major political failure— its failure to fully criticize the engines of either capitalism or institutionalized sexism as they gained momentum and power. The assumption both Hermione and Gerald make is that their complaint about social and political life is more valuable because it comes from them, agents not of feminism or enlightened industrialism but of noblesse oblige.

Allotropic Revision

I said earlier that Lawrence digested the Victorian novel; this section discusses the form of that absorption. By examining the typescripts of his Brangwen novels, it's clear that Lawrence wrote two and sometimes three versions of his novels at once. Lawrence (and often his wife Frieda) crossed each typescript with erasures and additions. He revised madly. Some pages are awash in fluid green ink (revision by rewriting); others have no marks at all; others still bear the signs of much "working through": testing word choice, tense, points of view, even vignette. These practices are striking—they are multiple, fluid, ongoing, rapidly shifting. And they are of a piece with much modernist typescript revision, which was radically altered by the development of the typewriter, carbon copies, and multiple editions.[12] What becomes clear when examining the versions of Lawrentian novels in typescript are his specific habits and patterns: his methods of including or removing repetition from text, his substitutions of certain concepts for others, erasures of loaded language, and the like.[13] Lawrence's alterations reveal his habit of revising phrasings not to adjust a plotting point or characterization simply but to reverse them completely. This aspect occurs across Lawrence's work, but it is of central importance in Lawrence's depictions of romantic and sexual entanglements.[14]

In a famous letter to Edward Garnett, we see a clear description of what it is Lawrence thinks he's doing with character:

> You mustn't look in my novel for the old stable ego of the character. There is another ego, according to whose action the individual is unrecognizable, and passes through, as it were, allotropic states which it needs a deeper sense than any we've been used to exercise, to discover are states of the same single radically-unchanged element. (Like as diamond and coal are the same pure single element of carbon. The ordinary novel would trace the history of the diamond—but I say "diamond, what! This is carbon." And my diamond might be coal or soot, and my theme is carbon.) (Kern 29–30)[15]

Here, the various elements of each character's plot are like an element's allotropes. They may appear to be quite different, but if broken down or distilled, their constitution remains the same. One way to think of this, formally, is to compare characters across the episodic stages of their plots. How is Gudrun of the "Pompadour" chapter different from Gudrun in "Snowed Up"? How can a reader connect Gudrun's almost puritanical response to Pussum and Halliday's affair to her attraction to Loerke? But one might also think of allotropes across versions of the novel. Unlike Hardy's major revisions, which took place after serial publication and which debowdlerized his work, Lawrence's major revisions took place in typescript, something I'll discuss in this and the following section. Lawrence's typescripts demonstrate connections between characters' points of view or aesthetic choices.

For instance, in one draft of a passage that, in the published novel, has been reduced to a complaint about Tennyson's sentimentalism, Lawrence embeds a complaint about sensational knowledge. Early in one of the *Women in Love* typescripts, Birkin rails at Hermione's Victorian sentimentalism, an awareness of which arises from her interpretation of a Tennyson poem. In full, the passage reads:

> "It's all that Lady of Shalott business," he said in his strong, abstract voice. He seemed to be charging her before the unseeing air. "You've got that mirror, your own fixed will, your immortal understanding, your own tight conscious world, and there is nothing beyond it. There in the mirror, you must have everything. And because you've found all your leading ideas become stale, circumscribed as they are by your mirror frame, you turn round against intellectualism, against thought, against any expression of abstract truth, you want only sensationalism, which means your senses in your head. You want merely the <u>knowledge</u> of a certain set of reactions in your senses. But it is the mental, conscious experience you want, in your head. An animal—back, you want to look at yourself in the mirror, like Shah Johan—you want to see your own animal actions in a mirror—your accursed Lady of Shalott mirror, which you've got in your head—and which is <u>you</u>, the beginning and the end of you—a fixed consciousness, an innumerable set of fixed conceptions, old, clear and final, and bound round by your will into one perfect round mirror in which the world takes place for you. But you would die, die rather than know that the world <u>doesn't</u> take place within your mirror, according to your universal consciousness. You'd die rather than know that your perfect consciousness doesn't stretch to the bounds and limits of the universe. You'd have to die, in the knowledge. And you're tough, you're tough, you won't die. You'll take your precious mirror to the grave with you, as if it were your own immortality. And there it will lie, the tuppenny ha'penny thing, like the combs and fibulas that come, rather tattered, out of the Saxon women's graves." (TS 2, 57, Lawrence's emphases)[16]

In the published novel, Lawrence cuts everything after "There in the mirror, you must have everything," losing Birkin's idiosyncratic reading of the poem in the process. The poetic allusion rests on a connection between the web the Lady weaves and art, with the mirror standing in as a tool for artificial mediation. One question the reference to the poem might raise, then, is what the proper relationship might be between art and the world. The poem could be read as implying either that the better art would be unmediated (that is, that the Lady had never been forced by the curse to use the mirror) or that the mediation of the mirror somehow protects the Lady from the violence of the world. There are obviously many ways to read the assemblage of Lady, mirror, and web, but Birkin's adjustment here, that the mirror is Hermione, unsettles the idea of these things in relation, instead asserting an identity between two elements. Birkin's complaints about sensation, too, place Hermione in an aesthetic lineage that begins with the reception of the early Tennyson and continues into Pater's *Renaissance*.[17] Birkin sutures the aesthetic religion of sensation to hyperactive self-regard. His complaint is not simply that Hermione, borrowing a method forced on the Lady of Shalott, uses the mirror to "see" the world but also that the mirror acts as a conduit to self-obsession. Lawrence drops the turn to the specific form of Hermione's self-regard in the final version of the novel, along with his heterodox reading of Victorian aesthetics. In erasing this passage, he diminishes the criticism of earlier modes of aesthetic thinking while also stabilizing his depiction of Hermione as the novel's most oppressive figure. In the novel's published version, Hermione's self-obsessed personality develops from something like instinct rather than through her reading of nineteenth-century thinkers. That aggressive self-regard thus becomes a feature of her baseline personality rather than either a mark of her aesthetic education or a sign of late Victorian aesthetic failures.

This is only one of a number of alterations that shows Lawrence in a long process of altering both the novel's Victorian framing and its representation of idealized relationship. Many of these adjustments take place as Lawrence explores the differences between the Brangwens and Hermione. For example, later in the same typescript, as Ursula and Hermione discuss Birkin's proposal to Ursula, Lawrence alters a verb in a way that further underscores the difference between the Victorian prehistory of the novel's characters and their modernist representations. In the first typescript, Ursula says, "He wants me really to submit to him in marriage," while in the published version of the novel, the verb is "accept," not "submit." In the same revision, Lawrence adds the sharply critical explanation of Hermione's response to Ursula's revelation: "Hermione shuddered with a strange desire. Ah, if only he had asked *her* to subserve him, to be his slave—She shuddered with desire" (TS 1, 539).[18]

A page later, Lawrence continues his revisions with an eye to erasing his characters' Victorian antecedents. In the following parenthetical phrase, Ursula recognizes that Hermione does not understand the kind of sexual life Birkin proposes when Hermione turns to complain about Birkin's desire for an "odalisk":

> "Yes," said Ursula vaguely.—After all, to do him justice, he did <u>not</u> want an odalisk, he did not want a slave. Hermione would have been his slave—there was in her a passionate desire to prostrate herself before a man—the same desire that was so plain and so horrible in Charlotte Bronte. Ursula shuddered, and realized that she was betraying Birkin. (TS 1, 360)

Lawrence revises "betraying" into "belying," softening the possible complaint one might make of Ursula's agreement with Hermione. In the first version, Lawrence suggests that her acceptance of Hermione's terms (especially the damning term "odalisk") is a betrayal; the revision takes into account Ursula's parenthetical thought—that Hermione misunderstands Birkin and does not do him "justice." In the initial form, Lawrence's verb "betray" does indeed imply the kind of tight relational control that Hermione says is Birkin's aim. As he revises, though, he complicates both Ursula's understanding of what Birkin asks and her assessment of Hermione's inability to understand those aims. In the published novel, the allusive little passage alters even further:

> "Yes," said Ursula vaguely.—After all, the tiresome thing was, he did *not* want an odalisk, he did not want a slave. Hermione would have been his slave— there was in her a horrible desire to prostrate herself before a man—a man who worshipped her, however, and admitted her as the supreme thing.—He did not want an odalisk. He wanted a woman to *take* something from him, to give herself up so much that she could take the last realities of him, the last facts, the last physical facts, physical and unbearable." (Cambridge edition 295)

Of course, the most substantial revision in this passage is the deletion of the reference to Charlotte Brontë's supplicating heroines and Hermione's desire to "prostrate herself before a man." Embedded in this reference is the narrator's own view of Brontëan submission—it is both "so plain" and "so horrible": not only distasteful but also so obvious that it comes to define Brontë as a writer for this narrator. What's stunning about this revision is that it troubles the fine line between masochistic supplication and dominant display. Lawrence adds, in place of the explanatory reference to Brontë, "a man who worshipped her, however, and admitted her as the supreme thing," a revision that not only reverses the concept of prostration but, when considered in relation to the initial reference, dramatically alters the force of that comparison. First, it adds man's sexual worship to the general notion of womanly prostration: a woman on a pedestal necessarily supplicates herself. More loosely, if we think of this revision as somehow taking the place of Lawrence's strange Brontë reference, we can see how this description of an idealized figure of manly worship of a faultless woman connects itself to the high Victorian sadism familiar to readers of *Villette* and *Jane Eyre*. If we think about this, again, loosely, in terms of the aesthetic and political differences between Ursula and Hermione, we see how Ursula imagines Hermione not only as like the narrator's imagined Charlotte Brontë but also as a woman interested in a relation that both places her on a pedestal and keeps her there: Hermione, for all of her supposed interest in women's political rights, is turned on by the patriarchy.

By examining such revisions—primarily substitution revisions—made in typescript, an indexical narrative emerges. Over the course of revising, Lawrence downplays his general indebtedness to the nineteenth-century novel while at the same time investing certain characters with catchphrases, ideas, and aesthetics lifted from the high Victorian period. And these unpleasantly Victorian characters, perhaps Hermione Roddice and the Pompadour club's Pussum most explicitly, are also the characters most closely connected to the use of sexual power for hierarchical gain. In Lawrence's world, sexual power grounds most relationships, but when a character uses domination to stabilize erotic connection, the result is disastrous, and the connection fails.

Further, given the centrality of authentic sexual and romantic connection to much feminist criticism, many of the negative critical evaluations of Lawrence fault him in comparison not to his forbears but to his descendants. Much of this criticism finds its first impulse in Kate Millett's important book *Sexual Politics*. Millett's analysis—pointed, trenchant, and often damningly right—puts Lawrence in (bad) company with Norman Mailer and Henry Miller: visionary devotees of "sexual violence and ruthless exploitation" (138).[19] Only, Lawrence's version of this exploitation is limpid, pathetic, and, in its final version in *Lady Chatterley's Lover*, transmuted into a wincingly oblivious cult of the phallus. Millett presents a Lawrence counter to the technician and class warrior Leavis and Williams admire. Lawrence's failures thus become failures of his sexual imagination, an imagination that Millett claims is stuck in the very "Arthur Donnithorne" habits he roundly criticized: "Birkin had in fact wanted Gerald's virginity, if one may refer to such a quality in a rich Lothario to whom sex had been an exploitative hunt carried out against lower-class women, Minnette [*sic*] for example, with whom his rank and money assure him an easy dominance over a slavish prey" (267). Except, of course, that Gerald never dominates the Pussum; he engages in dominating, sexual games with her, but she remains distant from him, aloof (*Women* 81). If we disarticulate the play of sexual domination from the politics of the novel, we see Lawrence's mode depends on a core assumption of equality, flexible though that equality may be.[20] The mistake in Millett's vision of sexual life is that equality between the sexes would manifest as a social and romantic equipoise. This is not the case. And, over the course of Lawrence's two Brangwen novels, we see power as a vital exchange among the characters.

Revising Lawrence

Thus far, I've been focusing on Lawrence's strategies for depicting characters' interactions and alterations. I turn now to a longer discussion of Lawrence's revision strategies to bolster my account of his writing's vitalist logic. As I suggested in the previous section, his revision strategies alter over the transition from manuscript to typescript to proof. For example, in the *Women in Love* manuscript pages that remain ("The Sisters" holograph pages), Lawrence sometimes strikes through whole passages, though his attention tends to focus on individual word choice. In the typescripts, both Lawrence and Frieda make numerous changes, some massive (requiring pages of handwritten new text) and some minute (a word change here or there). Some of the large-scale revisions are of interest here, but my focus will be on smaller changes, substitution changes. It's my contention that some of these changes—especially changes made while the text was in typescript form— demonstrate a feature of Lawrence's writerly practice that is essential to my claims about his form of fiction. In the revisions I examine, the spatial scaffolding of the scene does not change. What alters is what I will call the allusive ground of the scene. By adjusting, for example, adjectival description, Lawrence alters the allusive ballast against which his scenarios play out. Additionally, Lawrence's writing, if we allow ourselves to compare it over the course of the revisions, sharpens his critique on nominally Victorian thinking.

Most of these revisions can be seen only in the Cambridge edition, which allows one to examine both typescripts in comparison. Some, though, fall out of even that volume. These revisions never rise to the level of an independent version because they are embedded in the process of a single iteration of the revised typescript. Genetic critics argue that this kind of revision really only arrives at the moment in publication history when authors had the capacity to work through typed copies.[21] Hannah Sullivan makes a version of this point: "The consequence was exposure, from an early stage, to two visually very different forms of text. Manuscript became a place for freewheeling fast composition; typescript, which was scarcer, a space for correction and revision" (39).[22]

As in the passages that began this chapter, a short example from the second *Women in Love* typescript helps demonstrate a number of these revision strategies. In a discussion with Hermione early in the novel, Birkin challenges her mode of thinking, one he connects to a harsh critique of Victorian sentiment:

> "You are merely making words," he said; "knowledge means everything to you. You don't want to <u>be</u> an animal, you want to be conscious of your own animal instincts, to get a thrill out of them. It is all purely secondary—and more decadent than the most hide-bound intellectualism. What is it but the worst and last form of intellectualism, this love of yours for passion and the animal instincts? (TS 2, 56, emphasis Lawrence's)

Many of the typescript revisions in this passage are substitution revisions; "be conscious" is marked through, altered into "observe," "instincts" is altered into "functions." Lawrence adds a word, "mental," to qualify "thrill." The revision thus reads, " 'You are merely making words,' he said; 'knowledge means everything to you. You don't want to be an animal, you want to be conscious of your own animal instincts, to get a thrill out of them.' " The passage in the Cambridge edition reads, " 'You are merely making words,' he said; 'knowledge means everything to you. Even your animalism, you want it in your head. You don't want to *be* an animal, you want to observe your own animal functions, to get a mental thrill out of them' " (41). These adjustments are, again, minor, but they accumulate toward a harsher assessment of Hermione's attitudes. And the stages of this revision demonstrate how cautiously Lawrence alters a number of elements in his depiction of Birkin's quarrel with Hermione. Perhaps most clearly seen in the substitution of "instinct" for "function," Lawrence diminishes the possibility of a lived, empirical response from Hermione: the allusive ground shifts from a focus on biology to a focus on form. "Instinct" retains a connection to a true animality, one that has been perverted, but "function" turns Hermione into a processing machine. Perhaps most bizarrely, though, if one reads these typescripts into one another (a practice impossible until one has both the typescripts and the published book in hand), one sees the trajectory of Lawrence's thinking through the substitutions. Not only does he add the sense that her use of "animal" motivations is self-aware ("conscious"), it is also curiously distanced from the self ("observe"). Of course, this strategy of reading could happen only outside of the novel's period of initial publication; but, when examined this way, a pattern of revision emerges. By reading in this ahistorical way, one might float all of Lawrence's versions of Hermione's problem simultaneously. Then, she becomes both warped "instinct" (animal, but perversely so) and "function" (so un-animal as to be mechanistic). In these compounded phrases, we here see Lawrence oscillating between a frustration with Hermione's failed animality and one based on her absence of animality.

Again, these observations can happen only when we compare the versions of the novel to one another. And, given the editorial necessity to consider only the final versions of each round of revision, some of these choices become invisible. Even the Cambridge edition can show only each stopping point, each whole set of revisions. And if partial revisions of the sort I'm describing happen over much of Lawrence's typescript, the ones upon which I've focused below all cluster around Hermione Roddice, the *Women in Love* character I've discussed as most closely connected to a nasty Victorianism. Hermione's connections to exquisite masochism come, primarily, from her self-presentation early in the novel. But what happens to her character when her masochistic investments tip into violence marks a shift in the power imperious women have in the twentieth-century novel.

Hermione's status as a villain emerges early in the novel, at the moment of her introduction:

> This was Hermoine Roddice, a friend of the Criches. Now she came along, with her head held up, balancing an enormous flat hat of pale yellow velvet, on which were streaks of ostrich feathers, natural and grey. She drifted forward as if scarcely conscious, her long blanched face lifted up, not to see the world. She

was rich. She wore a dress of silky, frail velvet, of pale yellow colour, and she carried a lot of small rose-coloured cyclamens. Her shoes and stockings were of brownish grey, like the feathers on her hat, her hair was heavy, she drifted along with a peculiar fixity of the hips, a strange unwilling motion. She was impressive, in her lovely pale-yellow and brownish-rose, yet macabre, something repulsive. People were silent when she passed, impressed, roused, wanting to jeer, yet for some reason silenced. Her long, pale face, that she carried lifted up, somewhat in the Rossetti fashion, seemed almost drugged, as if a strange mass of thoughts coiled in the darkness within her, and she was never allowed to escape. (*Women* 9–10)

This small passage offers a wonderful example of Lawrence's habits of character development: he fixes Hermione's character through her aesthetic choices and her strangely rigid movements, but minor adjustments in the phrasing shift the emphasis in this character study from Hermione's Victorian mien to her willful contemporariness.[23] Initially, Hermione's "red brown" hair might connect her to Lizzie Siddal or other titian-haired pre-Raphaelite women "in the Rossetti fashion." But Lawrence erases this coloring, leaving only the heaviness of her now "fair" hair. Erasing the internalized reason for her attitude, Hermione's face is now "blenched" rather than "thought-clenched." Dropping the French affectation of "déhanchement," Lawrence substitutes "fixity of the hips," limiting both Hermione's lopsidedness's movement and the aural chime of "haunch." The longest passage of revision here turns Hermione's appearance from "a vision," "covered with beauty, and unnatural, unholy," into something "macabre, like lovely horror," reaffirming both her material presence (she is a "horror," not a "vision") and dismissing her threat to the religious order (she is no longer "unholy") and transforming it, instead, into a threat to sense more generally (she is "lovely horror"). The final substitution here tamps down the menacing energy of Hermione's thoughts—they are no longer "writhing" like serpents, but "coiled" instead "in the darkness within her." The threat Hermione presents is no longer one of chaotic energy but one of poised threat.[24]

But if these revisions slightly diminish Victorianism's hold on Hermione's characterization, her villainy surpasses any alterations Lawrence might make. Why, for example, does Lawrence specify the movement of Hermione's hips, a decision that seems to point to her sexual possibilities, if only to shut down their flexibility so completely? More, though, when we get access into people's response to Hermione, we get one of the strangest descriptions of interaction in Lawrence, a description that models the evocative oscillation that marks Lawrentian life: "[p]eople were silent when she passed, impressed, roused, wanting to jeer, yet for some reason silenced." The syntax implies a general positive response as it gets going, people are "impressed" and "roused." But Lawrence revokes that sense with his last term in the sequence—people who encounter Hermione "[want] to jeer" at her. Thus, the middle term, "roused," takes on a dramatically new meaning. Rather that catalyzing desire, Hermione catalyzes anger in her watchers. This "rousing" implies sexual want less than it connects to political excitement. Lawrence's sentence produces a crowd whose encounter with Hermione shifts from desire for her to a desire to supplant her unwelcome authority. If Hermione's characterization connects to the exquisitely masochistic heroines I've discussed in previous chapters, it is in her self-presentation and in her assumption of a distanced, cold demeanor. What's changed, though, is the broader social world's assessment of her masochistic aesthetics—no longer is her rigid self-presentation appealing. Similarly, Hermione's desire to dominate everyone around her, sexual objects and any other person who happens to be in her path, disregards one of the central facets of the masochistic dyad: its closure from the broader social world.

Most of all, though, what is it about Hermione that "silences" the people who want to "jeer" at her? The "silences" that bookend this passage are surprisingly distinct from one another. The first, so proximate to "impressed," implies an awed quiet, one in accord with Hermione's status and position as the "most remarkable woman in the midlands." The second silence carries with it the ghost of a silent jeer that meets Hermione wherever she goes. We hear the muffled residue of these taunts at every subsequent passage that develops Hermione's depiction. We also note that there is a menace in Hermione that forbids the angry jeering she inspires. Status no longer guarantees respect, clearly, but Hermione's disturbing qualities go far beyond those afforded by her social position.

Hermione's particular threat to Lawrentian life appears more clearly if we examine her views on almost any aesthetic or political thought introduced into the novel. John Marx reads Birkin's copy of Hermione's Chinese drawing as modernist, "[abstracting] the object from the domestic context in which he finds it," but I will argue that Hermione's aesthetics are remainders and reminders of masochistic aesthetics.[25] It's clear that Lawrence wants to register a greater investment in Rupert Birkin's worldview than in Hermoine Roddice's, but her placement in the novel links her, and the critique her presence develops, to the masochistic aesthetics I've been discussing. And that relationship—between Hermione's vision of the good life and Birkin's— makes for some of the most combative passages in the novel. For Marx, *Women in Love*'s ideals confirm an almost Hardyan Anglo-primitivism:

> Lawrence weighs in by revising a warning that appeared in mass market and scholarly publications about the point when human beings became over-civilized. Progress was not guaranteed, the argument went, and the very institutions that made British people comfortable tended to make them weak. But degeneration was not inevitable, according to Lawrence. He reasoned that contact with exotic societies had made English culture strong, and that its future lay in capitalizing on a long experience mediating among the world's places, peoples, and things. Instead of ambivalence, he offered his readers conviction that uncovering a repressed but crucial link between home and colony was a promising development. Far from presaging degeneration and national peril, Lawrence portrayed the primitivism of English culture as a sign of renewal. (123–24)

In Marx's view, Lawrence lays out a plan to join aesthetics to politics in a form that supposedly recharges, in an imperial vein, English authority without depending on military might or imperial overthrow. The term that Marx develops, "connoisseurship," emphasizes the curatorial, the aspects of cultural life that work as ballast against the "degeneration" that imperial expansion had apparently wrought on English art. In this view, the characters' retreat from obvious social or political engagement into an aestheticized home life develops a model for politicized connoisseurship. This retreat implies that the proper political frame is, in fact, the domestic one, a move that aligns Lawrence with quietist impulses in the years between the wars. Characters that do not develop these skills fail to thrive. But Marx notably avoids discussion of Hermione's aesthetics. Lawrence's worst connoisseur, she holds a position in this novel removed from but adjacent to Birkin and Ursula's modernist style. Hermione's old-fashioned habits are old-fashioned because they are focused on a domination that looks imperial. The model of this imperial authority draws its strength from its vectored relation to power. Imperialism leans on a growth model; if you aren't increasing power, it's slipping from your grasp. One curious element of this depiction is Hermione's own insistence on her connection to an avant-garde that denies her entrance. Where the sexuality Lawrence approves of is "primitive," dark and internal, Hermione's sexuality is superficial, and intensely orchestrated, and does not give her the access she demands.

But Hermione—one of Lawrence's most-discussed characters, probably owing to the litigious energies of Hermione's real-life avatar, Ottoline Morrell—is not a *general* portrait of a feminist or a New Woman.[26] We should read Lawrence's condemnation of Hermione as a condemnation not of her political views but of her particularly political personality. Hermione is a tyrant. And her tyranny comes from her misunderstanding of how power works. In Lawrence's new world, power is not unidirectional or unchanging. Instead, the characters who are given special privilege in these novels— Ursula, Birkin, to some extent Gudrun—are flexible creatures. Birkin's aggression, especially at the novel's outset, and especially directed toward Ursula and Gerald, is soothed by marriage as much as Ursula's lassitude becomes more concentrated after her marriage. Lawrence connects generative femininity to the generation of new aesthetic ideas. Ursula and Gudrun, both implicated in reproductive plots, are "new" women in ways that Hermione cannot be. Hermione is beholden to the old ways, but the old ways, for Lawrence, are ideas only thirty years past their prime. Lawrence's major complaint about Hermione is her sterility. And, in Lawrence's view, fecundity is not necessarily linked to actual reproduction. While Gudrun's last turn in the first drafts of the novel is toward motherhood, motherhood does not salvage the Brangwen sisters entirely; Lawrence drops the point from the printed manuscript. Or, rather, it's not motherhood—or even the possibility of motherhood—that makes them fecund. The peculiarly Lawrentian fecundity comes from the Brangwens' availability to access many worlds (an access that is, to be sure, troubling at times). What saves Ursula and Gudrun from a fate like Hermione's is the Brangwen sisters' susceptibility to negotiation (and, most beneficially, *principled* negotiation) in relation to their careers, politics, or sexual lives.

Like Gems

I've been making a case for flexible characterization in Lawrence's fiction, that characters' views, social, political, personal, are always already negotiated with the views of the figures that surround them. Unlike most novel characters, Lawrence's people do not move through the events they

encounter in a vectored plot; plot alters and shapes character idiosyncratically, if at all. But this is not to say there is never a progressive vector at work
in Lawrence's form. In these final pages, I will show how Lawrence sketches
his fiction with a spatial and conceptual scaffold. But, importantly, this scaffold does not depend on its content to make meaning. Said another way,
while Lawrence's texts are rife with reference and context, neither of these
elements is at all essential to his novelistic aims. The passage upon which
I want to focus occurs two-thirds of the way through *Women in Love*, in
"Woman to Woman," the chapter that reintroduces Hermione after her rest
cure at Aix. This takes place well after Hermione attacks Birkin with her
lapis lazuli paperweight. While Hermione has been away, Ursula's connection with Birkin has become more intense, and this chapter directly pre-
cedes the erotic core of the novel, "Excurse." Despite her rest cure, Hermione's self, according to Ursula (and one suspects, the narrator) is still "all in
her head" (*Women* 292). Hermione's cerebral habits irk Ursula, and the
narrator dips subtly into Ursula's consciousness to give us her take on Hermione's failings. This passage is worked over in the typescripts, with a
number of Lawrence's revisions altering the allusive frame supporting the
paragraph.

If we separate out the revisions (see figure) into different iterations
(even if these alterations don't lead us to consider each revision a different
version), we see a pattern emerging. The typewritten copy reads:

> Hermione, whom [*sic*] brooded and brooded till she was exhausted with the
> ache of brooding, isolating thought, spent and ashen in her body, who gained
> so slowly and with such effort her hard and gem-like conclusions of knowledge,
> was apt, in the presence of this woman, whom she thought simply female,
> animal, spontaneous, to wear the hard conclusions of her bitter meditations
> like jewels in the esoteric centre of her life. (TS 1, 357)

The handwritten alterations to the typescript lead us to read the text as

> Hermione, who brooded and brooded till she was exhausted with the ache of
> her effort at consciousness, spent and ashen in her body, who gained so slowly
> and with such effort her hard and dead conclusions of knowledge, was apt, in
> the presence of other women, whom she thought simply female, to wear the
> conclusions of her bitter meditations like jewels which conferred on her an
> unquestionable distinction, established her in a higher order of life. (TS 1, 357)

357

and papers, and playing on the piano. Then Ursula arrived. She was

surprised, and very unpleasantly so, to see Hermione, of whom she had

heard nothing for some time.

" It is a surprise to see you," she said.

" Yes," said Hermione - " I've been away at Aix - "

" Oh, for your health?"

" Yes."

The two women looked at each other. Ursula *resented* could not bear Hermione's

long, grave, downward-looking face. There was something of the stupidity

and the unenlightened self-esteem of a horse in it." She's got a horse-

face," Ursula said to herself," she runs between blinkers." It did seem

as if Hermione, like the moon, had only one face turned to the world, *side to her for to her penny. There was no reverse observe.* as

if there were no reverse to the penny. She really ran between blinkers;

She stared staring out all the time on the narrow, but to her complete world of the

achieved consciousness. In the darkness, she did not exist. Like the

moon, one half of life was lost to her. *her was lost to life .* *self* Her life was all in her head,

she did not know what it was, spontaneously to leap with life, *run or move* like a

fish in the water, or a weasel on the grass. She must always know.

But Ursula could not see the pathos of this fate, she could only see *only suffered from Hermione's onesidedness* *only suffered underfelt*

Hermione's self confidence, which seemed to pull her down as nothing; the arrogance of knowledge, Hermione, who brooded and brooded till she

was exhausted with the ache of brooding, isolated thought, *her effort at consciousness,* spent and

ashen in her body, who gained so slowly and with such effort her hard *dead*

and positive conclusions of knowledge, was apt, in the presence of those *other women,*

women, whom she thought simply female, animal, spontaneous, to wear the

hard conclusions of her bitter meditations like jewels which conferred *an unquestionable distinction*

on her an order of higher merit, established her in the esoteric centre *a higher order*

of life. She was apt, mentally, to condescend to woman such as Ursula, *Whom she regarded as*

who were purely emotional. Poor Hermione, it was her one stronghold. *possession*

Typescript 1, volume 5. D. H. Lawrence, *Women in Love,* box 26, folder 2, p. 357.
Harry Ransom Center, The University of Texas at Austin.

And the final version, the one printed in the Cambridge edition, reads:

> Hermione, who brooded and brooded till she was exhausted with the ache of
> her effort at consciousness, spent and ashen in her body, who gained so slowly
> and with such effort her final and barren conclusions of knowledge, was apt, in
> the presence of other women, whom she thought simply female, to wear the

conclusions of her bitter assurance like jewels which conferred on her an unquestionable distinction, established her in a higher order of life. (292)

First, we might consider this passage in relation to the conversation between Birkin and Hermione from "Class-room," in which Birkin strongly
criticizes Hermione's adoption of what she claims is an "animal" vitalism.
On the one hand, some adjustments, such as erasing the term "animal"
from Hermione's assessment of Ursula, pull this characterization more in
line with the version of Hermione we've already come to know. By cutting
this qualifier, Lawrence leaves Hermione's character to engage in her self-
deluded version of "animal" vitality while characterizing her objection to
Ursula as related to her perception of Ursula's "femaleness."

But, on the other hand, there are some adjustments, to the allusive ground
of the passage, that both sharpen Lawrence's analyses of Victorian aesthetics and art while also disguising these complaints as personal to Hermione.
Among the alterations is one that all Victorianists will immediately recognize.
In the typescript revisions, Lawrence changes the adjectives qualifying Hermione's conclusions from "hard and gem-like," to "hard and dead." By the time
the novel is printed, though, Lawrence has reworked this phrase to "final and
barren conclusions." Along the way, we see one immediate substitution (of
"dead" for "gem-like") and a slower substitution ("hard" exists in both the
typescript and the holograph alterations Lawrence makes to that typescript).
In changing "hard" to "final," Lawrence exchanges a word referring to the quality of Hermione's conclusions to one signaling their temporal status. This
alteration locates Hermione's conclusions not only in terms of their internal
attributes or logics but also in terms of plotted time. "Final" refers both to her
conclusions' significance as signals of an ending (these are the last conclusions
Hermione will draw) and also to their certainty or doneness.

But this is not the most important alteration in the revisions. Over the
course of the typescript revisions, "gem-like" becomes "dead," which becomes, finally, "barren." "Gem-like" is an especially loaded word. If Tennyson
used it (in *Idylls*), Pater made it famous in his conclusion to *The Renaissance*,
the text that more than any piece of nineteenth-century aesthetic criticism
disconnected the work of art from morality. "Not the fruit of experience, but
experience itself, is the end," writes Pater. Then, "[t]o burn always with this
hard, gem-like flame, to maintain this ecstasy, is success in life" (188–89).[27]
The aim of the Paterian artist was to access "vital forces" in the present, to

fully, somatically engage with the world. And, to return to the passage from "Class-room," we find that Lawrence undergirds Birkin's aesthetic theory with this point. Again, Birkin's complaint of Hermione is that she speaks of this access to the vital real without actually having any experience that would denote true access. The printed edition of the book is absent the explicit Paterian chime of "gem-like." In its place, "barren" evokes not simply the death of the intermediate qualifier, "dead," but a version of deathliness connected explicitly to reproduction. It is a word most clearly connected to a woman's failure to produce a child. Earlier, I suggested that Lawrence connects new aesthetic ideas to a feminine generation that is not synonymous with childbirth. Here, we see an extension of that claim, with a twist. If we imagine the middle term as the term that encapsulates both "gem-like" and "barren," we might begin to see a connection between misreading Pater— that is, reading Pater for his fashionableness, not his argument—and sterility. Lawrence shows us, in the allusion to Hermione's forced Paterian life, a direct trajectory from foolishly adopting a principle you have no intention of living to conceptual, if not actual, sterility. And, given the emphasis on the fulfillment borne of generative life—Ursula's potential childbearing or Gudrun's sculptural work—we see Hermione as fully mistaken in her insistence that principle and concept are the grounds upon which character is built. Hermione's failure, then, is one of experience, even when she limply rests her principles on an aesthetics that demands experience. To circle back to the passage with which this chapter opened, Lawrence has transmuted Hermione's "hard, gem-like conclusions" into the actual hard gem she uses earlier in the novel: the "jewel stone" with which she strikes Birkin at Breadalby (*Women* 105). Thinking obliquely, the lapis lazuli is an allotrope of these now-hidden dead gems. And those hidden dead gems may, in fact, be allotropes of Ursula and Gudrun's stockings—"*Aren't* they jewels!"—a late symbol, in their blend of jewel-like surety of color and soft, silken flexibility, of the sisters' vital companionability even in the face of sincere political and social differences (436).

It must be said that Lawrence's vision of vitalism is vehemently anti-Pater.[28] Lawrence's version of Pater, for good or ill, is a writer dedicated to fixing living matter in place, on freezing vital life so that one might examine and relish its beauty.[29] While it's also likely that Lawrence's objections to Pater and Paterian aestheticism had much to do with his own ambivalent (to say the least) views about male homosexuality, his main complaint about Pater's vitalism appears to center on decadence's apparent desire to fix experience in preserving amber. The language of fixity will be familiar by now, but, to this concept of frozen or fixed action, Lawrence adds his own concept of consummation: in Lawrence's preface, the end of sexual congress, the orgasm, is implicated in decadent vitalism's desire for perfect, or "exquisite," form. In his short preface to his 1920 poems, Lawrence explains the dangers of this now old-fashioned kind of vitalism:

> The poetry of the beginning and the poetry of the end must have that exqui-site finality, perfection which belongs to all that is far off. It is the realm of all that is perfect. It is of the nature of all that is complete and consummate. The completeness, this consummateness, the finality and the perfection are con-veyed in exquisite form: the perfect symmetry, the rhythm which returns upon itself like a dance where the hands link and loosen and link for the supreme moment of the end. Perfected bygone moments, perfected moments in the glim-mering futurity, these are the treasured gem-like lyrics of Shelley and Keats.
>
> But there is another kind of poetry: the poetry of that which is at hand: the immediate present. In the immediate present there is no perfection, no consum-mation, nothing finished. The strands are all flying, quivering, intermingling into the web, the waters are shaking the moon. There is no round, consum-mate moon on the face of the running water, nor on the face of the unfinished tide. There are no gems of the living plasm. The living plasm vibrates unspeak-ably, it inhales the future, it exhales the past, it is the quick of both, and yet it is neither. There is no plasmic finality, nothing crystal, permanent. If we try to fix the living tissue, as the biologists fix it with formation, we have only a hard-ened bit of the past, the bygone life under our observation. (ii–iii)[30]

The immediacy that Lawrence wants "the poetry of the present" to reflect is distinguished from the frozen or fixed "gems" of the poetry of the past or future. Once poetry tips into comment about time's passage, it begins to imagine a wholeness (a "consummation") that could be described, catego-rized, and "treasured." In this short essay, we see Lawrence decoupling the category of bound movement from aesthetic beauty. He separates quivering life from exquisite objects. In Lawrence's view, as soon as we begin to con-cretize or crystalize an aesthetic object, we harden its quivering vitalism into something final. Counter to the plasm or running flame Lawrence evokes throughout this essay, crystalline gems have had their vital energies dimin-ished: buzzing stasis no longer has any appeal.

But all of this is lost in the final version of the passage. We must sense the gems set throughout Lawrence's novel by another means. Hermione's problem is relegated to the personal—her aesthetic training, her aesthetic categories are seen as nothing more than personal failings. And while Lawrence's characters frequently rail against Victorian moral standards, we here see a Lawrence who simultaneously adopts the pose of a Victorian aesthetic and criticizes that pose. By so doing, Lawrence offers us the possibility that Hermione is, actually, not a poor reader of Pater. And if she is a proper reader of Pater, Hermione's failings show us it's time for something new. As I've suggested already, Hermione is the character most explicitly tied to the version of masochism I've been charting throughout this book. She is imperious and domineering, and she expects fealty from the people who surround her. And, as we've seen in Catherine Earnshaw, Glencora Palliser, and Sue Bridehead, dominant women have a vexed relationship with generation. In all of the novels I've treated, women's relationships to sexual pain have a complex, usually negative, relation to their status as mothers. But Lawrence's view makes this connection more pronounced. Not only is Hermione here a "barren" figure because her sexual life can produce no children, but by embedding a ligature to Victorian aesthetic ideals in his initial formulations— specifically, to the centrality of immediate accessibility to aesthetic truth— Lawrence suggests there is a connection between masochism and aesthetic death. In the nineteenth century, masochism was the aesthetic shore upon which a refugee from reproductive futurity might find herself. But, by Lawrence's moment, we see masochism, typified by Hermione Roddice, fully, and irrevocably, connected to death. If the Victorian masochist was given an outlet, into aesthetic life, the Edwardian masochist had no such sanctuary. But she did have sex—actual, represented, diegetic sex.

Public Sex

As might be clear, there are lots of ways that what Lawrence prescribes for sexual life is limiting and strange. And, as I've suggested, Kate Millet and Christopher Craft are just two of the many critics whose observations about what is and is not allowed in Lawrentian sexual life offer corrections to his admittedly masculinist and heterosexist vision. But what I am marking out here is his interest in divesting sexual life from social and political frames as a way of salvaging sexual life's dislocating, unequivocal weirdness. In other words, Lawrence anticipates a disarticulation of sex (acts) from sexuality (organizing concept). What this moment shows us, once and for all, is how the language the novel uses for sexual life, words like "lightning," "bliss," "consummation," is always already metaphorical. Over the course of his career, Lawrence realizes he has to name names if he's going to dislocate sexual life from disciplinary bounds. The problem, of course, is that metaphor itself has an alternative capacity to dislocate, one that generates some of the most evocative scenes of sexual description in Lawrence.

It is this realization that spurs him on, in *Lady Chatterley's Lover*, his last finished novel, to use intimate, some might say obscene, words to name the actions and body parts of his characters. "What is cunt," Connie asks. To which Mellors replies, "An' doesn't ter know? Cunt! It's thee down theer; an' what I get when I'm i'side thee—an' what tha gets when I'm i'side thee—it's a' as it is—all on't!" (178).[31] Connie's ungrammatical question highlights the strangeness of Mellors's response. The capaciousness of the term is impressive—in Mellors's view, the meaning of "cunt" can include reference to both his and Connie's genitals, to the experience of sex itself, as well as the particular kind of achievement one partner gets from sex with the other: "what I get when I'm i'side thee." Mellors's explanation highlights the political power expletive has in *Lady Chatterley*, but it also draws attention to how conceptually fungible explicit language is for the characters who use it. The Lawrentian sexual revolution hinges on naming parts and actions but not exactly acts. (Things enter other things, body parts get named, and, through all of this, obscenity gains traction. But Lawrence never says, "This scene is a scene of anal sex.") Instead, the scenes themselves emphasize bodily interaction, while characters' discussion of events allows a different kind of explicitness to reign. Here is Lawrence's most widely discussed sex scene:

> It was a night of sensual passion, in which she was a little startled, and almost unwilling: yet pierced again with piercing thrills of sensuality, different, sharper, more terrible than the thrills of tenderness, but, at the moment, more desirable. Though a little frightened, she let him have his way, and the reckless, shameless sensuality shook her to her foundations, stripped her to the very last, and made a different woman of her. It was not really love. It was not voluptuousness. It was sensuality sharp and searing as fire, burning the soul to timber. (*Lady Chatterley* 246)

This passage slightly blends two kinds of explicit description. The dominant mode is hermeneutic ("thrills of tenderness," "her last," "foundations," "burning the soul to timber"). Lawrence limits the relational language to verbs: Connie is "pierced again." The imbalance between the descriptive strategies here demonstrates the difficulty in incorporating relational description into scenes, even though the language that makes up relational description relies on verbs and prepositions, words that mark out the actual placement and movement of bodies in an act. "Pierce" is itself a tricky word: it describes the act evoked here, Mellors anally penetrates Connie, but it has a metaphoric tinge to it, reminding the reader, perhaps, of cupid's arrow, of penetrations of all kinds.

A bit before this central scene, Mellors explains his marriage to Bertha Coutts to Connie:

> "Well, I married her, and she wasn't bad. Those other 'pure' women had nearly taken all the balls out of me, but she was all right that way. She wanted me, and made no bones about it. And I was as pleased as punch. That was what I wanted: a woman who *wanted* me to fuck her. So I fucked her a good un." (*Lady Chatterley* 201)

What's striking here is the scene's relational method. Mellors relies on an explicit verb, "fuck," to explain his married actions. And this conversational transparency becomes central to the functional power of Connie's relationship with the gamekeeper. Other characters don't fare as well under this new, transparent regime. In a letter to Connie, Ivy Bolton, Clifford's nurse, writes about Mellors's former treatment of Bertha: "[she] goes about saying the most awful things about him, how he has women at the cottage, and how he behaved to her when they were married, the low, beastly things he did to her, and I don't know what all" (263). "Low" and "beastly" are more euphemistic than hermeneutic, though they share some resemblance to the vague dazzlement of Connie's sexual awakening. Mellors's interest in anality is, in Ivy's eyes, something that connects him to animals. The logic of this observation isn't surprising, but, in a novel where characters like Mellors and Connie can talk about penises, cunts, and fucks, Ivy's euphemism stands out as conceptually impoverished. As old fashioned.

Lawrence's achievement is his simultaneous use of two oppositional representational strategies, the hermeneutic and the metaphorical, within one novel. More, that his most-loved characters, the features of the text wherein Lawrentian value might be said to reside, use both modes to explain sex's importance to them, and to describe the same kind of act performed at different times with different partners, that is to say, performed differently. And each example of each act has a discrete character within the frame of Lawrence's novel. It's true that there is a strange lag between the kind of depiction that can describe an act as it unfolds and a portrayal used to describe an act that has passed, but what's striking, and what I want to linger on as I end, is that in *Lady Chatterley* both regimes can be used fluidly by the same character. By showcasing Connie's and Mellors's descriptive capacities, Lawrence presents an implicit criticism of characters like Ivy Bolton, characters whose dependence on euphemism cannot expand to include expletive. Not because expletive is necessary but because the tension between the descriptive systems is. It is only by using both systems idiosyncratically that a space can open within description to evaluate each act on its own terms instead of organizing it into a hierarchy of activity or a categorical list. But the characters the novel most values, Mellors and Connie, use both kinds of description *in order that they might have* sexual conversations.

In *Lady Chatterley*, Lawrence's descriptive technology borrows from two widely adopted representational regimes. This exposes what can only be called a descriptive dialectic. And it is this dialectic that if it allows kinds of sex experience to be untethered from kinds of acts, also allows the space between marriage and sex to be made visible, exposing an important gap between the world of exchange and the world of sense. Lawrence's simultaneous deployment of both strategies shows there are ways of understanding a marriage plot that don't rely on evaluative assessments: Connie's relationship with Mellors is neither good nor bad; it is only human, by which I mean animal. It might seem like this final point argues for the ascendency of relational description, but the force of expletive needs the seductive confusion of the hermeneutic to approach the strangeness of lived experience. Sex, it turns out, always needs metaphor, always needs translation. And it needs it most when it's called most clearly by its name.

Conclusion

How to Read Exquisitely

One of the major difficulties with reading is that one must learn to inhabit a world in which something that pains you can also bring you great pleasure. In a special issue of *Representations*, Sharon Marcus and Stephen Best argue for a turn to "surface reading" to reinvigorate, and theorize, that pleasure. Much of what Marcus and Best argue for chimes with what I have said about the relationship between history and literary criticism, although Marcus and Best focus on the connection between radical progress and the literary critical sphere. They argue, "Criticism that valorizes the freedom of the critic has often assumed that an adversarial relation to the object of criticism is the only way for the critic to free himself from the text's deceptive, ideological surface and uncover the truth that the text conceals" (16–17).[1] In other words, one of the dangers of a politically minded criticism is its tendency to downplay or ignore formal and aesthetic qualities when a work's politics are suspect. In Trollope's case, for instance, his novels' investments in landed, embedded Englishness can make it difficult to perceive the volatile, cosmopolitan characters and plotlines at his novels' peripheries. But, more than that, his apparent conservatism makes it very difficult to notice these volatilities without assuming—or fantasizing—that their presence gives the reader access to Trollope's true radical within. Of course, the radicals in Trollope's novels are part of his representational strategy, one that can be fully appreciated only when we come to see the sincerity *and* the skepticism about Liberalism blended in his narrative voice.

By imagining that our first responses to a literary text must be either affiliation or rejection, we limit the complexity of our response to a literary object. In this I agree with Marcus and Best, who write that their aim in developing surface reading as a practice is "to suggest that there might be ways of studying culture that would neither attack nor defend it." But does their solution to this problem work? They continue, "[We propose] that rather than evaluate culture as masterworks of genius or documents of barbarism, we instead define what is unique about the disciplines that study culture [as] their interest in human artifacts, in contrast to the sciences, which focus on processes beyond our creation and control" (17). This sounds a lot like Susan Sontag's plea against "Interpretation," in which she suggests that description might be a more laudable critical aim than plumbing a text for "meaning" (9).[2] But both of these arguments, offered decades apart, point to the difficulty in articulating a criticism that feels politically engaged and literarily accurate.

Sometimes, our jobs are politically simple. For instance, when we read Emily Brontë's vision of love's brutality, we can't help but feel sorrow for a world in which such violence can be unremarkable because institutionalized. Because we sympathize with Isabella's plight at Heathcliff's hands, we also sympathize with Brontë's depictions, which is, in part, to expose the brutality to which all wives are subjected. *Wuthering Heights* uses a calculatedly vicious example to draw attention to the violence of the norm, and it is a norm we readers also reject. But for novelists like Trollope and Lawrence, the critic finds her job more difficult. These novelists clearly don't condemn violence and cruelty, and contemporary readers find their positions hard to parse. Should we not condemn violence and brutality, especially when it is leveled against those whose positions are precarious? Or can we imagine a progressive criticism in which political failures may be acknowledged but that trains its explanatory energy on formal qualities?

These kinds of difficulties have become, in the past decades, easy to dismiss as formal or technical insufficiency: the reason Lawrence is so objectionable is that he is a bad—especially a lazy—writer. The reason Trollope is boring is he wrote too quickly. But in neither example is this the case, or is it precisely the case. Lawrence's manuscripts show a writer struggling with revision, working out his sentence's rhythms and his novel's plots. And though Trollope's ideas about revision don't correspond to our own, it is not necessarily the case that revision alone produces formal complexity. One can write complexly on a strict timetable. So, have these authors' politics become a good excuse for ignoring their forms?

The first thing we miss when we read primarily for politics is the formal invention that writers can and do produce when they are building a world from words. The second thing we miss, and this may be more significant, is the way that even a relatively clearly spoken politics may be sharply at odds with the literary object a writer produces. For example, Trollope's conservatism is most easily secured by reading his *Autobiography*. In that text, the author roundly criticizes the characters the contemporary reader might most like—Madame Max, Lizzie Eustace, even Lady Glencora Palliser are all cut down to size, whereas the Roger Carburys and Planty Palls of the world are elevated as prime examples of the English imperial gentleman. This is only part of the picture. One of the great benefits of the realist novel is its desire to reflect an entire representational world. This means that though a novelist might, indeed, play favorites, she still must represent things that don't accord with her political or social aims. More than this, as readers, we have the freedom to read against our own political perspectives when we read fiction. Do we lose anything by turning novels and poems into machines made of words, not worlds made of words?

Reading against one's political perspective has not been a particularly laudable aim over the last few decades in literary criticism. And much of the personal justification for reading and writing about literature of the past comes from a sense that such careful study will yield contemporary political spoils. But what aspects of literary texts do we miss when we focus on the political? Description offers us one example of a kind of prose fictional technique that can be difficult to read within political frameworks. In *The Antinomies of Realism*, Fredric Jameson dilates on Emile Zola's descriptive catalogs, which pad out the dire plots of his novels with visceral, charged detail.[3] But, Jameson suggests, these catalogues are not simply doing the work of the real: they aren't just there to present us with the world in all its dense, vital material. Instead, while the lists give name to objects with intense precision—a fish head here, a slinking eel there—they, says Jameson, disarticulate the verbal from the visual, pressing with an "ecstatic dizziness" onto the reader. Jameson continues:

> The unexpected result is that far from enriching representational language with all kinds of new meanings, the gap between words and things is heightened; perceptions turn into sensations; words no longer take on a body as prey to its nameless experience. Finally the realm of the visual begins to separate

from that of the verbal and conceptual and to float away in a new kind of autonomy. Precisely this autonomy will create the space for affect: just as the gradual enfeeblement of named emotions and the words for them opened up a new space in which the unrepresentable and unnameable affects can colonize and make their own. (54–55)

Like Jameson, we are often perplexed by what it is critics should do with patches of dense description. As critics, description often seems to get in our way. It is, after all, not plot; indeed, it may slow us down or even throw us off plot's path. Nor is it, exactly, character, though it often does the work of telling us everything we need to know about one. Passages of description, bright and enticing though they may be, feel like places where an author gets carried away, describing a room or dress with details that seem extraneous, excessive, and sumptuary. Such passages can be difficult to explain. As I suggested at this book's outset, we might marshal a historical account of descriptive prose, connecting discrete elements to a specific aesthetic mode—that detail is indicative of Decadence, this other one, of Anglo-Catholicism. Sometimes, descriptive passages signal an author's aesthetic investments or her cultural allegiances—we can tell what side of an aesthetic debate an author found herself on by noticing the kinds of wall-hangings or sofas with which she decorated her imaginary rooms. But how do we explain the ways description works formally, especially description about characters and their interactions? How do we explain the way description slows down narrative time, forcing us to read slowly, with careful attention to sensation and space? Why is it that a passage of description can often feel like a turning point in a novel, even when nothing happens—nothing that could be called an action or an event, in any case?

There are ways to unlock descriptive pileups—methods, like those I've used in this book, that don't look to, say, the uses of ferns in nineteenth-century Parisian home furnishing but instead look to similar scenes, other such clots of thick description. Zola offers a perfect example of the appeal of these scenes, his novels thick with excessive detail. These scenes feel overdone, with each instance of finer and finer exactitude pushing the power of descriptive prose further and further afield from representation into something like abstraction. In *The Kill* (*La Curée*), for instance, Zola writes of the piquant pleasures experienced by two characters embarking on an incestuous affair:

They spent a night of passion. Renée was the man, the ardent, active partner. Maxime remained submissive. Smooth limbed, slim, and graceful as a Roman stripling, fair-haired and pretty, stricken in his virility since childhood, this epicene creature became a girl in Renée's arms. He seemed born and bred for perverted sensual pleasure. Renée enjoyed her domination, bending to her will this creature of indeterminate sex. For her this relationship brought continued experiments, new sensations, strange feelings of uneasiness and keen enjoyment. She was no longer certain: she felt doubts each time she returned to his delicate skin, his soft neck, his attitudes of abandonment, his fainting fits. She then experienced an hour of repletion. By revealing to her new forms of ecstasy, Maxime crowned her mad outfits, her prodigious luxury, her life of excess. He ingrained into her flesh the high-pitched note already singing in her ears. He was a lover who matched the follows and fashions of the age. This pretty young man, whose frail figure could be seen by his clothes, this effeminate creature that strolled along the boulevards, his hair parted in the middle, with little bursts of laugher and bored smiles, became in Renée's hands one of the most corrupting, decadent influences that, at certain periods among rotten nations, lead to the exhaustion of the body and the unhinging of the brain. (158)[4]

In this scene, erotic power and its role reversal are obvious centers of the narrative attention, but Zola's description also borrows from categories that might elude our notice if we weren't reading him alongside other writers. With its emphases on both the neurasthenic destruction that hedonism brings and the precision of the aesthetic choices Maxime and Renée make, this passage reads as a more explicit version of the British masochism I have described in this book. What's more remarkable about this passage, though, is that Zola tells us the pair is incestuous in the first chapter, a point that alters the force of these later, descriptive revelations, which continue to describe Maxime and Renée's encounter, in almost excruciating detail, in Renée's hothouse. There is no way this passage offers a surprise about the plot or a revelation about these characters. So what is it doing here? Considering the passage's structural uselessness, this is the kind of description I have called, at various points, "dense," "thick," or "decadent": it is hard to parse and difficult to understand as anything other than indulgent, virtuosic language.

While the last term—"decadent"—is often used to denote the specific, cosmopolitan Aesthetic movement that culminated in the late part of the nineteenth century, in the texts I have treated, the word evokes the clotted, sensual passages that come from describing textures and surfaces in great detail. Decadence signals the material, sensual frames upon which masochistic scenes play out—descriptions of clothing, furniture, ambient light, scent, and physical sensation all contribute to the overwhelming atmosphere that such scenes demand. For the Zola passage above, plants, described in vivid detail, become metaphors for the lovers' bodies, but, more than that, they become beacons that warn the lovers of the dangers their excesses will produce. The language here fixes the material world Zola describes, not the figurative world Zola writes. His heavy use of noun and adjective combinations develops the description by employing more concrete elements, which creates a suffocating atmosphere while also minimizing the action of the scene. Like many scenes of exquisite masochism, not much moves in Renée's hothouse. Stasis breeds its own kind of enticements.

Perverse Formalism

In thinking about the method of reading I have argued for in this book, I've had recourse to some reading habits developed in conversation with vastly different texts. Angus Fletcher's concept of the "daemonic agent," although drawn from explicitly allegorical texts, helps explain how descriptive scenes might relate to the novel's more obvious structural engines, like character and plot: "[w]hatever area these abstract ideas come from, these [daemonic] agents give a sort of life to intellectual conceptions; they may not actually create a personality before our eyes, but they do create a semblance of personality" (25–26).[5] Fletcher's account, which connects a symbolic mode to the creation of character, may explain why masochistic tableaux produce such an eerie feeling in the reader. The realist framework upon which the novel is drawn expects a relationship between a character's interior thoughts and feelings and his or her action—that psychological experience has some bearing on the story that develops. In these narrative environments, the masochistic tableau feels slightly out of place. In passages like the ones I've discussed in this book, when representations of plot and the life of the mind are diminished, the realist mechanisms that guide stories toward their endings halt, and developed character flattens into something like symbolic character. Masochistic tableaux have the capacity to function as what Fletcher calls "allegorical machines" (53–57), hovering in the interstices between representation and symbol. This isn't to say masochistic characters don't have interiors. More, that in these moments—in which plot and context drop away and the pair acts in a kind of ritualized scene—interior isn't central, embodiment is. This has the added effect of making the contours of the masochistic scene—whatever aesthetic or sartorial elements with which the dyad has chosen to upholster its fantasy—take on symbolic meaning and produce a sense of conceptual wholeness. The masochistic scene has the flavor of idealized perfection. These are some of the reasons that masochistic tableaux feel more connected to symbol than to story or character.

Michael Clune puts a similar point into different terms: "[t]ime is fully spatialized" by writers in an effort to arrest readerly perceptions and "[plunge the reader] into a different perceptual matrix" (25).[6] "The Kantian aesthetic object," Clune writes, "is not simply that which produces an immediate sense of perpetual vitality in me. It is also the object which I *sense* as having the capacity to *extend* this vitality" (40, Clune's emphasis). The aestheticized scene thus has the capacity not only to freeze time within its frame but also to give insight to the reader into how she might extend that frozen attitude into her life. When considered in light of Clune's claims, masochistic tableaux work as art objects writ small within the novel. It is no mistake that these scenes are often the most aestheticized in any given novel. By virtue of their static presentation, they force greater readerly attention to their constitutive elements—that is, to form. These are passages that might drift below readerly notice in part because the most obvious devices of novelistic form—plot development and contextual character—drop away, and instead features that we more readily associate with allegory and poetry—potent, symbolic description—rise to the textual surface.

Literary history has too often been beholden to history first and literature second. But the best reason to read novels is because they are aesthetic gems to be held up for our pleasure and interpretation. At least since Sontag's "Against Interpretation," these two values can feel opposed in literary criticism: interpretation has to do with a text's content or meaning, while pleasure can, in Sontag's terms, truly come only from avoiding interpretive impulses, in reading with an immersion in what she calls "form." She writes, "Interpretation takes the sensory experience of art for granted, and proceeds from there" (13). The concern here, in Sontag's view, is that interpretation—pulling apart texts for meaning—limits the sensory enjoyment we can take in them, not by dismissing it but by normalizing it. This, again according to Sontag, limits the truly radicalizing experiences that an engagement with art can bring. But her definition of meaning is quite narrow: "[f]or decades now, literary critics have understood it to be their task to translate the elements of the poem or play or novel or story into something else." That "something else" is meaning—a method that unlocks the images or symbols or history in a novel or poem and translates them into something understandable. What I have tried to do in this book is to interpret form. While there are historical and symbolic similarities between many of the scenes I've discussed, the central factor that makes these scenes masochistic is their shape, their form. I have described the formal scaffold that structures these scenes, that makes them similar, and, by so doing, to explain, in part, why they cause difficulty for or anxiety about interpretation. Interpreting the relationships between characters is as valid an aim as interpreting the characters themselves. We can unlock the aesthetic markers that explain what kind of character Sue Bridehead is, and we can think about the marriage law that leads Glencora Palliser to consider her options, but these analyses don't land on what makes Sue's clinch with Jude or Glencora's dance with Burgo so evocative and weird. But formal analyses can.

I understand that there is, at its core, a perversity to my method. Usually, a perverse reading is one that is illogical, contrary, foolish, or wrong. But there is another way to read perversely. To read not just against the grain (as we are all taught to do) but against what counts as reason, against what counts as evidence. In my readings, I have not looked to the political or cultural matter that prompted the authors to write in the ways they did, though there is value in that project. Nor have I assumed that that these novels' central value lies in showing contemporary readers how nineteenth-century people understood the complex institutional medium in which they lived, though there is value in that project, too. Instead, I have argued that the novel offers special kinds of evidence—aesthetic evidence, formal evidence— that present us with more modest argumentative spoils. To return for a moment to "Surface Reading": in "[trying] to describe texts accurately" (16), Best and Marcus leave open the forms that accuracy can take. Again, this call reminds me of Sontag's plea for description to make a viable return to criticism (13), but is description alone enough to counteract symptomatic reading, no matter how careful that description may be? As I've been suggesting, this book reads not only the elements that appear on a text's surface but also elements that barely warrant the name. The scenes I've described as "exquisitely masochistic" read very differently depending on which author writes them, which poses a problem for any reading that looks for evidence made manifest. And this, in turn, puts a lot of pressure on the hunt for inchoate elements, for atmosphere and feeling, to help the critic identify sites of interest. If both depth reading and surface reading imagine an ideal world in which, armed with, respectively, either enough research or enough text, any critic could fruitfully approach a novel, what I am describing here works differently. And, some might say, what I am calling perverse formalism will not work for everyone.

I've been arguing for an interpretive mode that develops from form. Caroline Levine makes a case for a capacious definition of form, one that sutures together the political and the aesthetic, arguing that one may be "nested inside" the other, "and that each is capable of disturbing the other's organizing powers (16–17).[7] I agree that by considering these two kinds of forms as separate, we limit the ways we understand aesthetic life to alter and ramify in political life, and we particularly ignore the ways political and aesthetic forms tend not to alter in smoothly rational, uncomplicated ways (Levine 46). Too often when the political becomes the root cause of and rationale for inquiry into the aesthetic, we do a disservice to the power the aesthetic has. But, even in this view, there is an authority granted to the political that the aesthetic has very little chance of resisting. There should be space to conceive of form to the side of the political, too. Such interpretation does not demand that the critic forms an ethical or political attachment to or detachment from a text, just that she forms a readerly attachment to the text. And it may seem flimsy and untethered from the real; but its flexibility, its critical lightness, allows formal interpretation to do heavy conceptual work. So the interpretations I've given offer insight not into how to read these novels historically but into how to read these novels. We must read as Dorothea reads, "under a new current of feeling," in the bright moment before she tips back into doctrine, back into history: "How very beautiful these gems are!" (13).[8] But we must not mistake an interpretation of a jewel's beauty for complacency. Interpretation allows us to see a lapidary object for what it is: something beautiful, but something carefully made, as well. We must read like Gudrun and Ursula read their stockings, with unhinged joy: "*Aren't* they jewels! *Aren't* they lambs!" (Lawrence 436, Lawrence's emphasis).[9]

Close, formal attention to literary objects yields knowledge, but how do we understand that knowledge? This knowledge is necessarily partial and limited. It is not knowledge about the world or about history. It is not knowledge about what we usually call "truth," in that it is not truth about the world. But it is truth, nevertheless. This knowledge may not be fully extractable or portable. Reading perversely may not tell us much about how most women in nineteenth-century England encountered marriage law. It might not tell us how most people of the period understood the risks attendant in premarital sex or how they understood love or jealousy. But each novel I have treated here gives us an instance of how one person might encounter these kinds of problems. Characters are not people, and novels are not worlds, but they are examples of how one man or one woman imagined worlds might be. They are exercises in thought, arranged in patterns and forms as a poem is. And perverse reading can produce a scansion, so we might better be able to read the meter a novel can beat.

Notes

Preface

1. Joss Marsh discusses the development of explicit language in *Word Crimes* (Chicago: U of Chicago P, 1998). The story Marsh tells, of changes in novelistic representations of blasphemy, is connected to a similar development in novels that detail explicit sexual acts. Detailing the power transparent representation gave to Hardy's most (sexually and religiously) explicit novel, Marsh writes, "In short, *Jude the Obscure* commits blasphemy with a vengeance that can have left the perpetrator in no doubt, despite his disclaimers, of the full stop it would put to his fiction career. The *Pall Mall Gazette*'s outraged summary of the action—'dirt, drivel, and damnation' (Lerner and Holstrom 111)—was not mere glib alliteration but a grimly accurate picture of the blasphemous text that closed the book on Victorian fiction, and opened readers' eyes to the shock of the modernist new" (170–71).

2. Elsie Michie's *The Vulgar Question of Money: Heiresses, Materialism and the Novel of Manners from Jane Austen to Henry James* (Baltimore: Johns Hopkins UP, 2011) describes one potent symbol of this threat, the wealthy woman. For Michie, the figure of the wealthy woman is positioned against the poor, virtuous woman as a way of developing the novel's broad investments in good character and demonstrable self-worth.

3. Emily Brontë, *Wuthering Heights*, ed. Richard J. Dunn (New York: Norton, 2003),

4. The *Oxford English Dictionary* definitions of "exquisite" include exquisite torture, "elaborately described," and exquisite qualities, which can be good or bad but which are "cultivated to a high degree of intensity; consummate, extreme." The sixth definition reads, "Of pain, pleasure, etc.: Intense, acute, keen." *OED Online* (Oxford University Press, December 12, 2014 <http://dictionary.oed.com/>).

Chapter 1. Making Scenes

1. The central text on the relationship between the marriage plot and the novel form is Nancy Armstrong's *Desire and Domestic Fiction: A Political History of the Novel* (Oxford: Oxford UP, 1987). Armstrong explains this shift: "Literature devoted to producing the domestic woman thus appeared to ignore the political world run by men. Of the female alone did it presume to say that neither birth nor the accouterments of title and status accurately represented the individual; only the more subtle nuances of behavior indicated what one was really worth. In this way, writing for and about the female introduced a whole new vocabulary for social relations, terms that attached precise moral value to certain qualities of mind" (4). Tony Tanner's *Adultery in the Novel: Contract and Transgression* (Baltimore: Johns Hopkins UP, 1979) draws attention to the way the novel shifts, in the eighteenth century, from representing "potentially disruptive or socially unstabilized energy that may threaten, directly or implicitly, the organization of society" toward a focus on marriage "and the securing of genealogical continuity" (3–4). One of the side effects, Tanner claims, is that

the marriage plot then begins to "gain its particular urgency from an energy that threatens to contravene [the] stability of the family upon which society depends," an energy from adulterous threats to the marital order (4).

2. Lawrence Stone's *The Family, Sex and Marriage in England 1500–1800* (London: Penguin, 1990) details this as a historical shift. Perhaps the central novel of the period, George Eliot's *Middlemarch* (1871–72), is, among other things, an extended rumination on what misery marital mistakes can bring.

3. To give a few examples of pertinent events, this period loosely covers the destruction of the law of coverture with a series of acts designed to stabilize women's equality in and around the institution of marriage. For example, the Custody of Infants Acts in 1839 and 1873 allowed for maternal contact with and care of minor children in the case of divorce or separation; the Matrimonial Causes Act of 1857 allowed divorce through courts instead of private act of Parliament; the Married Women's Property Acts of 1870 and 1882 (and the 1874 amendment to the 1870 act) eventually allowed married women to own and control property after marriage. Finally, in 1918 women over thirty were given the vote, and in 1928 this right was extended to all women over twenty-one. Stephanie Coontz's *Marriage, a History: How Love Conquered Marriage* (New York: Penguin, 2006) offers an eminently readable history of the major alterations in marriage.

4. Emily Brontë, *Wuthering Heights*, ed. Richard J. Dunn (New York: Norton, 2003); D. H. Lawrence, *Women in Love* (New York: Penguin Classics, 2007).

5. Also in this period, protofeminism's investment in dislodging the rule of coverture and its attendant inequalities gives way to agitation for women's suffrage. As legal changes disbanded coverture (the legal and financial primacy of men after marriage) over much of the nineteenth century, an aesthetic focus on the cultural aftereffects remained. For an evocative account of these aftereffects, see Ablow's *The Marriage of Minds: Reading Sympathy in the Victorian Marriage Plot* (Stanford: Stanford UP, 2007).

6. Anthony Trollope, *Phineas Redux* (Oxford: Oxford UP, 1983).

7. From Anthony Trollope, *Phineas Finn* (Oxford: Oxford UP, 1973). All subsequent references are to this edition.

8. For an excellent account of the geographic specificity of Phineas's parliamentary ambitions, see Elaine Hadley's "The Irishness of Liberal Opinion," *Living Liberalism: Practical Citizenship in Mid-Victorian Britain* (Chicago: U of Chicago P, 2010), 229–90.

9. In a wonderful passage of early description, Trollope writes, "Her eyes were large, of a dark blue colour, and very bright,—and she used them in a manner which is as yet hardly common with Englishwomen. She seemed to intend that you should know that she employed them to conquer you, looking as a knight may have looked in olden days who entered a chamber with his sword drawn from the scabbard and in his hand" (1:25).

10. See Anderson, *The Powers of Distance* (Princeton: Princeton UP, 2001), in particular the chapter "The Cultivation of Partiality: George Eliot and the Jewish Question" (119–46), which makes the case that the "deracinated Jew [Daniel Deronda] who comes slowly to learn of, and affirm, his cultural heritage" gives Eliot a coherent form upon which to develop her "cosmopolitan ideal" that imagines that "critical detachment" gives insight into not only the self but also political and social attitudes (119).

11. Here, I have in mind the point Viktor Shklovsky makes in "Art as Technique" *Rus-*

sian Formalist Criticism: Four Essays (Lincoln: U of Nebraska P, 1965), 3–24, that "[t]he more you understand an age, the more convinced you become that the images a given poet used and which you thought his own were taken almost unchanged from another poet. The works of poets are classified or grouped according to the new techniques that poets discover and share, and according to their arrangement and development of the resources of language; poets are much more concerned with arranging images than with creating them" (7).

12. See Richard von Krafft-Ebing, *Psychopathia Sexualis*, trans. Franklin Klaf (New York: Arcade 1998), 87. The model of masochism I am developing adjusts both Freud's early description of masochism as sadism turned on the self in "Beyond the Pleasure Principle," *The Freud Reader*, ed. Peter Gay (New York: Norton, 1989), 594–625; and his later account of moral masochism in "The Economic Problem of Masochism," *The Standard Edition of the Complete Psychological Works of Sigmund Freud*, vol. 19 (London: Hogarth, 1991), 161–70.

13. For an account of anticipation's centrality to masochistic scenes, see Gilles Deleuze and Leopold von Sacher Masoch, *Masochism* (New York: Zone, 1991). All subsequent references are to this edition. For Sade's connection to utilitarianism and action, see Frances Ferguson, *Pornography, the Theory: What Utilitarianism Did to Action* (Chicago: U of Chicago P, 2004), 57–95.

14. For more on the centrality of negotiation to masochistic scenarios, see Gilles Deleuze's essay, "Coldness and Cruelty," in *Masochism*, particularly 161–70. Deleuze's argument, which develops an account of a single-subject masochism in which the male orders and orchestrates the scenes of his humiliation, departs from my own account, which focuses on the necessity of two agents in developing scenic surprise.

15. Deleuze notes the repeating images of coldness in the masochistic scene in "Coldness and Cruelty." According to Deleuze, the aesthetics of masochism feature the dense, northern furs to metaphorically connect the dominant woman to the cold, marble statue of which she appears to be an avatar but also to remind the masochist of the warm flesh beneath the dense pile. Deleuze writes, "Masoch's [written] art . . . [relies] on [visual] art and the immobile and reflective quality of culture. In his view the plastic arts confer an eternal character on their subject because they suspend gestures and attitudes. The whip or the sword that never strikes, the fur that never discloses the flesh, the heel that is forever descending on the victim, and the expression, beyond all movement, of a profound state of waiting" (70).

16. For more on womanly authority and fictional heroines, see Janice A. Radway's *Reading the Romance: Women, Patriarchy, and Popular Literature* (Chapel Hill: U of North Carolina P, 1984); Nina Auerbach's *Woman and the Demon: The Life of a Victorian Myth* (Cambridge: Harvard UP, 1982), Sandra M. Gilbert and Susan Gubar's *The Madwoman in the Attic: The Woman Writer and the Nineteenth Century Literary Imagination* (New Haven: Yale UP, 1979), Kathy Alexis Psomiades's *Beauty's Body: Femininity and Representation in British Aestheticism* (Stanford: Stanford UP, 1997); and Mary Jean Corbett's *Family Likeness: Sex, Marriage, and Incest from Jane Austen to Virginia Woolf* (Ithaca: Cornell UP, 2008). In her blend of Proppian analysis and ethnography, Janice Radway suggests the opposite: readerly attention develops from character rather than plot. Radway covers a contemporary literary formation in *Reading the Romance*: "To begin with, the ideal heroine is differentiated from her more ordinary counterparts in other romance novels by unusual intelligence or by an

extraordinarily fiery disposition. Occasionally, she even exhibits special abilities in an un-usual occupation. Although the 'spirited' heroine is a cliché in romantic fiction, these ideal women are distinguished by the particularly exaggerated quality for their early rebellious-ness against parental strictures" (123). What's particularly striking about this is that current-day Romantic fiction seems to have fully jettisoned the anodyne Victorian heroine in favor of a figure much more closely aligned with the dominant woman. Kathy Psomiades and Nina Auerbach both discuss the ways this alteration is presaged in the Victorian novel. For Psomiades, the perverse, decadent versions of femininity contemporaneous with Aesthet-icism offer one clear example of the limited appeal of the Victorian milquetoast. And in Auerbach's seminal study, the "queenly" woman is part and parcel of Victorian feminine subject formation, working alongside the "victim" we may typically associate with the nine-teenth century. More recently, there have been a number of charging books from feminist critics that make the connections between women's cultural roles and changes in the novel form during the Victorian and early modernist periods.

17. The language of bodily oscillation—"quivering," "trembling," "shivering"—also con-nects this kind of masochism to the masochism Gilles Deleuze describes in "Coldness and Cruelty," where he suggests the language of the cold works in masochistic scenes to under-score the thin line between statue and actor that undergirds the tableaux that masochists enjoy. For Deleuze, the masochistic scene depends on the thrill of discovering that an ap-parently inviolate statue is, in fact, a living woman. See Deleuze and von Sacher-Masoch.

18. For an account of masochistic impulses in the nineteenth and early twentieth cen-turies that does *not* focus on sexual life, see John Kucich's *Imperial Masochism* (Princeton: Princeton UP, 2006). Kucich argues that masochistic structures underpin the British im-perial project's aims, in particular male subjectivity. His account separates psychoanalytic models of masochism from their sexualized context, arguing instead that limiting masoch-ism to erotic frameworks limits its "political legibility" in a period defined by fantasies of British omnipotence (20). While Kucich's book focuses primarily on the ways dominance and hierarchy shape the institutional and bureaucratic structures of British imperialism, Anne McClintock's *Imperial Leather: Race, Gender and Sexuality in the Colonial Contest* (Lon-don: Routledge, 1995) offers an account of the dominant place sexualized power played in the psychosexual imaginary of the nineteenth and early twentieth centuries.

19. In Deleuze and von Sacher-Masoch.

20. The word Sacher-Masoch uses is *übersinnliche*, which has been translated alternately as "extrasensual," "suprasensual," or, as I've chosen, in keeping with Deleuze's translators, "supersensual." In all of the English translations, what's kept is the notion of excessive sen-sual experience.

21. This term also connects the so-called supersensualist to the another novelistic stock character in an interesting way; we might imagine that stock figure, the neurasthenic, as an example of what happens once the supersensualist's nerves give out. We might then see evidences of supersensual pasts in characters from Collins's Mr. Fairlie to Wilde's Lord Henry. Even in the idyllic countryside of Hardy's Wessex, characters are described as "su-persensitive," the close cousin of "supersensual."

22. See Sigmund Freud, *Three Essays on the Theory of Sexuality: Essay One, Sexual Aber-rations, The Freud Reader*, ed. Peter Gay (New York: Norton, 1989), 247–53. Freud writes,

"The most common and most significant of all the perversions—the desire to inflict pain upon the sexual object, and its reverse—received from Krafft-Ebing the names of 'sadism' and 'masochism' for its active and passive forms respectively" (251). It's surprising how uniformly sadism and masochism are linked together even in more recent critical accounts. Freud's late career concept of moral masochism also aligns dramatically with the typical Victorian marriage plot: a submissive and martyred woman devotes herself, body and soul, to the man she loves. In this mode, both the submissive woman and dominant man are relegated to the realm of the ideal: creatures of unparalleled goodness and purity of mind that will remain inviolate paragons.

23. For a strong account of Masoch's single-subject masochism, see Deleuze and von Sacher Masoch. The initial connection between Masoch and the perversion his name came to describe appears in Krafft-Ebing.

24. In perhaps the most well-known version of this approach, the American writer Edith Wharton presents her heroine in an actual *tableau vivant*:

> Indeed, so skillfully had the personality of the actors been subdued to the scenes they figured in that even the least imaginative of the audience must have felt a thrill of contrast when the curtain suddenly parted on a picture which was simply and undisguisedly the portrait of Miss Bart.
>
> Here there would be no mistaking the predominance of personality—the unanimous "Oh!" of the spectators was a tribute, not to the brushwork of Reynolds's "Mrs. Lloyd" but to the flesh and blood loveliness of Lily Bart. She had shown her artistic intelligence in selecting a type so like her own that she could embody the person represented without ceasing to be herself. It was as though she had stepped, not out of but into Reynolds's canvas, banishing the phantom of his dead beauty by the beams of her living grace.

From *The House of Mirth* (London: Virago, 1990), 145–46.

25. This habit may be part of the reason nineteenth-century literary studies have had so many calls for a new way of reading. Their proximity to our own period may be slipping as time moves on, but the temptation to see the rapacious, unconcerned growth of early capitalism as an avatar for its contemporary child is quite powerful. See Amanda Anderson's warning against aggrandizement beginning in her "Victorian Studies and the Two Modernities," in *Victorian Studies* 47:2 (2005), 195–203; and later in *The Way We Argue Now* (Princeton: Princeton UP, 2005); Rita Felski's *The Uses of Literature* (London: Wiley, 2008) and its claim for "ordinary" reading; Stephen Best and Sharon Marcus's recent "Surface Reading: An Introduction," *Representations* 108 (2009), 1–21; and the V21 Collective's manifesto (v21collective.org).

26. We might think of a correlative in the way that methods borne of ideology critique often seem to forget that such tactics might as easily be applied to minor or benighted epistemologies (such as Marxism itself!), not just to dominant forms of knowing. Almost always, literature loses this battle.

27. In their introduction to *Disciplinarity at the Fin de Siècle* (Princeton: Princeton UP, 2002), Joseph Valente and Amanda Anderson describe the anxieties that motivate disciplinarity distrust of in our contemporary political climate, and they suggest that the late Vic-

torian period is of special interest in these regards because "this was the time that saw the emergence and professionalization of numerous disciplines or intellectual fields that might be broadly gathered under the rubric of the 'human sciences': aesthetics, anthropology, sociology, psychoanalysis, sexology, and economics" (1–2).

28. Interestingly, poetry doesn't have this problem, or it doesn't have this problem in the same way. Part of this might have to do with the necessary encounter one has with form when reading poems, or it might have to do with the catch-all quality of the realist novel, which is, among other things, interested in reflecting other modes of writing in its pages. A number of robust claims for the specific epistemological and philosophical power of poetry have appeared in recent years. Beginning with Frances Ferguson's *Solitude and the Sublime* (London: Routledge, 1992); Sharon Cameron's *Choosing, Not Choosing* (Chicago: U of Chicago P, 1993); and Isobel Armstrong's *Victorian Poetry: Poetry, Poetics, Politics* (London: Routledge, 1993), this line of thinking continues in more recent work like Yopie Prins's *Victorian Sappho* (Princeton: Princeton UP, 1999), Virginia Jackson's *Dickinson's Misery: A Theory of Lyric Reading* (Princeton: Princeton UP, 2005), and Simon Jarvis's *Wordsworth's Philosophic Song* (Cambridge: Cambridge UP, 2008).

29. In a clear example of this dynamic, Elsie Michie makes a similar point about the vivacity of Trollopean women in the "abstract" romance plots of his novels: "In using the rich woman to acknowledge history directly, Trollope underscores the economic implications of romance plots even as he stresses their romanticism" (*The Vulgar Question of Money* [Baltimore: Johns Hopkins UP, 2012], 109).

30. Sandra Macpherson, *Harm's Way: Tragic Responsibility and the Novel Form* (Baltimore: Johns Hopkins UP, 2010). See also Lisa O'Connell, "Marriage Acts: Stages in the Transformation of Modern Nuptial Culture," *differences* 11 (Spring 1999): 68–111.

31. See, for example, Amanda Anderson's *The Powers of Distance: Cosmopolitanism and the Cultivation of Detachment* (Chicago: U of Chicago P, 2001); and Elaine Hadley's *Living Liberalism* (Chicago: U of Chicago P, 2010). Both of these investigations offer important accounts of Victorian resistance to a liberalism borne of rigidity and inaction, emphasizing the full-throated, progressive aspects of both Liberal politics and aesthetics. But I'm invested in another model of negotiation and debate, one that focuses not on consensus building and growth but on stasis, suspense, and static intensities.

32. Think of Leavis's damning point that "there is an elementary distinction to be made between the *discussion* of problems and ideas, and what we find in the great novelists" (*The Great Tradition* [New York: Doubleday, 1954], 17; his emphasis).

33. Elisha Cohn's compelling work on the powers of reverie focuses attention on the self-generating qualities of states of mindlessness. See, in particular, "'No Insignificant Creature': Thomas Hardy's Ethical Turn," *Nineteenth Century Literature* 64 (March 2010): 494–520.

34. Sharon Marcus, *Between Women: Friendship, Desire, and Marriage in Victorian England* (Princeton: Princeton UP, 2007).

35. See Michie 107–09, for an account of this conceptual shift in nineteenth-century Britain as wealth from manufacturing declines and wealth from banking and investment increases. Michie writes, "Wealth, after midcentury, ceased to be defined as a substance and instead began to be regarded as an intangible force," a force that "enable[d] its possessor to be active and energetic, to make things happen" (108).

36. From Anne-Lise François, "Toward a Theory of Recessive Action," *Open Secrets: The Literature of Uncounted Experience* (Stanford: Stanford UP, 2008), especially 21–38.

37. Levine, Caroline, *The Serious Pleasures of Suspense: Victorian Realism and Narrative Doubt* (Charlottesville: U of Virginia P, 2003).

Chapter 2. The Grasp of *Wuthering Heights*

1. See Sandra M. Gilbert and Susan Gubar, *The Madwoman in the Attic* (New Haven: Yale UP, 1979), 248–308; Terry Eagleton, *Myths of Power: A Marxist Study of the Brontës* (London: MacMillan, 1975), 118–19; Robert Polhemus, *Lot's Daughters: Sex, Redemption and Women's Quest for Authority* (Stanford: Stanford UP, 2005), 173–96.

2. The peculiarity of Emily Brontë's central pair might be illuminated by a brief comparison to Charlotte Brontë's novels. For example, both *Jane Eyre* and *Villette* valorize a model of companionate marriage along pedagogical lines. More specifically, perhaps, Jane and Rochester's marriage at the end of *Jane Eyre* bears little resemblance to either Catherine Earnshaw and Heathcliff's relationship or Catherine the Younger's impending marriage to Hareton Earnshaw. A masochistic model in *Jane Eyre* might elevate Rochester's marriage to Bertha Mason to a place of value rather than condemning it as a block to Jane's upward mobility.

3. See Frank Kermode, "A Modern Way with the Classic," *New Literary History* 5.3 (1974): 415–34.

4. See J. Hillis Miller, *Fiction and Repetition: Seven English Novels* (Cambridge: Harvard UP, 1982), 42–72.

5. Emily Brontë, *Wuthering Heights*, ed. Richard J. Dunn (New York: Norton, 2003), 63. Subsequent citations appear parenthetically in the text.

6. Deleuze writes, "Disavowal, suspense, waiting, fetishism and fantasy together make up the specific constellation of masochism. Reality, as we have seen, is affected not by negation but by a disavowal that transposes it into fantasy. Suspense performs the same function in relation to the ideal, which is also relegated to fantasy. Waiting represents the unity of the ideal and the real, the form or temporality of the fantasy. The fetish is the object of the fantasy, the fantasized object par excellence." I will suggest that the anticipatory desire Heathcliff experiences throughout the course of his adult life with Catherine corresponds to this account. See Gilles Deleuze, "Coldness and Cruelty," in Gilles Deleuze and Leopold von Sacher-Masoch, *Masochism* (New York: Zone, 1989), 72.

7. Eagleton 118.

8. Recall Catherine's "I am Heathcliff" speech to Nelly early in the novel (*WH*, 64). See, too, Richard Dellamora, "Earnshaw's Neighbor/Catherine's Friend: Ethical Contingencies in Wuthering Heights," *ELH* 74 (2007) 535–55; and Polhemus, *Lot's Daughters*, 173–75.

9. Frank Kermode makes a similar claim in "A Modern Way with the Classic," 420.

10. Joseph Allen Boone, *Tradition Counter Tradition: Love and the Form of Fiction* (Chicago: U of Chicago P, 1987). Boone draws attention to Catherine and Heathcliff's difference from the gender norms in their world:

One needs to be careful, however, in applying the slippery term "androgyny" to these two characters. For readings that designate Heathcliff the sundered "masculine" component and Catherine the "female" half of a Platonic (or even "monstrous") whole mistakenly transform the nearly identical personalities of Catherine and Heathcliff into sexually defined opposites. This is precisely the conventional notion of love against which Brontë pits her vision. Rather, what one finds in the young Catherine and Heathcliff are states remarkably free of the constraints typically imposed by social constructions of "masculinity" of "femininity"; theirs is the place of difference vis-à-vis the exacting geography of gender mapped out by their world. (154)

11. Nancy Armstrong, *Fiction in the Age of Photography: The Legacy of British Realism* (Cambridge: Harvard UP, 1999). See also her *Desire and Domestic Fiction* (Oxford: Oxford UP, 1987), 186–202. Armstrong has recently argued that the novel's violence "erupts when [an] individual achieves identity, hence masculine identity, by subordinating and controlling femininity" (*How Novels Think: The Limits of Individualism from 1719–1900* [New York: Columbia UP, 2005], 87). Armstrong's accounts of *Wuthering Heights* emphasize male violence directed toward women victims. While this accurately describes some of the violence in the novel, my interest, at least for the purposes of adducing a masochistic model, is in the sexualized power women (principally the Catherines) have over men.

12. Ivan Krielkamp, "Petted Things: Wuthering Heights and the Animal," *Yale Journal of Criticism* 18.1 (2005), 87–110.

13. Susan Meyer, *Imperialism at Home: Race and Victorian Women's Fiction* (Ithaca: Cornell UP, 1996). Her account hinges on reading Heathcliff as the novel's central character: "[t]he novel is indeed not so much the story of Catherine as it is the story of Heathcliff: the need for the narration of a story is evoked by his arrival and ends with his death" (116). Patricia Spacks in contrast imagines Catherine as the novel's engine: "[a]lthough Heathcliff dominates the action of Wuthering Heights . . . Catherine more clearly exemplifies what the two of them stand for," projections of adolescent fantasy that cannot imagine a world beyond the self (*The Female Imagination* [New York: Knopf, 1975], 138).

14. Bersani further claims that Catherine is, "in psychoanalytic terms, the principle ego of the novel, the 'I' who, while not proving the narrative eye in the technical sense of point of view, nonetheless expresses most clearly the novel's psychological point of view on familial and nonfamilial identities. It is through Catherine's relation to Heathcliff that Brontë dramatizes most powerfully her children's exhilarating and terrifying confusion about what and where the self is in and beyond the family" (*A Future for Astyanax: Character and Desire in Literature* [Boston: Little, 1976], 204.)

15. For examples of single-character criticism, see Harold Bloom, ed., *Heathcliff* (New York: Chelsea, 1993). Heathcliff's role in the novel is indeed slightly different than Catherine's, as he occupies both masochistic and sadistic positions willingly, whereas Catherine often appears to resist the submissive role in which marriage places her. Bloom's introduction imagines Heathcliff as a character in need of a decoder, asserting that "[f]eminist criticism doubtless will help solve the dilemma of Heathcliff, when some day its instruments of analysis become more refined" (2–3). But, by trying to crack the symbolic codes of single characters, we ignore the centrality of intercharacter relationship in this novel.

16. For Deleuze, sadism and masochism feature different symptomatics:

Sade's secret societies, his societies of libertines, are institutional societies; in a word, Sade thinks in terms of "institutions," Masoch in terms of "the contract." The juridical distinction between contract and institution is well known: the contract presupposes in principle the free consent of the contracting parties and determines between them a system of reciprocal rights and duties; it cannot affect a third party and is valid for a limited period. Institutions, by contrast, determine a long-term state of affairs that is both involuntary and inalienable; it establishes a power or an authority which takes effect against a third party. (76–77)

See, for example, one of Dolmance's erotic tableaux in *Philosophy in the Bedroom*, wherein the arrangement of bodies features a number of active stage directions ("He bites her," "He slaps her," etc.). Marquis de Sade, *Justine, Philosophy in the Bedroom and Other Writings*, trans. Richard Seaver and Austryn Wainhouse (New York: Grove, 1965), 346.

17. Significantly, both Catherine the Younger and Isabella are remarkably satisfied with their curtailed existences within the Grange before Heathcliff absorbs them into the Heights. Both of these women align more securely with gendered convention than does Catherine the Elder, and both are dramatically (and negatively) altered by their lives at the Heights.

18. Strangely, we do not see the adult Catherine reenter the Heights after her marriage to Edgar. Brontë instead gives us the spectral waif who inhabits Lockwood's dream, a character whose age ("twenty years, I've been a waif for twenty years" [21]) corresponds more closely to the time of Catherine's convalescence at the Grange than to her actual death.

19. While this might be a change brought about by her proximity to the Lintons or to the "civilizing" effects of the Grange, Brontë makes it clear that much of the change is effected by Frances Earnshaw's "art" in restraining Catherine (41). A thorough outsider, Frances Earnshaw hopes to reform Catherine in her own image, but this alteration meets with only partial success. Frances restrains Catherine's wildness but does not eliminate it; when Hindley confines Heathcliff to the garret, for example, Catherine climbs through the skylight like "a little monkey" (47).

20. Meyer reads this as a "return of the colonial repressed." According to Meyer, Heathcliff's insurrectionary vengeance has the effect of "deflecting attention from the fully human status of female characters like Isabella, and more generally from women's problems in relation to the unjust distribution of social power" (119, 124).

21. Rachel Ablow, *The Marriage of Minds: Reading Sympathy in the Victorian Marriage Plot* (Stanford: Stanford UP, 2007).

22. Consider, for example, Isabella's comment to Hindley that "[i]t's well people don't really rise from their grave" (140) or Catherine's support of her father when "his soul departed" (217).

23. Also see Ablow 61.

24. Rachel Ablow makes a case for this kind of reading. Once Edgar refuses to "participate in his wife's moods," Catherine encounters her true status as a wife; she is only indulged, not in control (58–62).

25. Gilbert and Gubar make explicit the connection between reproduction and the increasing limitations on Catherine's willfulness. They see Catherine's hunger strike as a response to "being monstrously inhabited" (285–86).

26. See Georges Bataille, *Literature and Evil* (New York: Marion Boyars, 1985), 20.

27. Of course, Catherine slightly mischaracterizes her early relation to Heathcliff here: "Cathy, when she learnt the master had lost her whip in attending on the stranger, showed

her humour by grinning and spitting at the stupid little thing, earning for her pains a sound blow from her father to teach her cleaner manners" (30).

28. See, for example, Polhemus 178. Polhemus makes the convincing claim that Brontë's novel depicts the pair's self-created world as beyond gender. But I suggest that many of the masculine aspects of Catherine (including her imagined identity with Heathcliff in the "I am Heathcliff" speech) underscore her sexual dominance instead of her more fluid understanding of gender.

29. Ian Duncan, *Scott's Shadow: The Novel in Romantic Edinburgh* (Princeton UP, Princeton: 2007).

30. As Ivan Krielkamp has noticed, elsewhere in the novel Brontë describes Heathcliff's hair as a "colt's mane," and he is often linked to the novel's animal world. Here, Catherine's fixed grasp on him simulates a bridle. Where Krielkamp reads Heathcliff's animalism, and others read racialization, I read evidence of explicitly sexual submission. Krielkamp's argument emphasizes Heathcliff's connection to a particularly pet-like animality, arguing that Heathcliff is a version of Keeper, Emily Brontë's bulldog. At times like this, Catherine's power over Heathcliff indeed appears to be the power of an owner over a pet, but in Heathcliff's greater physical strength and his constant returns to Catherine's side, I also see evidence for his full engagement in his submission (Krielkamp 97–98; Dellamora 537).

31. Bersani's account persuasively models the kinds of relationship Catherine and Heathcliff engage in: "[t]hese sexless lovers are both too naïve and too important to be seductive with each other; each one merely pounces on or haunts the other in order to prevent the other from escaping" (213). The "pouncing" and "haunting" are integral to the difference between these two characters, as I explain below. But I disagree with Bersani that these scenes are sexless; instead, they are nongenitally sexual.

32. That fit features a similar bodily hardening: "she stretched herself out stiff, and turned up her eyes, while her cheeks, at once blanched and livid, assumed the aspect of death" (93).

33. Briefly, there is one other piece of evidence to support this claim. When Nelly lays out Catherine's body, she opens one of the windows to the death chamber "moved by [Heathcliff's] perseverance to give him a chance of bestowing on the fading image of his idol one final adieu." Nelly states that upon reentering the room she observes

> "on the floor a curl of light hair, fastened with a silver thread, which, on examination, I ascertained to have been taken from a locket hung around Catherine's neck. Heathcliff had opened the trinket and cast out its contents, replacing them by a black lock of his own. I twisted the two, and enclosed them together." (131)

This is a peculiar moment for Nelly. One expects her to replace the black hair with Edgar's blonde lock, but instead she binds the two together. Bizarrely, this counters Heathcliff's eventual machinations to get his and Catherine's coffins altered. If Heathcliff imagines his own body blending with Catherine's before Edgar's has time to decay, Nelly's twist here folds a scrap of Edgar's body into Catherine's dust. But while this seems in line with Nelly's view of Edgar's intense attachment to Catherine, I want to suggest that this action also demonstrates Nelly's understanding that both Heathcliff and Edgar are necessary to Catherine. Without Edgar's presence, and without her marriage to him, the relationship between Heathcliff and Catherine loses some of its masochistic tension. The frozen scenes I've been

Chronicle of Barset's Madalina Demolines, as well as the more obvious appeal of Lily Dale in both *The Small House at Allington* and the *Last Chronicle*, or the attention-seeking Signora Neroni in *Barchester Towers*). Even more than offering a "contrasting position," Trollope's heiresses share a potent, almost jolie-laide aesthetic frame that locates their powers of seduction in their self-display as much as in their financial power. See Deborah Denenholz Morse's "Broken English Pastoral" in *Reforming Trollope: Race, Gender, and Englishness in the Novels of Anthony Trollope* (Farnham: Ashgate, 1999), 13–37.

3. Trollope, *The Prime Minister* (New York: Dodd, 1918). Glencora's investments here expose her to Plantaganet's charge of vulgarity, but Glencora continues with her efforts because "[n]othing to her was so distasteful as failure" (235).

4. For an example of critical dissatisfaction with *Can You Forgive Her?*, see Henry James's 1865 review of the novel reprinted in *Anthony Trollope: The Critical Heritage*, ed. Donald Smalley (London: Routledge, 1969, 249–53). The unsigned *Spectator* notice included in the same volume remarks that the novel is "more than usually loose and straggling" and that "its central point is far more faint and colourless" than Trollope's other tales (248). I discuss James's complaints in detail below. Later critics such as Robert Polhemus have noted the asymmetry of the novel's plots: "the beautifully conceived story of [the Pallisers'] early life together is surrounded and partially spoiled by the longer Alice Vavasor part of the book" (*The Changing World of Anthony Trollope* [Berkeley: U of California P, 1968], 102). Of the novel, Mary Hamer says that Trollope "knew he had taken on a tough assignment" in portraying Alice in a sympathetic light (a portrayal Hamer diagnoses as flawed because discomforting to its author) and, further, that the "awkward" syntax of the novel's first sentence paves the way for its thematic awkwardness (*Writing by Numbers: Trollope's Serial Fiction* [Cambridge: Cambridge UP, 1987], 118).

5. Juliet McMaster traces an effortful masochism in "The Unfortunate Moth: Unifying Theme in *The Small House at Allington*," *Nineteenth Century Fiction* 26.2 (1976): 127–44. McMaster emphasizes Lily Dale's apparently irrational rejection of her suitors as evidence of her pleasure in suffering. Lily's prolonged refusal of even engagement marks her as peculiar even in Trollope's world—while her refusals preclude formal engagement, they have the effect of placing her in a perpetually almost-engaged position. Instead of thinking of Lily as "enamored of suffering," as McMaster claims, we might instead see Lily as enamored of refusal, and thus of suspension itself. See also McMaster's *Trollope's Palliser Novels* (New York: Oxford UP, 1978). Her "priggishness," as Trollope famously called it, links to her refusal to enter fully into the marriage market, a market in which, J. Hillis Miller claims, weddings are moments when English girls' identities are "fixed" to their new married personas ("Literature and a Woman's Right to Choose—Not to Marry" *diacritics* 35.4 [2005]: 45). James Kincaid has argued that the choices available to Trollope's heroines are limited in part by the drastic change marriage affords: "[w]omen are pressed either to abandon their selves or to plunge into some kind of private insanity," an insanity typified, for Kincaid, by Lily Dale's energetic refusals of Crosbie and Eames in *The Last Chronicle of Barset* (*The Novels of Anthony Trollope* [Oxford: Oxford UP, 1977], 177).

6. Rachel Ablow, *The Marriage of Minds: Reading Sympathy in the Victorian Marriage Plot* (Stanford: Stanford UP, 2007). Ablow suggests that this physical power, as well as the law, connects women to their husbands.

discussing suggest that one of the ways intensity develops in this relationship is through its untenability. Edgar helps to construct the boundaries of Heathcliff's intense feeling for Catherine and their mutual need for their grasping embraces. This also suggests that Nelly, the third (or fourth?) party in so many of the novel's frozen tableaux, has an investment in these scenes that goes beyond her simple moral piety or her self-serving surveillance.

34. Compare this formulation to what Martin Hägglund calls the "chronolibido" in *Dying for Time* (Cambridge, MA: Harvard UP, 2012), 6–14. Hägglund suggests that desire cannot coincide with a desire for immortality but rather must always be imagined as focusing on survival. To want something, one must always look for an extension of life. While the relationship I'm describing in *Wuthering Heights* might appear to be exactly what Hägglund criticizes, Catherine and Heathcliff's attention to dissolution—that is, to decay— squarely places them inside a libidinal economy that emphasizes death. Their approach to total annihilation (material, as well as vital, death and decay) is always asymptotic, it is true, but their shared vision appears to hinge on imagining their dust's mingling as (in Hägglund's terms) a kind of survival, not as a kind of immortality. In a strange way, Heathcliff's love for death is actually a desire for survival.

35. It is worth noting that Brontë also connects Linton Heathcliff to cats, but she characterizes him as a torturer: "[B]ut Linton requires his whole stock of care and kindness for himself. Linton can play the little tyrant well. He'll undertake to torture any number of cats if their teeth be drawn, and their claws pared. You'll be able to tell his uncle fine tales of his kindness, when you get home again, I assure you" (210). This repeats not only Linton's refusal to engage in any battle he might lose but also his vicious cruelty.

36. Perhaps most famously, Terry Eagleton suggests, "The culture which Catherine imparts to Hareton in teaching him to read promises equality rather than oppression, an unemasculating refinement of physical energy." But Eagleton also points to the "sentimental self-indulgence" of the pedagogical scene; it does not solve the conflict between Heathcliff and Catherine: "[t]he world of the Heights is over, lingering only in the figure of Hareton Earnshaw; and in that sense Hareton's marriage to Catherine signifies more at the level of symbolism than historical fact, as a salutary grafting of the values of a dying class on to a thriving progressive one" (118–19).

Chapter 3. Buoyed Up

1. Anthony Trollope, *The Way We Live Now* (New York: Penguin, 1994); and *Can You Forgive Her?* (New York: Penguin, 1972); hereafter referred to as *WWLN* and *CYFH* respectively.

2. Elsie B. Michie's *The Vulgar Question of Money* (Baltimore: Johns Hopkins UP, 2012) offers some insight into the ways Trollope's heiresses are different from those in other realist novels: "Working through, in an almost mathematical sense, the permutations and combinations of the marriage plot, Trollope reveals the way its "false" fictional oppositions can be used to deny or limit the social impact of forms of wealth that seemed, in their very intangibility, to be virtually limitless. . . . Though these rich women occupy a negative or contrasting position in relation to the novel's romantic heroines, they exceed that familiar binary even as it is involved" (109). The masochistic framework that I've been arguing for suggests another way of looking at these women, one that includes dramatically presented women who are not, or might not be, heiresses (think of the peculiar draw of *The Last*

7. Anthony Trollope, *An Autobiography* (London: Williams, 1946). Trollope also writes that in *The Way We Live Now* he "ventured to take the whip of the satirist into [his] hand" (308–09).

8. *The Way We Live Now* and *Can You Forgive Her?* are not the only Trollope novels that present a trio of women set on various forms of sexual domination. *The Small House at Allington* features Lily Dale's removal from the marriage market, a removal that continues into *The Last Chronicle of Barset*, wherein Lily aggressively campaigns to keep Grace Crawley from accepting a marriage proposal. In *The Eustace Diamonds*, Jane Carbuncle's efforts to marry off her niece Lucinda Roanoke end with a violent scene of paralysis as Lucinda is driven mad by the very idea of her wedding. Even the tyrannical Mrs. Proudie shares some aspects of sexual domination with these more socially rebellious characters. Some of Trollope's novels focus on these masochistic relationships—especially novels that focus on engagement as a suspended system of sexual relationship. But *The Way We Live Now* is peculiar in that it relegates these relationships to the periphery of an economic plot that also focuses on suspension, the speculative railroad Melmotte devises.

9. Here I am thinking particularly of the final scene in which Mr. Melmotte appears, wherein he is described as both "magisterial" and "audacious." Trollope writes, "But even he, with all the world now gone from him, with nothing before him but the extremist misery which the indignation of offended laws could inflict, was able to spend the last moments of his freedom making a reputation at any rate for his audacity. It was thus that Augustus Melmotte wrapped his toga around him before his death!" (*WWLN* 640). Not only does Trollope imagine Melmotte as poised between "the world" and "nothing," but also the connection between the disgraced financier and the fall of Rome indicates a kind of narrative admiration of the extent of Melmotte's villainy. Similarly, though he is violently sadistic, the narrator considers George Vavasor's merits: "[t]here must have been something great about [him], or he would not have been so idolized by such a girl as his sister Kate" (*CYFH* 73).

10. For more on lying and dishonesty in Trollope, see John Kucich, *The Power of Lies: Transgression in Victorian Fiction* (Ithaca: Cornell UP, 1994). Additionally, Michael Ragussis in *Figures of Conversion: "The Jewish Question" and English National Identity* (Durham: Duke UP, 1995) makes a claim that hinges on secrecy and opacity. Accounts like these argue that Trollope's "wicked" characters are in fact "wicked" and are to be read as delicious villains: interesting only because they are bad. I argue, however, that the most "villainous" figures in Trollope (Melmotte, Lizzie Eustace in *The Eustace Diamonds*, and even Reverend Slope in *Barchester Towers*) are given moments of narratological blessing. It's this kind of complex, situational narratological value that Ruth apRoberts comments upon in *The Moral Trollope* (Athens: Ohio UP, 1971). While it seems as though Trollopean novels hinge on a kind of ethical situationalism, as apRoberts claims, I suggest instead that there's a palpable narratological *investment* in wickedness. While Trollope argues against "a certain class of dishonesty, dishonesty magnificent in its proportions, [which has climbed] into high places" (*Autobiography* 308), within the novels there are moments of appreciation for, if not outright approval of, wickedness that seems at odds with the critical version of the writer as a spokesman for traditional ethical standards. For more on the ways Trollope's characters' psychologies are at odds with readings focused on vice and virtue, see Amanda Anderson's "Trollope's Modernity" (*ELH* 74 [2007]: 509–34), which argues that the "recalcitrant

psychologies" of Trollope's characters undercut any analyses that tend toward moral certitude (511).

11. In *Can You Forgive Her?*, Lady Glencora exposes her connection to violence most dramatically in encounters with her two "duennas," Mr. Bott and Mrs. Marsham.

12. What Mrs. Hurtle seems to be doing links her directly to the world of "natural acting" that Lynn Voskuil examines (*Acting Naturally: Victorian Theatricality and Authenticity* [Charlottesville: U of Virginia P, 2004], 1–19). Voskuil reexamines the assumption that Victorian culture placed "authenticity" in opposition to "theatricality." Instead, she demonstrates, a notion of natural acting, present from the time of Hazlitt, might enable Victorian characters to play-act an imagined or created character, while also producing believable gesture and tone, thus linking the seemingly oppositional terms of *theatricality* and *authenticity*. Furthermore, Voskuil claims that the critical attention to theatricality has produced a critical inattention to authenticity: "Because it is usually construed as the impenetrably coherent Other, it serves as the stable prop that an unruly theatricality requires in order to showcase its histrionics. The opposition between the two is thus securely maintained, because the causal relationship works both ways: if postmodern theatricality disrupts the coherence of authenticity, that same coherence authorizes the transgressions of theatricality. As a result, authenticity remains underdeveloped as a theoretical construct, and its cultural complexities are consistently underestimated, including those notions of authenticity so persistently attributed to the Victorians" (10). Taken in this light, Mrs. Hurtle's capabilities seem to indicate that the narrator's attention to her ability to imitate does not damn her as "inauthentic" but rather indicates her authentic theatricality. And one must note that it certainly takes Paul much of the novel's length to turn away from her capable scenes of seduction; one might argue, in fact, that Paul never turns away from a seduction scene, turning to "embrace" Mrs. Hurtle immediately after explaining his plan to marry Hetta Carbury (*WWLN* 745). Lady Glencora, as we shall see, becomes defined by her amusing expressions and her funny face. Her theatricality is an emanation linked, along these lines, to her candor.

13. There is one other striking moment of multiple letter writing in *The Way We Live Now*: Lady Carbury begins the novel by sending off three letters to three different editors in support of her *Criminal Queens*. In that case, though, Lady Carbury writes her letters quickly, without revision, and sends them without a second thought. In *Can You Forgive Her?*, Alice Vavasor's letter-writing practice works differently than does Mrs. Hurtle's and keeps both John Grey and George Vavasor at a distance, while Burgo Fitzgerald's secret letter to Lady Glencora acts as a talisman in her indecision over their possible elopement. According to Deleuze's account, writing, especially contractual writing, is integral to masochistic systems. Gilles Deleuze, "Coldness and Cruelty," in Gilles Deleuze and Leopold von Sacher-Masoch, *Masochism* (New York: Zone, 1989).

14. Laura Kipnis describes the problems masochistic sexuality can produce in contemporary culture (*Bound and Gagged: Pornography and the Politics of Fantasy in America* [New York: Grove, 1996]). In the course of the extensive interviews she conducted with Daniel DePew, Kipnis lands on one of the key problems of *United States v. DePew*. The prosecutors understand that DePew was interested in sexual relationships with unknown men and that those sexual relationships were often sadomasochistic, but they do not understand one of the key functions of DePew's need to spin out more and more outrageous fantasy plots in

his first encounters with the disguised officers. Kipnis explains DePew's rationale: "[i]t's a common practice in [DePew's] world for guys to get together in a hotel room, discuss their fantasies, and have sex" (37). DePew's case clearly demonstrates a key to understanding how masochistic scenes and contracts get actualized. As participants discuss their fantasies, they are also watching the other participants, registering the possibilities of enacting the scenes they're describing. In Trollope's case, Mrs. Hurtle expresses her desire to whip Paul in part to see how much of her dominance he will take. Paul's ability or interest in emotional suffering seems to indicate his possible inclusion in a masochistic relationship, but his refusal of the image of the whip firmly positions him in opposition to the kind of sexualized violence on which Mrs. Hurtle seems intent.

15. Paul's tameness aligns him with a Severin-like subservience, but Paul's reaction to her threat of violence proves that his breed of "over-civilized man" is not given to physical masochism. While Paul seems to respond emotionally to Mrs. Hurtle's scenes, to her ability to prolong their relationship in a pattern of pure waiting, he does not respond in a submissive way to her threat of the whip. This is the "profound state of waiting" that Deleuze discusses (70). Mrs. Hurtle and Paul could, in fact, continue their long relationship of scenes and waiting if Paul did not actually speak to Hetta Carbury about marriage.

16. Again, one might link this reading of Mrs. Hurtle's fears with Deleuze's reading of *Venus in Furs*. In the final masochistic scene of the novel, Severin is whipped by The Greek, a character who, Deleuze says, is a combination of the "new man" figure the novel seems to value and the cruel father who breaks the fantasy of the masochist. Deleuze writes that "in his sadistic role . . . [The Greek] represents the dangerous father who brutally interrupts the experiment and interferes with the outcome" (66). The third party becomes a problem in the masochistic scene because, in part, it reminds the dyadic masochistic partnership of their fantasy's outside.

17. This fixity of role is, of course, in direct contradiction to many of the critical theorists of masochism and sadomasochism (Pat Califia, *Public Sex: The Culture of Radical Sex* [Pittsburgh: Cleis, 1994]; and Leo Bersani, "Foucault, Freud, fantasy and Power" *GLQ* 2.1 [1994]: 11–34), who argue that one of the most progressive aspects of sadomasochistic sexuality is the reversibility of roles. These theorists mainly focus on a sadomasochistic sexual subculture that operates apart from the literary models I am discussing above, where I think the reader is supposed to read masochistic or dominant characters as being slightly out of step with the novel's normative sexual system. However, Bersani offers a critique of the notion that role reversibility offers practitioners a way of counteracting current "normative" versions of sexuality and appropriate sexual violence: "If there is some subversive potential in the reversibility of roles in S/M, a reversibility that puts into question assumptions about power inhering 'naturally' in one sex or one race, S/M sympathizers and/or practitioners have an extremely respectful attitude toward the dominance-submission dichotomy itself. Sometimes it seems that if anything in society is being challenged, it is not the networks of power and authority, but the exclusion of gays from those networks" (15). Bersani's argument is that if power adheres to gender, same-sex scenarios also negate the idea that dominance and submission are two key terms in sexual interaction. What is not being questioned in models that encourage role reversibility as a root of S/M pleasure is that there remains an assumed connection between submission and penetration, something

submissive-as-such that adheres to the body being penetrated, whipped, or injured. In Trollope, Mrs. Hurtle's reversal (she becomes a trodden-upon worm just as Paul refuses to submit to her will) signifies a kind of subjective collapse in part due to Mrs. Hurtle's dependence on masochistic scenarios in the construction of her sexuality. I mean here that she in some way demonstrates an *agreement* with Deleuze's premise of a single-subject masochism, but the body of that subjective self is reversed in Trollope's account.

18. The rhetoric of this scene is remarkably similar to the final proposal scene between John Grey and Alice Vavasor in *Can You Forgive Her?* In both, the "omnipotence" of the man problematically shuts down the suspended model the woman has heretofore engaged (772). One of the troubling side effects of Trollope's rhetoric of omnipotent power is an acknowledgment that coercion, specifically physical or moral coercion, may be part of a conventional marriage proposal.

19. I mean not only to trouble Kathy Psomiades's claim that Mrs. Carbuncle is Lucinda's mother but also to point to certain similarities between Carbuncle and Mrs. Hurtle. Both of these women are stuck in marriages whose contracts are in question: Mr. Carbuncle is always somewhere else, and Mrs. Carbuncle's relationships to other men are often in question. Similarly, Mrs. Hurtle deflects questions about Caridoc Hurtle by alternately insisting on his death, on her murdering him, and their divorce. See also Kathy Psomiades, "Heterosexual Exchange and Other Victorian Fictions: *The Eustace Diamonds* and Victorian Anthropology," *Novel: A Forum on Fiction* 33.1 (Fall 1999): 93.

20. Glencora actually appears in *The Last Chronicle of Barset*, but only as one of Conway Dalyrymple's paintings.

21. Women in Trollope tend to press men toward radicalism. This has something to do with their tendency to focus on the personal, not the political, but it also has to do with women investing themselves in politically radical aims (Alice's lobbying for the ballot, Glencora's claim for men and women's equality).

22. Miller discusses Trollope's tendencies to use a specific type of English femininity (girls with "tenderness, modesty, and freshness") for his heroines in "Literature and a Woman's Right" (45).

23. One wonders whether Glencora ever happily occupies her wifely status or whether it is always secondary to a primary, and quite often untenable, position (potential adulterer, hostess).

24. This is made explicit when we see Alice and Glencora cooing over the new edition to the Palliser fold: "'There's one comfort;—if my manikin lives, I can't have another eldest. He looks like living;—don't he, Alice?' Then were perpetrated various mysterious ceremonies of feminine idolatry which were continued till there came a grandly dressed old lady, who called herself the nurse, and who took the idol away" (*CYFH* 828). Romantic love is related to idolatry throughout the novel, perhaps most clearly in one of Alice's internal monologues about her earlier attachment to George: "He whom she had worshipped had been an idol of clay, and she knew that it was well for her to have abandoned that idolatry" (60–61).

25. It is curious that James's plot solutions for these two characters have a strong whiff of melodrama about them. Melodrama is, in my account, a peculiarly masochistic form, as it depends on the extension of suspense rather than plot solution. For a more Freudian

model of masochism's relationship to melodrama, see Ellen Bayuk Rosenman, "Mimic Sorrows: Masochism and the Gendering of Pain in Victorian Melodrama," *Studies in the Novel* 35.1 (2003): 22–43.

26. And here James might be critiquing (as he does elsewhere) Trollope's tendency to value comedic endings (marriages, births) over the tragic endings James prefers (death, either metaphoric or literal). I argue that Trollope's formal complexity allows him to avoid producing novel endings that are either solely tragic or comedic. As Kincaid has argued, in Trollope's world, the application of such generic distinctions is precarious (7).

27. Of course, James could not have foreseen Trollope's later incorporation of Lady Glencora, though the already ongoing chronicles of Barset give a good indication of Trollope's possible reintroduction of his characters in other novels. A corollary to this is that, even in novels with eponymous heroes or heroines, Trollope rarely focuses a plot on a single character. Compare this to James's *The Portrait of a Lady*, in which Isabel appears on almost every page.

28. For example, George Vavasor "vanishes from our pages" (752), and Burgo Fitzgerald is exiled in a line: "Here we must say farewell to Burgo Fitzgerald" (793). Alex Woloch points out how these directions rely "*both* on our ability to imagine a character as though he were a real person . . . and on our awareness of such a highly artificial and formal aspect of the narrative structure as chapter divisions" (*The One vs. the Many* [Princeton: Princeton UP, 2003], 13). In Woloch's example, the introduction of Mr. Slope is held off for a new chapter in *Barchester Towers*. Both George's and Burgo's removals are reduced to the bare minimum where Slope's introduction is teased out over the chapter break.

29. Kincaid has connected James's creation to Trollope's Alice Vavasor: "James, who wrote about the same dilemma exactly in *The Portrait of a Lady* should have known better. Perhaps he did. In any case, Alice, like Isabel Archer, is out to test the conditions and extent of her freedom" (183). Kincaid argues that Isabel and Alice are more similar than not, as both resist the recommendations of those who surround them.

30. Consider *Princess Cassimassima*, James's only extended treatment of a character introduced elsewhere in his fiction (New York: Penguin, 1987).

31. This, too, marks Alice's position as more conventional than Isabel's but, in some ways, as poignant. While Isabel's choice is unsettling, it is satisfactory as a choice—Alice's "choice" is not. As we shall see, Alice's consent to her marriage is problematized by what I characterize as John Grey's excessive domination. Instead, it seems that Isabel's choice to remain with Osmond remains a choice (as shown in her long night of seeing), while Alice's marriage does not. And while we might think Isabel's "Americanness" may be the root of her self-will, the fate of Lucinda Roanoke reminds the reader that Trollope's American women tend to end even more poorly than do his English girls. As a side note, Isabel Archer's discrete self is also reflected through her name. She may officially become Mrs. Osmond, but there's something unalloyed in her character by this name change. There remains, in both of these characters, a kind of permanent virginity. On the contrary, Glencora's maiden name, Glencora M'Cluskie, is rarely invoked, though she is known, at various times, as Cora, Lady Glen, and finally the Duchess of Omnium (Glencora Omnium, as she signs herself).

32. This moment squares with the account of decision that Miller describes in "Litera-

ture and a Woman's Right." Miller claims that marital decision in Trollope is instantaneous and dependent on the love the young woman does or does not feel for her suitor (54). At this point in the novel, Alice wants to bracket love from her equation, so she is able to choose in George's favor. In this section, Kate assumes that Alice loves George romantically, and Alice's firm reply that she has not yet been able to make her decision indicates that she is *not* in love with George. The difficulty comes in Alice's final reengagement to John Grey. Apparently Alice "loves" Grey, but, as we shall see, the dynamics of that relationship severely compromise her free consent. Compare, too, Alice's use of letters to foreclose decision making to Mrs. Hurtle's use of her trio of letters to confound her motivations.

33. This habit is perhaps best exemplified by her behavior after Mr. Palliser snubs her when he catches Alice and Glencora in the gambling salon. On this occasion, Alice threatens, "As I do not choose to undergo your displeasure, I will return to England by myself" (*CYFH* 713). Less pronounced versions of this kind of action occur throughout the text, often in response to pressure from Kate and George Vavasor or John Grey, but also in response to Lady Glencora's aggressive wit, for example: " 'If you talk such nonsense, I will not stay,' said Alice" (287). This is such a common response with Alice that it becomes normalized by the novel's end: "In answer to this, Alice made her usual protest, and Lady Glencora, as was customary, told her that she was a fool" (754).

34. Sigmund Freud, *The Standard Edition of the Complete Psychological Works of Sigmund Freud*, 24 vols. (London: Hogarth, 1991). See also Kincaid 187. Of Alice's refusals of Grey long after George is out of the picture, Kincaid writes,

> As long as she can maintain her grip on this guilt, she can, of course, elude Grey. But there are, I think, other less rational reasons; her sincerity is almost fierce in these passages of self-abasement. The suggestion is that the guilt derives from a secret "fault," not her love for George, which in truth she never felt, but the independent exercise of will. Forgiving herself for that fault would mean, in effect, renouncing that independent will. As long as she can hold on to her guilt, she can, ironically, protect the shreds of her freedom. Masochism, then, for her as for Isabel Archer, is the last defense of independence, the last pathetic proof that they were and are free. (186–87)

I am suggesting that, unlike Isabel Archer, Alice Vavasor's masochism allows her to occupy positions of submission *and* dominance throughout the novel. Alice's refusals reflect her desire to punish herself and her desire to put off decision—to suspend event. Grey's eventual triumph over her points to the typical novel-ending use of marriage to seal off possibility. In Trollope's novels, though, such shutting down of masochistically inflected engagements does not have the same effect; his desire to spin stories over multiple novels, alongside his tendency to focus on marriages caught in medias res, points to a conception of marriage as an extension of this model of engagement, not its conclusion.

35. Kaja Silverman, *Male Subjectivity at the Margins* (New York: Routledge, 1992).

36. And this moment also reminds the reader that Alice has earlier responded to both suitors with a "shudder." The narrator wants to distinguish between these shudders—George Vavasor's aggression makes Alice shudder with repulsion, while John Grey's voice makes "[h]er whole frame [shudder]" with its sweetness (*CYFH* 394). As Kincaid has argued, this points to the essential similarity between Grey and Vavasor: both press Alice to set a

date for their impending weddings because they want to possess her. And while both want sexual possession, Vavasor wants financial possession, but Grey wants moral possession.

37. A woman's ability to control some of her money after marriage is of importance in *Can You Forgive Her?* To stop the potential flow of money after her marriage unites their incomes, Mrs. Greenow trains Bellfield by giving him a moderate allowance. Similarly, when Mrs. Marsham tries to put Alice down by suggesting that perhaps Mr. Palliser's horses shouldn't be called out to take her home, Glencora "savagely" replies that the horses are hers to do with what she wants (*CYFH* 470). This speaks to a growing recognition that what might belong to a woman *before* her marriage may in some way belong to her even after she is absorbed into her husband's family. Mrs. Marsham's age, and her position as a would-be toady to Mr. Palliser, marks her as one who believes in the primacy of the husband in a married couple.

38. Mrs. Greenow's apparent skill for freezing or collapsing time is indicated by her frequent misprision of the date. At various times in the course of the novel, she imagines her husband has died much earlier than he has: this shows both her readiness to engage in sexual games and her desire to flout convention in actuality but not in name. The forms of widowhood are useful to her, but she controls their application. Unlike that famous widow Victoria, Mrs. Greenow speeds the mourning process along to allow her reentry into the sexual market.

39. This scene features a remarkable still-life of Oileymead's best produce: "The basket and cloth were there, in the sitting-room, and on the table were laid out the rich things which it had contained;—the turkey poult first, on a dish provided by the lodging house, then a dozen fresh eggs in a soup plate, then the cream in a little tin can, which, for the last fortnight, had passed regularly between Oileymead and the house in the Close. . . . Then behind the cream there were two or three heads of broccoli, and a stick of celery as thick as a man's wrist" (*CYFH* 229). Mrs. Greenow's response to this ("When gentlemen will be too liberal, their liberality must be repressed" [229]) is offset by her acceptance of the entire spread.

40. Later, we come to understand just how large a role her maid (Jenny, who is re-named Jeannette when the widow comes into her fortune) plays in these constructions:

> The widow was almost gorgeous in her weeds. I believe that she had not sinned in her dress against any of those canons which the semi-ecclesiastical authorities on widow-hood have laid down as to the outward garments fitted for gentlemen's relicts. The materials were those which are devoted to the deepest conjugal grief. . . . But there was that of genius about Mrs Greenow, that she had turned every seeming disadvantage to some special profit, and had so dressed herself that though she had obeyed the law to the letter, she had thrown the spirit to the winds. . . . Her kerchief was fastened close round her neck and close over her bosom; but Jeannette well knew what she was doing when she fastened it,—and so did Jeannette's mistress. (425–26)

As she does with the railway porters, Mrs. Greenow recruits Jeannette to assist in her tableaux.

41. Mrs. Greenow's carriage is itself peculiar in that it is a hired carriage made to look like her own. By adding a liveried attendant to a hired, and refitted, carriage, Mrs. Greenow

is able to perform her wealth more obviously than that wealth might allow (*CYFH* 416). Her frugality reveals itself again when she explains her strategy for reusing her old linen in her new home: she "converts [the linen] to Bellfield purposes." Although each piece is embroidered "Greenow," by turning the sheets around she can save money and keep up appearances (807).

42. Here I am thinking of Michael Fried's discussion of absorption in eighteenth-century French painting (see *Absorption and Theatricality: Painting and Beholder in the Age of Diderot* [Berkeley: U of California P, 1980], 7–70). Fried writes of Chardin's absorption in daily life, "The result, paradoxically, is that stability and unchangingness are endowed to an astonishing degree with the power to conjure an illusion of imminent or gradual or even fairly abrupt change" (50). What seems to be happening in Glencora's moments of absorption is a combination of the distinct absorptive models Fried ascribes to two painters— Chardin's model of absorption in the everyday task and Greuze's model of absorption in unique, aggressively momentous, occasions. Glencora's absorption with her decision has both physical and psychological aspects.

43. This engagement is always partial, but perhaps its partiality, in combination with Glencora's researches into other modes of absorption, allows her fulfillment of a kind. Plantagenet's decision to let Glencora do what she wants helps her expand her experience, although, as we see in *The Prime Minister*, this expansion is not without missteps.

44. See Ablow 118–44. Ablow suggests that Trollope's critique of Louis Trevelyan's intense absorption in his wife in *He Knew He Was Right* is tied to his critique of personal investment in literary work. For Trollope, impersonal alienation is a more tenable position, which contributes to the distance his narrator seems to have from his characters; Trollopean characters rarely present the same interior contours that an Eliotic character might. Instead, I argue that the sexual desires Glencora translates offer another version of this characterological distance. Rather than allowing readerly access into his character's interior self, Trollope often shows his characters experiencing an intense absorption that drastically separates their experiences from the reader's experience.

45. This goes some way toward explaining why Glencora is so invested in becoming the Mistress of the Robes in *The Prime Minister*.

46. See Mary Hamer, *Writing by Numbers: Trollope's Serial Fiction* (Cambridge: Cambridge UP, 1987), 116. The wildness of the river links with the wild romance George seems to offer, but Alice misrecognizes him. George's Byronic aspects (his bad reputation, his impulse to contrariness, even his emotive—and dangerous—scar) apparently connect him to what Mrs. Greenow later calls the "rocks and valleys" of romance while they actually draw attention to his murderous and vicious interior. George Vavasor is brutal, and his brutality takes no prisoners. Alice imagines the Rhine as seductive, so close "that in the soft half light it seemed as though she might step into its ripple" (*CYFH* 82–83). But this feeling comes in "half light," and Alice is mistaken about George.

47. This explains why Burgo's name repeats itself throughout the Palliser series while Burgo does not reassert himself as a threat.

48. See, for example, Trollope, *The Eustace Diamonds* (Oxford: Oxford UP, 1973): "Lady Glencora in her time had wished to marry a man who had sought her for her money" (156); or see Trollope, *The Duke's Children* (Oxford: Oxford UP, 1973): "[a]nd the Duchess referred

to her own early days when she had loved, and to the great ruin which had come upon her heart when she had been severed from the man she had loved" (1:10).

Chapter 4. Hideously Multiplied

1. Character purity in the face of the sexual act is the subject of Mary Jacobus's seminal essay on Tess, another Hardy character whose sexual impulses wrongly condemn her. "Tess: The Making of a Pure Woman," *Tearing the Veil: Essays on Femininity*, ed. Susan Lipshitz (London: Keegan, 1978).

2. See, for example, Kate Millett, *Sexual Politics* (New York: Doubleday, 1970), 129–33; Robert B. Heilman's "Hardy's Sue Bridehead," *Nineteenth-Century Fiction* 20.4 (1966): 307–23); and Kathleen Blake, "Sue Bridehead, 'The Woman of the Feminist Movement,'" *Studies in English Literature, 1500–1900* 18.4 (1978): 703–26.

3. Thomas Hardy, *Jude the Obscure* (New York: Penguin, 1998). All subsequent citations are from this edition.

4. Hardy's preoccupation with masochistic developments in sexual relationships appears throughout his corpus: in the poetry (the powerful beloved engulfed in flames in "The Photograph," the macabre capitalist's wife in "The Lady in Furs"), the short stories (the cruel Mop's musical power over the submissive Car'line in "The Fiddler of the Reels"), and the novels (Bathsheba Everdene's combination of wealth and hauteur in *Far from the Madding Crowd*, Tess Durbeyfield's submission to mental torture in *Tess of the D'Urbervilles*). But it is in *Jude the Obscure* that Hardy's masochistic versions find their fullest fruition: in Jude Fawley, Arabella Donn, and, perhaps most of all, Sue Bridehead.

5. Sandra Macpherson, *Harm's Way: Tragic Responsibility and the Novel Form* (Baltimore: Johns Hopkins UP, 2010).

6. See Gillian Beer, *Darwin's Plots: Evolutionary Narrative in Darwin, George Eliot and Nineteenth-Century Fiction* (Cambridge: Cambridge UP, 2000), 220–41. Beer's seminal assessment describes the power of generation to surpass the human scales of Hardy's novels: "[s]exual joy is always dangerous, not only because of the possibility of loss, but because it is linked to *generation*, the law which rides like a juggernaut over and through individual identity and individual life spans" (225).

7. This marks Hardy's significant difference from Deleuze's masochistic model: Deleuze notes that Masoch's masochists always invest energy in writing out their parodic sexual contracts. The contracts in Masoch often give the dominant female complete control—to the point of death—over the masochist. As I noted above, Hardy's couple, especially Sue, remains wary of the writtenness of any contract, which is one reason their relationship is described best as a *union*. See Gilles Deleuze and Leopold von Sacher Masoch, *Masochism* (New York: Zone, 1991), 92. All subsequent references are to this edition.

8. In this way, sexual suspense looks a lot like narrative suspense more generally.

9. Edelman claims that the futural rationale behind political engagement links normativity explicitly to child production. It is impossible, he argues, for a politics based on futurism not to elevate heterosexuality to a position of prominence: "[f]or politics, however radical the means by which specific constituencies attempt to produce a more desirable social order, remains, at its core, conservative insofar as it works to *affirm* a structure, to *authenticate* social order, which it then intends to transmit to the future in the form of its

inner Child" (2). Here, I will press Edelman's claim that a heterosexual couple is incapable of fully resisting reproductive futurism's claim—Hardy's couple maintains comfort only as long as it remains a couple, before Little Father Time enters the novel. I am arguing that the masochistic dyad, as it refuses genital sexuality and thus child production, exists as a heterosexual order resistant to reproductive futurism. This accords somewhat with the status of the salutary child (or its lack) in Stanley Cavell's seminal study on the Hollywood comedy of remarriage, *Pursuits of Happiness* (Cambridge: Harvard UP, 1981). Along the way, Cavell connects the ascendency of the new Hollywood woman (the game, chatty, clever dame) with anxieties about male potency and female sexual frigidity, noting that the "man's inability to claim the woman . . . goes with events that requite not merely the absence but the denial of the possibility of children for the marriage, and it means (consequently?) the withholding of sexual gratification during a dozen or so years of what is called the prime of life" (32–33). I am here drawing attention to the interrogatory "consequently?" While Cavell points to the seemingly logical connection between a state of evaporated sexual potency and childlessness in such comedies' initial marriage plot, he here quietly suggests that childlessness *may not be* commensurate with sexlessness.

    10. This is why we must be cautious of accounts of Hardy's novel that downplay attention to the interconnectedness of the sexual and educative plots. For instance, Raymond Williams's classic comment that we must be alert both to what is gained and what is lost "if we are let in [to Christminster] as Jude was not" (*The Country and the City*. [New York: Oxford UP, 1973], 198). Of course, this raises the gender question: Jude was not given entry, but neither was Sue.

    11. The generative work such imaginative other lives do is the subject of Andrew Miller's *The Burdens of Perfection: On Ethics and Reading in Nineteenth-Century British Literature* (Ithaca: Cornell UP, 2008), but Miller's account draws special attention to why child bearing and child rearing so often occupy what he calls the "optative mode." Children and child rearing "[occasion a] pressing sense that there are intimate lives that, so deeply akin to mine, are lives that I am not, in fact, living" (203). Miller continues, "That the thought of children provokes thoughts of lives unled shouldn't come as a surprise, I suppose: children are regularly thought of as sharing family likenesses, inheritances, features of their parents, uncanny iterations that trouble our notions of individual identities. The most familiar occasion on which the idea of a shared singularity—the occasion on which what it means to have one body, separate from others—is naturally and troublingly presented as pregnancy" (203–04). The life unlived, and the attendant anxiety contemplating that life brings, is also the subject of Adam Phillip's most recent book, *Missing Out: In Praise of the Unlived Life* (New York: Picador, 2012).

    12. When teaching this novel, I encountered some resistance to this central claim: How can we read the last third of the novel as Sue's return to a genitally disengaged sexual connection with Jude when her language locates her character's ideological shift so securely in a religious hysteria catalyzed by trauma? I'll map this out in what follows, but I'm indebted to a graduate student, Ben Wiebracht, who was able to signal the moment in the novel where his resistance to this claim broke down. In conversation with Widow Edlin, after their final, waffling kiss, Sue says, "Jude has been here this afternoon, and I find I still love him—O, grossly!" (394). The major argument of this chapter, that sexual sensuality oper-

ating to the side of genital engagement motors the novel's central romantic plot, unmistakably happens in this moment. Sue's love for Jude is here imagined as ongoing as well as "gross," that is, coarse, indecent, obvious, in a word *material* ("Grossly," *OED Online* [Oxford UP, May 27, 2010 <http://dictionary.oed.com>]).

13. Recall, too, that Arabella sells *her* photograph of Jude to a secondhand dealer: his particularity is not part of her attraction to him (72).

14. Painful experiences of sensation are a constant in *Jude*. Sue describes herself as "super-sensitive" when first requesting she be allowed to live apart from Phillotson (222), and Jude describes both her as "ever-sensitive" and the couple as a unit as "over-sensitive" (250, 320). The pair call themselves "horribly sensitive" (286) once they begin to separate themselves from social life, and the narrator labels them as "the supersensitive couple" (305).

15. See Peter Widdowson's "Arabella and the Satirical Discourse in *Jude the Obscure*," *On Thomas Hardy* (New York, Macmillan: 1998) for a discussion of Arabella's integration into the novel's satirical "carnival" (179). Widdowson suggests that the strong critical tendency to focus attention on Sue's cerebral New Womanhood obscures Arabella's plot-level "obtrusiveness" in the novel, an obtrusiveness that, in turn, points to Arabella as the locus of Hardy's satirical voice (181).

16. Some readers, such as D. H. Lawrence, dismiss Arabella's power as negatively instinctual, preferring Sue's antinomian stance and intellectual draw. Lawrence writes, condemningly, that "instincts . . . fling Jude into the arms of Arabella, years after he has known Sue" (*Study of Thomas Hardy and Other Essays*, [Cambridge, Cambridge UP, 1985], 94). J. Hillis Miller points out in *Distance and Desire* (Harvard UP: Cambridge, MA, 1970) that most of Hardy's novels take up the stories of their protagonists *after* the protagonists have already pledged themselves to another and found that other lacking, and here *Jude* is no exception (165).

17. This dependence on scenes might mark Sue's sexual exquisite masochism most clearly. Sue initially claims to shy away from sexual contact, which leads to readings of her as frigid or sexually cold, but she eventually explains that her sexual desire takes a cruel form: "I did not exactly flirt with you; but that inborn craving which undermines some women's morals almost more than unbridled passion—the craving to attract and captivate, regardless of the injury it may do the man—was in me. . . . But you see, however it ended, it began in the selfish and cruel wish to make your heart ache for me without letting mine ache for you" (353). And, even earlier in the novel, when Jude questions Sue about her involvement with the undergraduate in London, she offers an erotic reading of her refusal to submit sexually to him: "People say I must be cold-natured,—sexless—on account of [never yielding]. But I won't have it! Some of the most passionately erotic poets have been the most self-contained in their daily lives!" (149).

18. The difficulty in securely establishing Sue's sensual needs also hovers over the end of the novel. A word Hardy repeatedly uses to further secure Sue's tentativeness is "ethereal," indicating her lack of material desire. She is an "ethereal creature," and Jude sees her "spirit . . . trembling in her limbs" (187). As Sue expresses regret for the genital turn their erotic relationship took, Jude disagrees with her, both asserting that her "natural instincts" are "perfectly healthy" but also saying she is the "most ethereal, least sensual woman" he has ever known (344). In these passages, Hardy is juxtaposing Sue's ethereal qualities to

Arabella's voluptuous embodiment, but, again and again, the narrative doubles back and questions Sue's commitment to spirit over substance. Recall she calls herself "The Ishmaelite" when Jude initially questions her on her sensual desires (139). Even at the novel's end, as Jude complains that Sue is "a sort of fay or sprite—not a woman!" Sue denies it, saying that although at first she wanted only to make Jude devoted to her, eventually her "heart ached" for him (352–53).

19. In this light, Sue might be seen as a kind of "natural actress," with gestures and expressions that hover between the real and the performed. See Lynn Voskuil, *Acting Naturally: Victorian Theatricality and Authenticity* (Charlottesville: U of Virginia P, 2004).

20. Remember, too, that we see Sue buying classical statuary well before we see her interact with Jude (95), a gesture that indicates her paganism. She buys the Venus and Apollo from an itinerant image maker, indicating both these pagan inclinations and a connection to Masoch's own Roman focus, Venus. Sue's proclivity for reciting Swinburne, too, seems to link her to an obsession with classicism and its decadent nineteenth-century iteration. *Venus in Furs'* Wanda admires the "serene sensuality of the Greeks" (159), and Sue is likened both to figures in a Parthenon frieze and Ganymedes (144, 154).

21. See Miller, *Distance and Desire* 166.

22. At a key moment in their relationship's development, the married Sue revisits an apparently ended conversation with Jude through a window frame: "I can talk to you better like this than when you were inside" (205). At this moment, it's clear it's not simply distance that prompts Sue's speech but the barrier of the framing device.

23. I stress here that Jude and Sue's relationship is sexual even before they become sexually intimate. That their familiar relationship obscures their sexual relationship is peculiar, given the number of cousinly marriages even in late Victorian novels.

24. Another example of the impossibility of carving out private space is evident in the passages about Sue's pagan statues. Sue mistakes her room in the religious reliquary as private (or at least capable of hiding objects from Miss Fontover's scrutiny) when she brings home the plaster statues. When Miss Fontover discovers the statuary and crushes them under her heel, she offers a Christian critique of Sue's pagan impulses but also maintains the impossibility of truly private space in a social world (93–95, 103). See Joss Marsh's "Hardy's Crime," which situates the novel in relation to contemporary debates about blasphemy's depiction; in Marsh's account, the reader can't help but perceive the obscenity of Sue's final religiopolitical position (*Word Crimes: Blasphemy, Culture, and Literature in Nineteenth-Century England* [Chicago: U of Chicago P, 1998], 273). But, rather than imagining the pair as *exchanging* positions by the novel's end (272), I instead want to emphasize the volatility of their religious and political adjustments. Read in this way, the force of Sue's propulsion from her freethinking position matters as much as her position itself. Somewhat relatedly, Amanda Claybaugh's illuminating account of *Jude*'s debts to the "novel of purpose" suggests Hardy yearns for a communitarian answer to his protagonists' mounting problems. But, again, the peculiarity of the cousin's marriage keeps their case from becoming typical and, as such, from becoming a representative for the ills of contemporary marital or educational standards (*The Novel of Purpose: Literature and Social Reform in the Anglo-American World* [Ithaca: Cornell UP, 2007]).

25. Sue's repeated use of "sordid" as a qualifier for "contract" points to the major prob-

lem, in *Jude* and indeed in Hardy's authorship, with marriage as a binding treaty. Again and again, characters come up against the impossibility of binding bodies to behave in a certain way through linguistic or legal means. The strikingly somatic root for "sordid" highlights the cancerous or ulcerous pressure marital contract has on relationship ("Sordid," *OED Online* [Oxford UP, December 29, 2009 <http://dictionary.oed.com>]).

26. Throughout the novel, the Fawleys are positioned, as a family, as living slightly beyond the pale. For example, Jude's early ambitions to become a scholar are discussed at length by the people of Marygreen, and Jude is the last to know his family's history of sexual and domestic violence (13, 282).

27. Another strange thing about Little Father Time's appearance is that he operates like Arabella's false pregnancy, over a longer period of time. While Arabella compels Jude into marriage with a fake pregnancy, Little Father Time implores his "parents" not to marry with the same insistence. Only when the "child" is removed does the full problem appear: when Arabella reveals she is not pregnant, Jude realizes he has married her on false pretenses; when Little Father Time kills the other children, Sue realizes that the genital sexuality in which she and Jude were engaged had supplanted the (successful) masochistic sexuality they had earlier constructed.

28. See, for example, Penny Boumelha's *Thomas Hardy and Women: Sexual Ideology and Narrative Form* (Sussex: Harvester, 1982). Boumelha argues that Sue's seeming frigidity is linked to her wish for both "a non-sexual love and [a] non-marital sexual liaison" with Jude (143). I want to press on Boumelha's notion that Sue's behavior after the children's deaths is a retreat from or "repudiation of" her sexuality. See also John Goode's "Sue Bridehead and the New Woman," in *Women Writing and Writing about Women*, ed. Mary Jacobus (London: Croom Helm, 1979), which takes up Hardy's representation of Sue's self-mortification.

29. Jude's lack of sentiment is made explicit immediately after the children's deaths, when Sue adopts the position of the grieving mother ("O my babies, my babies . . .") and Jude analyzes their deaths critically, quoting from *Agamemnon*: "'Nothing can be done,' he replied. 'Things are as they are, and will be brought to their destined issue'" (339). Jude is willing to continue in his unmarried life with Sue after the children's deaths, but, once she removes herself from their shared life, he begins to resist his impulse to reconstruct their suspended sexuality. The contract's flexibility and changeability is abandoned once the children expose the relationship's full contours.

30. Perhaps the clearest examples of the nongenerative in Hardy are Tess's violation and the birth and death of her unwanted infant in *Tess of the D'Urbervilles* (1891), but similar plotlines can be found in *The Mayor of Casterbridge* (1886), *The Return of the Native* (1878), and *Far from the Madding Crowd* (1874).

Chapter 5. Dead Gems

1. Raymond Williams is the loudest of these voices (see *Culture and Society: 1780–1950*. [New York: Columbia UP, 1983]), but F. R Leavis's laudatory *D. H. Lawrence: Novelist* (Chicago: U of Chicago P, 1955) also fits the bill.

2. *The Rainbow* (Penguin, New York: 1989) and *Women in Love* (New York: Penguin Classics, 2007).

3. Leo Bersani, *A Future for Astyanax* (Boston: Little, 1976). See also James Cowan's

D. H. Lawrence and the Trembling Balance (State College: Pennsylvania State UP, 1990) for an account of Lawrentian flux.

4. For more on the strange other worlds mobilized in novels by such moments of decision, see Andrew Miller's *The Burdens of Perfection: On Ethics and Reading in Nineteenth-Century British Literature* (Cornell UP: Ithaca, 2008), especially pages 202–05.

5. Kate Millett is perhaps the strongest voice in this cohort, but Katherine Anne Porter makes a similar claim about Oliver Mellors in "A Wreath for the Gamekeeper," published just as *Lady Chatterley* began to see the light of day after its censorship (*Shenandoah* 11.1 [Autumn] 1959).

6. See Elisha Cohn, "'No Insignificant Creature': Hardy's Ethical Turn," *Nineteenth-Century Literature* 64.4 (March 2010): 494–520.

7. This is not to say that all homosexual loves in Lawrence fail nor that they might be attributable to false self-concept. See, especially, the appeals, strikingly erotic in their tactics, that Struthers and Kangaroo make to Richard Somers in *Kangaroo* (1923). In fact, all of this novel's romances dovetail with Craft's suggestion that sexual expression is connected to death and abjection (Christopher Craft, *Another Kind of Love: Male Homosexual Desire in English Discourse, 1850–1920* [Berkeley: U of California P, 1994], 168). In a stricken passage of the typescript, Somers makes a case for a mystical erotics built on actual enslavement: "It would be as in Egypt, say, when the mysteries of the gods and the temples and the divine kings stimulated all kinds of life-responses in the people, which we have lost. They had infinite sensations and feelings and strange answerings in their soul, an endless changing throb, because the world of getting-on had never been invented, and the world of barren dreariness of a so-called educated democracy. I'll bet you a slave in Egypt had a myriad-fold subtle vibrations and responses to things which for us don't even exist." *Kangaroo*, original typescript with the author's holograph emendations, The Henry W. and Albert A Berg Collection, NYPL, 260–01.

8. Richard A. Kaye also notes Lawrence's attempts to develop a Whitmanian "adhesiveness" in "Lawrence's *Women in Love* and the Homosexual Sublime" in *The Flirt's Tragedy: Desire without End in Victorian and Edwardian Fiction* (Charlottesville: U of Virginia P, 2002), 200–06.

9. See Craft.

10. Frances Ferguson has written extensively on Lawrence's class critique in *Pornography, the Theory: What Utilitarianism Did to Action* (Chicago: U of Chicago P, 2004). In Ferguson's essay, Mellors's challenge to Clifford is, primarily, a class challenge focused on Clifford's (false) assertion of his permanent rights to his property, property that, in Clifford's view, includes "game" Connie (139–45).

11. Kate Millett, *Sexual Politics* (New York: Doubleday, 1970).

12. In my thinking about medial intervention, I have been especially grateful for the work of media theorist Friedrich Kittler, especially *Discourse Networks 1800/1900* (Stanford: Stanford UP, 1992); and *Gramophone, Film, Typewriter* (Stanford: Stanford UP, 1999). In an essay on the specific medial shifts occasioned by a new capacity for repetition, Kittler writes, "In any case, the discovery of prose, this infinite irreversible movement, was a scientific and technical revolution which made Europe's old art forms look old in one fell swoop. Yet neither flesh nor entropy allow for mathematically closed solutions. Computers

are machines with a finite number of resources which run in a world of finite resources. They cannot get around admitting that poetry is right." *ReMembering the Body: Body and Movement in the 20th Century* (Stuttgart: Hatje Cantz, 2000), 268.

13. In a long, revised sequence of the *Kangaroo* typescripts, for example, each revision of erasure—where the word "connection" drops off the page in the course of two versions—is eventually resolved by small additions to the page, wherein synonyms for "connection" are slowly but surely turned back into "connection."

Later still in the *Kangaroo* typescript, Lawrence produces a crystalline version of this oscillation of narrative temperament. In the typewritten version, Lawrence writes: "Richard was silent. He knew it was true. And he hated the truth. But true it was." But, the alterations revise the text to read: "Richard was silent. Perhaps it was true. And he hated such a truth" (382). It's hard to overestimate how radically these alterations change Richard Somers's characterization. Not only do the changes reframe the truth claim's purchase ("it was" becomes "perhaps"), but they also adjust Richard's relationship to truth more broadly. No longer is he an enemy of truth per se, now he is skeptical of *such* truths.

14. Michael Levenson comments on this synonymic habit in "'The Passion of Opposition' in *Women in Love*: None, One, Two, Few, Many": "[t]raditionally, the paragraph has been regarded as that verbal unit which makes development possible, which allows the individual sentence to unfold its implications, mingling with other sentences to form a higher unity" (*Modern Language Studies* 17.2 [Spring, 1987]: 27). But, in *Women in Love*, Levenson claims, events expand to fully absorb each moment that could be imagined as an impetus. The strange result of this expansive writing style is a blockage in anything like forward momentum in plot.

15. Letter 732: To Edward Garnett, 5 June 1914. See also Stephen Kern, *The Modernist Novel: A Critical Introduction* (Cambridge: Cambridge UP, 2011, 29–30).

16. Typescript 2, Lawrence, D. H., *Women in Love*, Box 28; Folder 1, Harry Ransom Center, University of Texas, Austin, Texas.

17. See Isobel Armstrong's *Victorian Poetry: Poetry, Poetics and Politics* (London: Routledge, 1993), especially 11–13, 23–65.

18. Typescript 1, Lawrence, D. H., *Women in Love*, Box 26, Folder 2, Harry Ransom Center, University of Texas, Austin, Texas.

19. See both Millett, *Sexual Politics*, and a more persuasive account of the ways vision connects to feminist violence, Linda Ruth Williams's *Sex in the Head: Visions of Femininity and Film in D. H. Lawrence* (Detroit: Wayne State UP, 1993).

20. This chimes with Daniel Albright's discussion of the Dalcroze movement in the early years of the twentieth century. Recall that Ursula and Gudrun produce a Dalcroze-inspired dance in "Water-Party." In a discussion of Nijinsky's choreography, Albright explains, "Nijinsky told his dancers to follow the private count that he called out backstage, not the rhythm of the conductor's baton—partly because the dancers couldn't follow Stravinsky's meters, but also in obeisance to Dalcroze's ideal of the autonomy of living plastic, its refusal to submit to the role of mere accompaniment to music" (105). In other words, in many of Lawrence's erotic scenes, one finds a commitment to a difficult, dissonant "living plastic." For a full discussion of *gestus*, the corporeal hieroglyphs of the modernist moment, see Daniel Albright's *Untwisting the Serpent: Modernism in Music, Literature and the Other Arts* (Chicago: U of Chicago P, 2000), 101–37.

21. Lawrence takes great pleasure in typing his own work, until he makes himself ill typing out *Women in Love* and turns to others to help finish the typescripts and revisions: "It is great fun" (*The Letters of D. H. Lawrence*, vol. 2, ed. George J. Zytaruk and James T. Bolton [Cambridge, Cambridge UP, 1981], 5, 645) quoted in Craft 165).

22. See Hannah Sullivan, *The Work of Revision* (Harvard UP, 2013).

23. The initial typescript version reads:

The bridesmaids were here, and yet the bridegroom had not come. Ursula wondered if something was amiss, and if the wedding would yet all go wrong. She felt troubled, as if it rested upon her. The chief bridesmaids had arrived. Ursula watched them come up the steps. One of them she knew, a tall, slow, reluctant woman with red brown hair. This was Hermione Roddice, a friend of the Criches. Now she came along, with her head held up, balancing an enormous flat hat of pale yellow velvet, on which were streaks of ostrich feathers, natural and grey. She drifted forward as if perfectly aimless, her long, pale, thought-clenched face lifted up, not to see the world. She was rich. She wore a dress of silky, frail velvet, of pale yellow colour, and she carried a lot of small rose-coloured cyclamens. Her shoes and stockings were of brownish grey, like the feathers on her hat, her hair was tawny and heavy, she drifted along with a peculiar déhanchement, trailing, drifting. She was impressive, in her lovely pale-yellow and brownish-rose, like a vision, something covered with beauty, and unnatural, unholy. People were silent when she passed, impressed, roused, wanting to jeer, yet for some reason silenced. Her long, pale face, that she carried lifted up, somewhat in the Rossetti fashion, seemed almost drugged, as if a strange mass of dark thoughts writhed in the darkness within her, and she was never allowed to escape. (11)

24. Linda Williams also discusses Hermione's connection to violence in "Sadism and the Female Gaze" in *Sex in the Head*. She writes that Hermione's detached gaze is "[a symptom] of degenerate sexuality" (41) that connects Hermione's dependence on the visual frame with her "'pornographic' (for which read narcissistic, self-referential, mentally and visually enclosed) relationship with herself, with the *inside*" (42, emphasis Williams's).

25. See John Marx, *The Modernist Novel and the Decline of Empire* (Cambridge: Cambridge UP, 2005).

26. Because of her connection to the real-life Morrell, Hermione has a pride of place in biographical criticism. See John Worthen's *D. H. Lawrence: Life of an Outsider* (New York: Counterpoint, 2007); and Morrell's own memoirs, *Ottoline: The Early Memoirs of Lady Ottoline Morrell* (New York: Faber, 1963).

27. Walter Pater, *The Renaissance: Studies in Art and Poetry*, ed. Donald L. Hill (Berkeley: U of California P, 1980), 188–89.

28. I'm grateful to Alex Murray for his suggestions on Lawrence's anti-Paterian aesthetics.

29. Both Gerald Monsman and Carolyn Williams have written evocatively about the relationship between Pater's aestheticism and his form. See Monsman, *Walter Pater's Art of Autobiography* (New Haven: Yale UP, 1980); and Williams, *Transfigured World: Walter Pater's Aesthetic Historicism* (Ithaca: Cornell UP, 1989). Linda Dowling's *Hellenism and Homosexual-*

ity in Victorian Oxford (Ithaca: Cornell UP, 1994) describes the homosexual ethos against which Lawrence was railing thirty years later (98–103).

30. D. H. Lawrence, preface, *New Poems* (New York: B. W. Huebsch, 1920), i–xx.

31. D. H. Lawrence, *Lady Chatterley's Lover* (New York: Penguin Classics, 2006).

Conclusion

1. Marcus, Sharon, and Stephen Best. "Surface Reading: An Introduction," *The Way We Read Now*, Spec. issue of *Representations* 108.1 (Fall 2009): 1–21.

2. Susan Sontag "Against Interpretation," in *Against Interpretation* (New York: Picador, 1966).

3. Fredric Jameson, *The Antinomies of Realism* (New York: Verso, 2013).

4. Emile Zola, *The Kill*, trans. Brian Nelson (New York: Oxford World Classics, 2004). The original passage reads:

> Ils eurent une nuit d'amour fou. Renée était l'homme, la volonté passionnée et agissante. Maxime subissait. Cet être neutre, blond et joli, frappé dès l'enfance dans sa virilité, devenait, aux bras curieux de la jeune femme, une grande fille, avec ses membres épilés, ses maigreurs gracieuses d'éphèbe romain. Il semblait né et grandi pour une perversion de la volupté. Renée jouissait de ses dominations, elle pliait sous sa passion cette créature où le sexe hésitait toujours. C'était pour elle un continuel étonnement du désir, une surprise des sens, une bizarre sensation de malaise et de plaisir aigu. Elle ne savait plus; elle revenait avec des doutes à sa peau fine, à son cou potelé, à ses abandons et à ses évanouissements. Elle éprouva alors une heure de plénitude. Maxime, en lui révélant un frisson nouveau, compléta ses toilettes folles, son luxe prodigieux, sa vie à outrance. Il mit dans sa chair la note excessive qui chantait déjà autour d'elle. Il fut l'amant assorti aux modes et aux folies de l'époque. Ce joli jeune homme, dont les vestons montraient les formes grêles, cette fille manquée, qui se promenait sur les boulevards, la raie au milieu de la tête, avec de petits rires et des sourires ennuyés, se trouva être, aux mains de Renée, une de ces débauches de décadence qui, à certaines heures, dans une nation pourrie, épuisent une chair et détraquent une intelligence.

La Curée (Charpentier et Cie, Paris: 1874), 208–09.

5. Angus Fletcher, *Allegory: The Theory of a Symbolic Mode* (Princeton: Princeton UP, 2012), 24–68.

6. Michael Clune, *Writing against Time* (Stanford: Stanford University Press: 2013).

7. Caroline Levine, *Forms: Whole, Rhythm, Hierarchy, Network* (Princeton: Princeton UP, 2015).

8. George Eliot, *Middlemarch* (Penguin: New York, 2003).

9. D. H. Lawrence, *Women in Love* (New York: Penguin Classics, 2007).

Index

Index   197

— works: *Far from the Madding Crowd*, 185n4, 189n30; *Jude the Obscure*, 90–113; *The Mayor of Casterbridge*, 99, 189n30; on reproduction, 93, 94, 95–96, 111, 112, 186n9; *Return of the Native*, 190n30; *Tess of the d'Urbervilles*, 99, 185n4, 189n30
Harm's Way (Macpherson), 92
He Knew He Was Right (Trollope), 83
history, 19
homosexuality, 127, 130–31, 132, 149, 190n7

idolatry, 180n24

Jackson, Virginia, 170n28
James, Henry: *The Portrait of a Lady*, 74, 181n27, 181n29; *Princess Cassimassima*, 181n30; on Trollope, 73–74, 180–81nn25–29
Jameson, Fredric, 157–58, 193n3
Jane Eyre (C. Brontë), 171n2
Jarvis, Simon, 170n28
Jude the Obscure (Hardy), 90–113; Arabella Donn character in, 187nn15–16; causal plot of, 92–93; children's death in, 19, 107, 109, 110, 189n29; children's presence in, 96, 103, 108–9, 111, 113; embodiment in, 92, 112; genital sexuality in, 95, 104, 106–7, 112, 189n27; Hardy postscript to, 92; Jude Fawley-Arabella relationship in, 93–94, 102–3, 106, 107, 111, 189n27; Little Father Time in, 94, 95, 105–6, 107, 108, 189n27; marriage depiction in, 92, 95, 104–5, 112–13, 188–89n25; masochistic dyad in, 94, 95, 107, 109–10; Sue-Arabella relationship in, 100–101, 187–88n18; Sue Bridehead character in, 90–91, 97, 98, 99–100, 188n19; Sue-Jude expulsion from community in, 103–4, 105; Sue-Jude relationship in, 2, 24, 90–91, 94, 95–96, 97–98, 102, 103, 104, 105, 106–7, 108, 109–10, 111–12, 188nn22–23; Sue's marriage to Phillotson in, 90–91, 103–4, 109, 110; Sue's masochism in, 100, 102, 198n17; Sue's "paganism" in, 98–99, 188n20, 188n24; Sue's sexuality in, 90–91, 98, 100, 187–88n18, 189n28; suspense and suspension in, 94, 95–102, 109, 110–11

Kangaroo (Lawrence), 119, 190n7, 191n13
Kaye, Richard A., 190n8

Kill, The (Zola), 158–59, 193n4
Kincaid, James, 176n5, 181n29, 182n34
Kipnis, Laura, 178–79n14
Kittler, Friedrich, 190–91n12
von Krafft-Ebing, Richard, 167n12, 169nn22–23
Kreilkamp, Ivan, 33–34, 172n12, 174n30
Kucich, John, 168n18, 177n10

Lady Chatterley's Lover (Lawrence), 116, 119, 152–53, 154
Last Chronicle of Barset, The (Trollope), 60, 175–76n2, 177n8, 180n20
Lawrence, D. H., 114–54; character treatment by, 115, 123–24, 126–27, 129–30, 131, 133, 142, 145–46; class critique by, 190n10; critical evaluation of, 114, 138, 189n1; discursive style of, 114, 119, 124–27; dominant women in, 133, 151; on Hardy, 187n16; on homosexuality and homoeroticism, 127, 130–31, 132, 190n7; on marriage, 115, 119; politics of, 126–27; sex act depiction by, 24, 116, 119, 127–28, 150, 151–54; sexualized social order in, 24, 115–16, 119, 132–33; Trollope compared to, 118; typescript revisions by, 133–35, 139–40, 156, 191n13, 192n21; on Victorian aesthetics and art, 148–49; and Victorianism, 115, 135, 136, 138, 142, 148; vitalism in, 121, 129, 139, 148, 149–50
— works: *Kangaroo*, 119, 190n7, 191n13; *Lady Chatterley's Lover*, 116, 119, 152–53, 154; *New Poems*, 150; *The Rainbow*, 115, 118, 119–22; *St. Mawr*, 125–26; *Women in Love*, 2–3, 115–18, 122–23, 126–33, 139–49, 151, 163
Lawrence, Frieda, 134, 139
"Lawrentian Stillness" (Bersani), 116
Leavis, F. R., 20, 123–26, 138, 170n32, 189n1
Levenson, Michael, 191n14
Levine, Caroline, 23, 163, 193n7
liberalism, 20, 170n31
Life of Charlotte Brontë, The (Gaskell), 25
Little Dorrit (Dickens), 3

Macpherson, Sandra, 19, 92–93
Mailer, Norman, 138
Marcus, Sharon, 21, 155–56, 162, 169n25, 193n1

35–36, 173n18; Catherine the Elder's power in, 36–37; Catherine the Younger in, 35, 51–52, 173n17; Catherine the Younger-Linton marriage in, 53–54; death in, 26–27, 30, 37–38, 42–43, 47–49, 54, 174n34; exquisitely masochistic scenes in, ix–x, 44–45, 48–49; Heathcliff character in, 25, 34, 36, 44–45, 172n15, 174n30; Heathcliff-Isabella relationship in, 39–41; as historical novel, 42–43; Linton Heath-

cliff in, 53–54, 175n35; marriage depiction in, 27, 28–29, 31–32, 37, 39, 50–55; masochistic dyad in, 25–26, 30, 41, 43, 48, 53; pain and suffering in, 33, 38; sadism in, 31–32, 36, 39–41, 53, 54–55; suspense and suspension in, 26–27, 28, 30, 32, 35, 38–39, 51; violence in, 25, 28–29, 39–41, 49–50, 51–52, 156, 172n11

Zola, Emile, 157–59, 160, 193n4